7

6

5

4

3

18

2

1

D0492969

The Palmer Course

THE RYDER CUP COURSE LAYOUT

RYDER CUP IRELAND

RYDER CUP
Ireland

BRIAN COX

NEW
ISLAND

Ryder Cup Ireland
First published 2006
by New Island
2 Brookside
Dundrum Road
Dublin 14
www.newisland.ie

ISBN 1 905494 36 X

Front and back cover: The K Club © Aidan Bradley www.golfcoursephotography.com
Darren Clarke © Getty Images
Author photograph © Valerie Cox
Front and back endpaper image kindly supplied by The Golf Business Ltd.

Printed in the UK by Athenaeum Press Ltd., Gateshead, Tyne & Wear

10 9 8 7 6 5 4 3 2 1

Contents

This book is dedicated to my brother, David

Foreword

by John O'Donoghue, TD, Minister for Arts, Sport and Tourism

Of the many international sporting events which have taken place in Ireland over the years, none will surpass Ryder Cup 2006 in terms of prestige, worldwide interest and true sportsmanship.

Ireland is honoured to host this major world event, with its proud history stretching back to 1927. Over many epic encounters, Irish golfers from Fred Daly in 1949 to Padraig Harrington, Paul McGinley and Darren Clarke in 2004 have played pivotal roles. Who can forget the heroics of Christy O'Connor, Sr., who played in ten successive Ryder Cups, winning eleven matches between 1955 and 1973? Or indeed, the never to be forgotten two-iron approach shot by Christy O'Connor, Jr. to the eighteenth green at the Belfry in 1989, which clinched a win over Fred Couples of the US and was vital to Europe retaining the trophy.

These and the international performances of our elite professional golfers have helped Ireland to become recognised as a major golf destination. This country has much to offer the competitive and leisure golfer. More than 30 per cent of the world's genuine links courses are to be found on this island, many of which have been hosts to golfers for more than a century. More recent times have seen the development of a bountiful array of parkland courses, many of which have been designed by some of the foremost golf architects and players in the world, including Arnold Palmer, Jack Nicklaus, Seve Ballesteros and our own Christy O'Connor, Jr. These courses, carved from the scenic Irish landscape, are in tune with nature while providing formidable challenges to golfers of every standard. The development of this golfing infrastructure has facilitated the attraction of major international championships to Ireland, such as the 2002 American Express Golf Championship, which was won by Tiger Woods, the European and Irish Open Championships and, of course, the Ryder Cup.

Ryder Cup Ireland makes a valuable contribution to the store of knowledge associated with the Ryder Cup and the contribution of Irish golfers to the matches over the years. The author, Brian Cox, has used his great love for the game and his talents as a researcher and writer to uncover a rich vein of facts, anecdotes and memories dating back to the origins of this great competition. He records heroic Irish performances, captures the reminiscences of many Ryder Cup players and outlines the campaign that resulted in the 2006 Ryder Cup coming to the K Club.

This book will expand the knowledge of every reader interested in the history of the Ryder Cup and in the remarkable contribution this country has made to the series through its players, its golfing administrators and now as host to Ryder Cup 2006.

This historic event will make an enormous contribution to raising the profile of Ireland as a holiday destination for golfers. We now welcome more than 140,000 golfing visitors to our shores annually. These visitors generate more than €142 million in revenue for our tourism industry, but more significantly, I believe, a great majority become ambassadors for Ireland, its golf, its scenery and the welcome of its people.

In writing this excellent book, Brian Cox has made his own valuable contribution to the promotion of Ireland as a golfing destination as well as creating a volume that will be a treasured memento of Ryder Cup 2006.

An Brollach

le John O'Donoghue, TD, Aire Ealaíon, Spóirt agus Turasóireachta

B'iomaí ócáid idirnáisiúnta spóirt a bhí ar bun sa tír seo in imeacht na mblianta ach béarfaidh Corn Ryder 2006 barr bua orthu sin go léir as a chlú agus a cháil, as an spéis dhomhanda ann agus as cothrom na Féinne.

Is mór an onóir d'Éirinn an ócáid mhór dhomhanda seo atá faoi réim sa stair ó 1927 i leith, a reáchtáil. D'imir galfairí Éireannacha a gcuid féin i roinnt mhaith cluichí éachtacha dúshlánacha, daoine mar Fred Daly sa bhliain 1949 agus Pádraig Harrington, Paul McGinley agus Darren Clarke sa bhliain 2004. Cé a d'fhéadfadh gaisce Christy O'Connor, Sr. a ligean i ndearmad mar gur imir sé deich n-uaire i ndiaidh a chéile i gCorn Ryder agus mar gur bhuaigh sé aon chluiche dhéag idir 1955 agus 1973; nó go fiú an gaisce iontach a rinne Christy O'Connor, Jr. lena gharbhuille iarann 2 chuig an 18ú plásóg ar Ghalfchúrsa Belfry sa bhliain 1989 nuair a chinntigh sé bua ar Fred Couples na Stát Aontaithe agus gur coinníodh an corn san Eoraip de dheasca an bhua sin.

Is ceann scríbe cáiliúil don ghalf í Éire anois mar thoradh ar na héachtaí sin agus mar thoradh ar an saothrú atá curtha díobh go hidirnáisiúnta ag scoth ghalfairí gairmiúla na tíre seo. Tá buntáistí móra ag an tír seo don té a bhíonn san iomaíocht i gcúrsaí gailf agus don té a bhaineann leas fóillíochta as an ngalf. Tá os cionn 30 faoin gcéad d'fhíor-ghalfchúrsaí duimhche an domhain le fáil ar an oileán seo agus bhain roinnt mhaith galfairí úsáid astu le breis is céad bliain anuas. Forbraíodh lear mór galfchúrsaí ar fhearann páirce le tamall de bhlianta anuas. Dhear roinnt d'ailtirí agus d'imreoirí iomráiteacha gailf an domhain go leor díobh. Áirítear Arnold Palmer, Jack Nicklaus, Seve Ballesteros agus Christy O'Connor, Jr. na tíre seo ar na daoine sin. Tá luí nádúrtha leis na galfchúrsaí seo agus iad greanta i dtírdhreach na hÉireann ach is dubhdhúshlán do ghalfairí iad chomh maith pé caighdeán atá ag na galfairí sin. Ba mhór an chabhair an fhorbairt seo ar infreas-truchtúr an ghailf mar gur chuidigh sí le Craobhchomórtais mhóra idirnáisiúnta gailf a mhealladh go hÉirinn leithéidí Craobhchomórtas Gailf an American Express 2002 a bhuaigh Tiger Woods, na Craobhchomórtais Oscailte Eorpacha agus Éire-annacha agus ar ndóigh Corn Ryder.

Cuireann *Ryder Cup Ireland* leis an stór breá eolais faoi Chorn Ryder agus faoi pháirt na ngalfairí Éireannacha sna cluichí thar na blianta. D'fhigh an t-údar, Brian Cox, an gean atá aige ar an gcluiche leis na buanna atá aige mar thaighdeoir agus mar scríbh-neoir chun teacht ar dhíolaim théagartha d'fhíricí, de scéilíní agus de chuimhní a théann siar chomh fada le tús an chomórtais cháil-iúil seo. Breacann sé síos éachtaí móra na nÉireannach, cuireann sé cuimhní cinn roinnt mhaith d'imreoirí Chorn Ryder ar pár agus tugann sé cuntas ar an bhfeachtas gur dá bharr a bheidh Corn Ryder 2006 ar siúl sa K Club.

Cuirfidh an leabhar leis an eolas atá ag na léitheoirí úd gur spéis leo stair Chorn Ryder agus gur spéis leo gach a bhfuil déanta ag Éirinn don tsraith trína himreoirí, a riarthóirí gailf agus anois mar ionad do Chorn Ryder 2006.

Cuideoidh an ócáid stairiúil seo go mór chun aird a tharraingt ar Éirinn mar cheann scríbe saoire do lucht imeartha gailf. Tagann breis is 140,000 cuairteoir a mbíonn baint acu le cúrsaí gailf chun na tíre seo gach bliain. Gintear os cionn €142 milliún d'ioncam do thionscal na turasóireachta mar go dtagann na cuairteoirí seo chugainn ach ní hé sin amháin é creidim, mar cibé áit a dtéann siad molann a bhformhór an tír seo, a galfchúrsaí, a radharcanna áille agus an fháilte fhlaithiúil a chuireann mhuintir na hÉireann rompu.

Chuir Brian Cox a chuid féin le cur chun cinn na hÉireann mar cheann scríbe don ghalf nuair a scríobh sé an leabhar seo. Is leabhar é a choinneofar i gcaoinchuimhne Chorn Ryder 2006.

Introduction

In the late 1950s, I was still a pupil at St Paul's secondary school in Raheny on Dublin's north side. I took part in all the sports provided by the Vincentian fathers: rugby, cricket, basketball and tennis. In fifth year, in 1960, I got a part-time summer job at Sutton Golf Club, the home of three-time British Amateur Champion, the late J.B. Carr. At the time I was totally clueless about and ambivalent towards the game of golf. However, being constantly exposed to it over a three-month period, my views gradually changed.

Golf enthusiasts will remember the Canada Cup (now the World Cup of Golf) being played at Portmarnock in June of that year. There was a week-long heat wave at the time, resulting in record attendances at this famous links venue. I saw many of the world's greats, including Player, Palmer and Snead. I followed South African Gary Player when he shot his record 65, a rarity on this long, challenging stretch. The fairways were scorched and this encouraged a lot of run on the ball, thus facilitating low scores. Throughout the international event, my friends and I spent our free time marvelling at the skills of these great golfers.

However, it wasn't the world's greats that impressed me like one of our own did. Representing Ireland in the Canada Cup were Northern Ireland's Norman Drew and our own Christy O'Connor, Sr. There was something magically absorbing about O'Connor. He had a graceful, rhythmic swing that was sheer poetry in motion. The intensity of his concentration was written all over his tight-lipped face. I was in total awe of this magnificent ball striker who consistently propelled his tee shots into space with a precision that had to be seen to be believed. I was his fan for life.

The intensity of that experience would trigger what was until then my latent passion for golf. I joined Sutton Golf Club soon after and took up the sport seriously. Over a few short years, I played to a four handicap and my thoughts were invariably directed towards the professional game. The thought struck me as to how I was to realise this indulgent passion. It meant working by day for three years at Industrial Gases (IFS) in Bluebell, Inchicore and studying in the evening. The long-term goal was still golf oriented, with a short-term focus on either a legal or teaching career to achieve it. Teaching seemed to be more commensurate with the 'Royal and Ancient' game. Long summer holidays beckoned – the three-month stretch would afford me ample opportunity to grace the undulating fairways of the world's links courses.

After graduating from University College Dublin I began my teacher training at De La Salle College in Ballyfermot, a growing suburb not far from Dublin's Phoenix Park. Two years later I took up a position at Notre Dame des Missions secondary school, where I would spend a large part of my life – thirty-six years, in fact – before retiring as school principal at the end of August 2005. It was a career, or as it was then called, a vocation, in which I was deeply immersed.

Teaching was meant to be a launching pad for me embarking on a career as a professional golfer. What I hadn't reckoned on was how little time there was at my disposal to pursue my original dream. Coupled with that was my love of teaching. I loved the fact that I was involved in moulding young people's lives. I welcomed the challenge and obvious rewards the profession offered in those early days. The rewards were by no means financial. I had already jettisoned a well-paid job in industry to find more 'human rewards', and I had discovered and embraced these as a teacher.

A few years afterwards, I got married and settled down. My wife and I had five children. It was a new phase in life that demanded all the family focus and attention that you would expect. Golf went into cold storage for a considerably long period before resurrecting itself when the children were grown and embarking on their own careers – although I did engage them as caddies when they were young enough. Having retired, that love affair with golf has been rekindled and has prompted me to write this book on the Ryder Cup.

As a youngster, my golfing ambition was to join the professional ranks and win the Open Championship. However, the ambition to play in the Ryder Cup was uppermost in my thoughts. Neither materialised, but the passion – though kept very much at bay – was there and intensified over time. Now it has surfaced in another guise, hence my year-long pleasure in writing this book, which has been a most rewarding adjunct to my retirement from the teaching profession.

There is absolutely no doubt that the September Ryder Cup event at the K Club will be a huge success. Dr Michael Smurfit is to be congratulated for having this prestigious event staged there. Many will say it would never have come to Ireland were it not for him. The occasion will certainly turn out to be a uniquely personal triumph for all his dedication and commitment over a long number of years in realising a dream. In addition, successive Irish governments, along with Bord Fáilte (Fáilte Ireland), are to be congratulated for bringing the biennial series to our shores. The occasion will certainly raise Ireland's profile as an ideal golfing destination.

I am dedicating this book to my brother, David, who died in October 2005. One of my cherished golfing memories is associated with him. It was summer 1963, when I won the Sutton Cup. It was quite large and David shared in that memory by collecting the 'two of us' on his BSA motor bike to be welcomed home to a family celebration.

Brian Cox
May 2006

SECTION 1

Condensing
the
History

CHAPTER 1

Early Period

I often wondered where the game of golf originated. Modern thinking puts Scotland to the fore. However, forerunners of the game of golf include *chole*, a cross-country event played in northern France and Belgium using a ball the size of tennis ball hit to a distant target, such as a pillar or door. The Dutch had *kolven*, using something resembling a cricket ball and played on frozen ice. In Ireland, Cork seems to lay claim to a sport like *chole*. Corkonians call this traditional game *boules*, where the player throws a ball to a target that is a considerable distance away, such as a local county boundary. Perhaps the Cork game might be associated with the modern-day game of bowles.

Some say the game began in Holland, while others claim it was in China, but those most conversant with the traditions can point a legitimate finger to Scotland as being the home of golf. However, it was America that subsequently donned the mantle and its exponents became the sole masters of the sport for many decades – and, arguably, still are.

The Ryder Cup's humble beginnings officially began in 1927, but its origins can be traced back a few years prior to that. Before it became Europe versus the US in 1979, it was known as the Great Britain Team versus the US from 1927 up to and including 1937. There were no games played during the period of the

Second World War. It became the Great Britain and Ireland team (or as some would insist, the Great Britain and Northern Ireland team) in 1947 when Northern Ireland's Fred Daly made the first of his four consecutive appearances.

Who reigned supreme, the British or the Americans?

Enthusiasts on both sides of the Atlantic felt head-to-head encounters would be the final solution as to which country would produce the best golfers in the world. Before the outbreak of the First World War, informal matches existed between teams of professional golfers from France and the US. Many people don't realise how formidable a golfing nation France was in these early years. In America, an Ohio businessman, S.P. Jermain, was a major driving force in inviting two prominent English professionals, Harry Vardon (of 'Vardon grip' fame) and Ted Ray, to compete in the 1920 US Open. The Vardon grip technique involved the little finger of the right hand overlapping the index finger of the left hand, resulting in a 'marriage' of the two hands. This is the grip most golfers use today.

James Hartnett, circulation manager of the US golf magazine *Golf Illustrated*, was, along with the great American golfer Walter Hagen, very much in favour of overseas players pitting their golfing wits against their US counterparts. In those early days, the ultimate intention was to send an American team to Britain and to have the return matches on American soil. Needless to say, there was a considerable cost factor involved. Hartnett had a commercial interest in the venture, but in fairness to him he began a fundraising campaign to finance his country's visit to Britain. He didn't manage to realise sufficient monies, but the USPGA met to endorse Hartnett's idea of an international challenge and also his moves to fundraise for the event.

Some serious questions had to be addressed before embarking on the venture. Who should play for America? Americans, of course! But what about British professionals who jettisoned the land of their birth to look for work in the US? This concern led to the USPGA passing a motion stipulating that such players who wished to participate for their adopted country had to have lived in America for not less than five years. In addition, they had to signal their commitment and intention to take out US citizenship. Once this procedure was set in motion, the green light was given for the international challenge match to go ahead. Each player would be given $1,000 to defray travel and any other incidental costs associated with the trip. The next matter of concern was a suitable venue. The location was to be the Kings Course at Gleneagles at Perthshire in Scotland. This was a magnanimous American gesture, for it acknowledged their sense of history associated with this great game. James Braid arranged for *The Glasgow Herald* to sponsor the international challenge match between the British and American professionals. The Gleneagles course was also a convenient venue, as the event was being run in conjunction with the very lucrative *Glasgow Herald* 1,000 Guineas tournament, which had attracted many of the finest American players of the day.

The ten-man Great Britain team, captained by John Henry Taylor and with Emmett French at the helm, crushed the visitors by 10½ to 4½. Six-time British Open Champion Harry Vardon was a strong member of the winning home side. Also on the same team was Abe Mitchell, whose figurine was to adorn the Ryder Cup trophy in 1927.

However, I recall hearing the challenge matches came in for stiff criticism. Many said the fairways and greens on this new links course didn't meet with the highest of standards. Likewise, the bunkers were targeted for abuse – the sand was too gritty and was full of shells. Spectators were few and far between. There was a lack of enthusiasm and atmosphere that one would expect at an event like this. Despite this, Walter Hagen, two-time US Open champion and member of the visiting team, was anxious that this challenge match be repeated. Perhaps it was due to the fact that he was a member of the vanquished side who harboured thoughts of revenge at some future date. Credit was given to *The Glasgow Herald*, which arranged to have commemorative gold medals made for the occasion. A little more prestige was added when the American ambassador presented a medal to each member of the two teams.

Another informal Great Britain/US clash was arranged for 1926. It was to coincide with the leading Americans visiting our shores to qualify for the Open Championship. This spectacle resulted in a whitewash for Great Britain under Ted Ray as captain. His team trounced Walter Hagen's side by 13½ to 1½. The Americans still nourished further hope for a chance to compete again and to have the balance redressed.

'THE SEED WAS SOWN ONLY TO YIELD FRUIT A HUNDREDFOLD'

Sam Ryder was born in 1858. He was the son of a Manchester corn market entrepreneur. Professionally, he was a seed merchant who made his fortune from selling penny packets of seeds to an enthusiastic gardening public. He was a deeply religious individual who became a church deacon. His first sporting love was cricket. In his early fifties he was advised by his church minister to forego the game on health grounds and take up golf instead. This tall, thin, bushy-moustached church deacon took up golf around the age of fifty. He was to become a total fanatic of the game. He would not, however, play golf on the Sabbath, as it was totally alien to his religious and spiritual values. I wonder what he might think of the final day's play in today's Ryder Cup matches.

His seed company sponsored a number of tournaments in the early 1920s. He befriended Abe Mitchell, whom he regarded and respected as the consummate golf professional. He employed him as his own professional tutor and mentor at what was believed to have been an annual salary of £500 plus expenses of £250. His one wish was to see Abe relieved of many of the club chores that had precious little to do with golf. In so doing, Abe would find time to devote his talents to playing more tournament golf, and to playing the Open Championship in particular. He always regarded his friend as one of the very best golfers of his time never to have won a major championship.

Irish golfers might attribute the same sentiments to Christy O'Connor, Sr., who was regarded by his Irish fans and fellow professionals as being one of our great golfing exponents never to have won the Open Championship. Constant golf conversation between Sam and his close friend, Abe, always centred on which of the two great golfing nations was the better. Wentworth would host the second official international challenge matches in 1926. Abe Mitchell played. Sam Ryder was there and was taken in by what he saw. Above all, he admired the skills of the players, their integrity as individuals and the infectious atmosphere of the occasion. It was an appropriate time to put this matter to the test.

After the 1926 matches, Samuel Ryder had tea with British team members George Duncan and Abe Mitchell. Also present were Walter Hagen and Emmett French from the visiting team. It was Duncan, the 1920 Open champion, who suggested to Sam that he should provide a trophy for a regular series of matches between Great Britain and the United States. Sam's passion for golf was translated into action.

It is believed silversmiths Mappin and Web were comissioned to make a 'golden chalice' for the planned 1927 Ryder Cup. The effigy incorporated on the lid is said to be that of Abe Mitchell. Perhaps it was because of his religious fervour that his trophy would resemble a chalice and be made from pure gold. Gold was precious and unique. It was something to treasure and be used only on special occasions. Its tabernacle would be in the safe keeping of the PGA.

I was at the 1997 European Open at the K Club just outside Ireland's capital city, Dublin. It was a little while before the Ryder Cup matches at Valderrama in Spain. Those golf enthusiasts who were at the European event will recall that the Ryder Cup trophy was on display in the tented village. It was on a stand against a huge backdrop of white. I couldn't help but marvel at the likeness of the scene to an ecclesiastical setting. There it was, 'the chalice on the altar of repose' commanding the utmost of attention and respect. Standing on the 'bridge over troubled waters' leading to the Belfry's eighteenth green, 2002 Ryder Cup captain Sam Torrance held the same trophy in celestial reverence for all to see following Europe's great victory over the Americans in 2002. You could forgive golfers' reactions at feeling a compulsion to genuflect in admiration and awe of this magnificent piece of treasure steeped in symbolism and history.

This trophy received its initiation ceremony at the inaugural Ryder Cup biennial matches in 1927 at Worcester, Massachusetts.

1927 WORCESTER COUNTRY CLUB, MASSACHUSETTS, US

The British team set out for New York on the *Aquitania* without Sam Ryder and his intended captain, Abe Mitchell. Shortly before they sailed out on the week-long voyage to America, Abe fell ill. It was appendicitis and this ruled him out of any Ryder Cup matches. Ted Ray stepped into the role.

The 1927 estimated team expenses amounted to circa £3,000. An appeal for donations to cover the huge financial outlay met with a lukewarm response. The appeal was made to some 1,700 golf clubs in Britain, with just over 200 donating. Sam Ryder made up the difference.

Once they docked in Manhattan, they were whisked off by a small motorcade to the exclusive Westchester Hotel. An informal golf competition, a cocktail party and dinner were all part of the welcoming activities that awaited them. In addition, the British team were special invitees at a baseball game to see the New York Yankees play the Washington Senators at Yankee Stadium.

Sam Ryder wanted the Ryder Cup matches spread out over two days, with day one devoted to foursomes and day two's format to concentrate on singles. The usual stipulations about the national pedigrees of individual team members along with respective memberships of their professional golf associations were strictly adhered to. Unlike earlier unofficial international clashes between the two nations, the Americans inflicted a convincing defeat on the British side by 9½ to 2½. Walter Hagen's revenge was realised at an official level, as the original encounters had been informal.

The inaugural 1927 Ryder Cup matches had the legendary Gene Sarazen on the American team. Ted Ray was the British team captain, with Walter Hagen in charge of the US squad. The golfing gauntlet had been thrown down. The biennial matches between Britain and the US continued up to and including the 1937 event at Southport, but because of the Second World War didn't resume until 1947, when the matches were played at Portland, Oregon.

The question of Ireland being part of the team to face the mighty Americans wasn't resolved until 1947, when Northern Ireland's Fred Daly made his first of four appearances, the others being in 1949, 1951 and 1953. Our very first representative from Southern Ireland was Harry Bradshaw in 1953 in Virginia. The team was known as the Great Britain and Ireland Team up to and including the 1977 Ryder Cup matches at England's

Royal Lytham and St Anne's. From 1979 onwards, the team to face the US would be known as Europe.

Until 1959, Ryder Cup matches included four foursomes (Americans call these alternate shots) on the first day and eight singles on the second and final day. The format changed in 1961 to allow for four 18-hole foursome matches on the morning of day one and a further four in the afternoon. The second day was devoted to sixteen singles matches. The format was changed again in 1963 and 1977. In 1963 there were eight foursomes on day one, eight fourballs on day two and sixteen singles on day three. In 1977 the matches were played at Royal Lytham and St Anne's, when there were five foursomes on day one, five fourballs on day two and ten singles on the final day.

AMERICAN SUPREMACY

The Americans conveyed an aura of supreme confidence, both on and off the course. Those fans who were there will remember how impeccably turned-out the American contingent was: scarlet pullovers embellished with a gold-embroidered emblem displaying the Union Jack and the Stars and Stripes. It was a mind game that worked against the home side, which lost the 1977 Ryder Cup to them in convincing fashion.

The 1979 Ryder Cup in West Virginia would incorporate yet more changes to the existing format. Day one incorporated four foursomes, morning and afternoon; day two had four morning foursomes and four fourball matches in the afternoon; while the third and final day had six singles in the morning and six singles in the afternoon.

The 1979 match also saw a monumental change of a different kind. No longer would it be the Great Britain and Ireland team, but rather Europe versus America. The thinking down the years since the inaugural Ryder Cup in 1927 was that the series was a very one-sided affair. The US players and the American public at large were totally indifferent to the event. However, on this side of the Atlantic there was huge interest in these biennial international clashes. I recall as a youngster in my late teens anxiously looking forward to radio and newspaper reports on the progress and outcome of the matches. In fact, at the time I had contemplated pursuing a career in teaching, law or perhaps professional golf. The one overriding ambition I privately indulged in was to be a member of the Great Britain and Ireland Ryder Cup Team. Naturally, the Open Championship and the US Masters at Augusta were also on the agenda, but they paled in significance when compared to the Ryder Cup.

As stated, there was continued disinterest in the event from an American viewpoint because the encounter was lacklustre and one-sided. George Duncan, Abe Mitchell, Henry Cotton, Harry Bradshaw and Christy O'Connor, Sr. knew exactly why the Americans were constantly outperforming their opponents – the Americans excelled at the short game. From under 100 yards out, they were masters. In addition, they were totally supreme on the greens. They also exuded an air of invincibility, a mindset which affected their opponents.

Between 1927 and 1977, the US won eighteen times and the Great Britain and Ireland team won three times, with one halved match in 1969. When it became Europe versus America from 1979 onwards, the balance was redressed. From the Ryder Cup inaugural 1927 matches up to the conclusion of the 2004 matches (the 2001 matches were postponed because of 9/11 and resumed again in 2002), the US had twenty-four wins and Great Britain and Ireland/Europe had nine wins, with two ties.

There were suggestions on both sides of the Atlantic that fundamental changes had to be made in order to ensure the continuance of the Ryder Cup, especially after the home defeat at Lytham in 1977. Backing the call for change at an early stage was the legendary Jack Nicklaus, who called for a 'European team' versus America.

Jack Nicklaus approached Lord Derby. He told him the Ryder Cup was not a competition as much as he would like it to be a competition. It was, he felt, a bitter pill to swallow, but if a fundamental change wasn't implemented sooner rather than later, the biennial matches would die a quick death. The harsh reality, Nicklaus explained to Lord Derby, was that the Americans had almost a total monopoly of wins in the series. The British and Irish players play the European circuit – why not, then, have a European team to play against the US?

THE CHANGE THAT PROVED PIVOTAL

Lord Derby agreed to think about Jack's proposal. There was initial reluctance, mainly from this side of the water, to the idea. However, common sense prevailed. The forward thinking resulted in Brian Huggett and Peter Butler going to the 1978 Augusta Masters to put the 'European' idea to the PGA of America. Lord Derby made a fresh agreement with them to have the original team 'broadened'. There was all-round support for the change. There would now be a fair balance of abilities in future encounters and the new process would inculcate more interest in the biennial event among the American players and supporters.

Before all of this was legitimised, both the PGA of America and the British PGA encouraged Sam Ryder's heirs to change the deed of trust to include players from Continental Europe to contest the 1979 Ryder Cup matches against America. There was unanimous support for the recommendation. There was no doubt but Sam himself would have wholeheartedly endorsed the request.

Despite the profound change to the articles of association, the European contingent under captain John Jacobs was beaten by Billy Casper's side. The result was Europe 11, US 17. Antonio Garrido and Severiano Ballesteros were the first players from Continental Europe on Team Europe. They had mixed fortunes against the might of the Americans in West Virginia. In the morning fourballs on day one, they were beaten 2 and 1 by Lanny Wadkins and Larry Nelson. They won 3 and 2 against Fuzzy Zoeller and Hubert Green in the afternoon foursomes. On day two they suffered another devastating blow from Wadkins and Nelson in the morning foursomes and also lost to the same American pair in the afternoon fourball match. The symbolism of this profound change in team structure would prove to be massive.

1929 MOORTOWN GOLF CLUB, LEEDS, YORKSHIRE, ENGLAND

The 1929 Ryder Cup event at Moortown Golf Club in Leeds, Yorkshire was noted for Sam Ryder's insistence on British players being 'native-born citizens' of the nation they represented. The Ryder Cup was still in its infancy, with the general golfing public regarding the encounters as no more than glorified exhibition matches. Nevertheless, the Americans had little difficulty in raising some $10,000 from donations to fund their trip to Britain. The money mainly came from equipment manufacturers and exhibition matches back home. Another half-hearted appeal for financial support in Britain resulted in a mere £806, according to some.

The event had yet to fire the imagination. Much criticism seemed to point a finger at the custodians of the Ryder Cup, the British PGA, on the grounds of poor organisation. Some went so far as to suggest that the Royal and Ancient could take future responsibility for Sam Ryder's dream, otherwise the biennial occasion would disappear into thin air.

The home side beat their American opponents 7 points to 5. The inclement weather certainly didn't favour the visiting team. But the Cup was back! The singles matches will be remembered for Henry Cotton's crushing 4 and 3 defeat of Al Watrous. Although of German origin, Watrous was a native-born American who it was claimed practised more than his contemporaries, much in the same way as Harrington and Singh today are exemplary when it comes to work ethic. Watrous was inquisitive as to the composition of the golf swing. He was taken in by the manner in which 'the plane or the slot' of the swing could be accurately achieved and repeated. I recall hearing it led him on at least one occasion to stand naked in front of a mirror and observe the swing in motion; he paid very close attention to muscle movement.

1931 SCIOTO COUNTRY CLUB, COLUMBUS, OHIO, US

Discord was a feature of the 1931 matches, held at the Scioto Country Club in Columbus, Ohio. The event wouldn't be graced with the presence of Henry Cotton, who was omitted on a technicality. The rule of the day was that players had to be resident in the country they were born in so as to be eligible to represent it in the Ryder Cup. Cotton was not. For the same reason, Percy Alliss (father of the BBC golf commentator Peter Alliss) was left out, as he was a pro attached to the Wannsee Golf Club in Berlin. The British team was then at a considerable disadvantage at not having these two fine players on the team, which lost the 1931 matches by 9 points to 3. In the modern game in recent years, similar concerns were aired when there was a danger that some of our great European players who played for long spells on the US tour might be deemed ineligible to represent Europe in the Ryder Cup. However, common sense prevailed, with the creation of a World Tour.

The British team was exposed to the sweltering heat of June temperatures in Ohio. The result of the 1931 matches was the US 9, Great Britain 3. Strong pressure from the British PGA ensured that all other American venues would have a September date in the future.

1933 SOUTHPORT AND AINSDALE GOLF CLUB, SOUTHPORT, ENGLAND

Southport and Ainsdale Golf Club was the 1933 venue, when the result of the Ryder Cup result was more acceptable. Great Britain won, albeit by the slimmest of margins. The home team was captained by the formidable J.H. Taylor, who took his captaincy very seriously. His intention was to mould his team into a winning unit. He was well aware of the hiding that was meted out to the British when last they played on American soil. He employed a physical fitness guru from the British Army to lick his players into shape. Early morning runs on the beach followed by compulsory 'rub downs' to loosen the players' muscles were the order of the day for the younger and more 'advanced' members of Britain's Ryder Cup Team. Sixty-two-year-old Taylor led by example by joining the squad on their daily beach runs. It paid positive dividends. On this occasion, Great Britain beat the US by 6½ to 5½.

Abe Mitchell pulverised his American opponent, Olin Dutra, by 9 and 8, despite the fact that Abe was three down after nine holes (keep in mind that matches were over thirty-six holes then). What clinched the result for Great Britain was the unexpected but most welcome of wins from the last singles match out on the course on the final day. The match situation was that both teams were level at 5½ points each. Syd Easterbrook and his American opponent, Densmore Shute, went down the eighteenth hole all square. The enthusiastic crowds thronged the final fairway, adding to the excitement and sense of a British victory.

Both players found sand off the tee. The inexperienced Easterbrook played out safely, while Shute dared to go for the green but ended up in a second bunker. The sand explosion left him about twenty feet from the hole, just outside his opponent. The British pro left himself with a nasty left-to-right four footer. US team captain, Walter Hagen, secretly prayed that his player would just nudge his putt near to the cup to ensure what would be a tied result for the visiting team. Hagen knew the Americans would then retain the Cup, but to everyone's huge dismay, it ran some six feet past. To add insult to injury, Shute failed with the return. In McGinley-like fashion, Easterbrook calmly holed out to win his match and also the Ryder Cup for Great Britain.

1935 RIDGEWOOD COUNTRY CLUB, NEW JERSEY, US

We will recall that when it came to playing all future Ryder Cup matches in America, the calendar date would be September. This was to avoid the visiting team being exposed to the extremes of summer heat. Despite this, the British side suffered a humiliating defeat, going down to their opponents by 9 points to 3. They were totally outclassed by the US players, captained yet again by Walter Hagen. The 1935 matches will be remembered for yet another reason. For the first time, there would be three Whitcome brothers on the visiting team. Playing captain, Charles Whitcome, was regarded by Henry Cotton as the best of the brothers, endowed with a natural ability for the game. He had played in the inaugural Ryder Cup matches in 1927 and in a further five. Ernest played in three Ryder Cup events, while Reginald represented Great Britain on one occasion.

1937 SOUTHPORT AND AINSDALE GOLF CLUB, SOUTHPORT, ENGLAND

The Ryder Cup had already been held here in 1933, when Great Britain recorded that exciting one-point win over the ever-menacing American contingent. Naturally, the home mood was buoyant, especially since the great Henry Cotton was now deemed eligible to play. The last time he'd played in the matches was in 1929, but had ruled himself out of contention for the next three Ryder Cup events as he was a professional residing abroad. He was now at home.

On board the *Manhattan* with the American Ryder Cup squad that left New York on 16 June was Byron Nelson, newcomer to the Ryder Cup. Along with Ed Dudley, he was responsible for a crushing defeat of Henry Cotton and Alf Padgham in the first foursomes on the opening day. Nelson was later to become one of the greatest exponents of golf, but he was to suffer a Ryder Cup baptism of fire in the singles against the fiery, strong-willed and dogged Welshman, Dai Rees, who beat Nelson 3 and 1.

In the singles there was a very convincing win, this time for Cotton when he accounted for the 5 and 3 scalp of Tony Manero. However, boasting players like Sam Snead and Gene Sarazen on their side, the US captain, Walter Hagen, was to lead his team to an eventual 8 points to 4 victory over a despondent home side. This American win would mark the first time in Ryder Cup history they beat their opponents on British soil.

Due to the outbreak of the Second World War in Europe on 3 September 1939, there were no Ryder Cup matches until 1947.

CHAPTER 2

Middle Period

1947 PORTLAND GOLF CLUB, OREGON, US
THE GREAT BRITAIN AND IRELAND (NORTHERN IRELAND) TEAM

The war years took a toll on both Britain and America. The devastation was particularly acute in Britain. Many golf professionals were members of the armed forces and found little or no time to devote to the game from 1940 to 1945. Post-war rationing of food and petrol contributed to the difficulties of life's normal readjustment after the war, and golf on this side of the Atlantic suffered immensely. Following such a lengthy absence, many home players had to practically relearn the game. The appetite wasn't really there to resume and the Ryder Cup wasn't foremost in people's minds. There were more serious and pressing concerns that needed attention. This widespread belief didn't augur well for the future of the Ryder Cup.

However, the fact that the last event had been staged in England meant that the 1947 matches were due to be played in America. Behind-the-scenes USPGA negotiations were stepped up a gear to help rescue the situation. The Association's executive director, Fred Corcoran, had been involved in numerous rescue efforts with a wealthy American wholesale grocery businessman,

Robert A. Hudson, whose company regularly sponsored the Portland Open. Not only did Hudson agree to top up the meagre USPGA funds, but magnanimously covered the expenses of both teams. This was a very welcome gesture, especially for the overseas travelling team. In addition, each member of the visiting team was given a complimentary phone call home after the matches.

FRED DALY

Fred Daly became the first player from Ireland (Northern Ireland) to play in the 1947 Ryder Cup. That summer, he won the Open Championship at Hoylake (the venue for the 2006 event) and was the player very much in form.

The *Queen Mary* docked in New York and the visiting team was whisked off to a welcoming banquet hosted by Hudson. It was then down to serious business on 1 November. After a three-day train journey from New York right across America to the West, it would be time to focus on their mission. Despite the extremely wet weather, arguably favouring the British players, it was a daunting task for the visitors, as the US team included playing captain, Ben Hogan, Byron Nelson and Sam Snead. It proved just that, for the American side almost recorded a whitewash result: 11 points to 1 in favour of the US. They won all the matches on the first day and on day two won the first seven of the eight singles, with the eighth being won by British player, Sam King. It seemed the future of Sam Ryder's dream was under threat yet again.

1949 GANTON GOLF CLUB, SCARBOROUGH, ENGLAND
INELIGIBILITY CLAUSE

Harry Bradshaw should have been a member of the 1949 Ryder Cup team as well as the 1951 team. His pedigree was never in question. I met with Harry Junior and his sister, Breda, in the summer of 2005 to talk about their famous dad. 'He was the only player from the Republic of Ireland to have tied for the 1949 Open Championship, forcing a play-off with, and losing to, South Africa's Bobby Locke,' said Breda. At the time, there was an ineligibility clause that defied all logic and ruled Harry out of the 1949 and 1951 teams. According to the British Professional Golfers'

Association of the day, Harry Bradshaw was not a fully fledged member of their association – he was only an overseas member. Incredibly, though, Harry represented the British PGA as a member of a four-man team that officially played in South Africa over the six-month 1950–51 Irish winter period.

Six months before the Ryder Cup at Ganton, Ben Hogan was involved in an almost fatal road accident. The chances of him ever returning to the game were highly doubtful, but his strength of character and mind overcame 'the slings and arrows of outrageous fortune'. (For those readers interested in this period of Ben Hogan's life, look out for the splendid film *Follow the Sun*, with Glen Ford playing the leading role.)

Even though Ben could hardly walk, the American PGA honoured Ben with the captaincy of the US side at Ganton. The result of the 1949 Ryder Cup confirmed the supremacy and dominance of America as a world force in golf yet again – they won by 7 points to 5. Fred Daly won his foursome matches with Ken Bousfield but lost out to Lloyd Mangrum by 4 and 3 in the singles.

1951 Pinehurst Country Club, North Carolina, US

From an American viewpoint, interest in the Ryder Cup had been waning over the years but was now reaching an all-time low. Sam Ryder's dream was nice in theory but didn't meet with his expectations. I'm sure he looked forward to reasonable encounters with American opponents while at the same time wanting the Ryder Cup 'to promote a cordial, friendly and peaceful feeling' (Malcom Hamer, *The Ryder Cup, The Players*, Kingswood, p. 7) throughout the entire world, but with the harsh reality of a total imbalance between the abilities of the two teams, this aspiration was rendered meaningless.

The US players drove the ball generally straighter and longer than their counterparts. They could manipulate a draw or fade at will. Their short game from around 60 to 70 yards out was far superior, and above all, they excelled when it came to holing out. Americans oozed an air of total confidence and invincibility. This psychological mindset was transmitted to their opponents; it unnerved them and generally shattered their self-esteem as individuals and as a team.

Even the Americans' dress code, which was of a very high standard, undermined visiting players. They felt inferior and I believe this interfered with their standard of play. By contrast, the American 'feel good' factor permeated players individually and collectively and so brought the very best out of them. US players were constantly exposed to the cut-and-thrust of regular competition from one end of the year to the next. They learned to experience pressure, live with it and conquer it in order to be successful on the circuit.

This is not to say our players on this side of the Atlantic weren't very good players, but in the early years of international competitive play they, with a few exceptions, didn't manage the pressure element associated with top-class performance. Perhaps this realisation has been slowly dawning on our players, especially in the modern game, now that we have a world tour. It has come as no surprise to us to have observed in recent years how some of our gifted players have paid more attention to playing the American circuit. The same players have become beneficiaries of their significant learning curve.

Harrington, Clarke, McGinley and McDonald are four good examples to support this theory. Other European players are – and have been – doing likewise. It can only pay huge, positive dividends over time. Looking at performance statistics in Ryder Cup matches since 1983, it is abundantly clear that our performance levels have stepped up considerably. Many matches are now going down the eighteenth.

In 1951, then at Pinehurst, it was no surprise to see the visiting side go down to the might of the Americans by a margin of 7 points. The Great Britain and Ireland (Northern Ireland) team was beaten by 9½ to 2½ points. Fred Daly was responsible for the half point in his match against Clayton Heafner.

1953 WENTWORTH GOLF CLUB, SURREY, ENGLAND
THE GREAT BRITAIN AND IRELAND TEAM

Two headlines grabbed the world's attention in the 1953 series of Ryder Cup matches. One was the coronation at Westminster Abbey and the second was when Edmund Hillary climbed Mount Everest. As for the Ryder Cup, there was nothing unusual about the result. What can be said was that it was another victory for America, albeit a slender one. The psychological and allied differences between the two teams in the 1951 Ryder Cup were borne out yet again and caused a great deal of concern for non-playing captain, Henry Cotton. Tony Jacklin would refine this dimension during his own unique style of captaincy in 1983, 1985, 1987 and 1989 (discussed in more detail in Chapter 10).

Cotton was by nature a very disciplined and methodical individual. He knew exactly what the Ryder Cup entailed. For his part at Wentworth, he was to insist on the very best for the players under his charge. The five-star Kensington Palace Hotel, London was where Lloyd Mangrum's US team stayed and were exposed to the ultimate in luxurious surroundings with the very best of attention. To begin with, Cotton provided his team with the very best of hotel accommodation and brought them to a performance of *Guys and Dolls*. Receiving the best would ensure giving the best. Togetherness was an essential component of his Ryder Cup strategy. It was imperative that his players gel as a unit and function as an effective team. In his team discussions, he would constantly stress the need to focus on their sole mission: to defeat the opposition.

HARRY BRADSHAW ENTERS THE FRAY

1953 was a significant date for the Republic of Ireland. It was the first time that the Americans played against the Great Britain and Ireland team. Southern Ireland's Harry Bradshaw would play alongside his Northern Ireland colleague, Fred Daly. They actually played together in the foursomes on day one and easily disposed of their US opponents, Walter Burkemo and Cary Middlecoff.

The Irish players were also successful in their singles matches in 1953. It was the same year BBC golf commentator Peter Alliss made his inaugural Ryder Cup appearance, being narrowly beaten in the singles by Jim Turnesa. Cotton had put so much into the contest only to be disappointed by the result. It was another American success. However, his team had been beaten by the narrowest of margins: US 6½, Great Britain and Ireland 5½. It can be said that Cotton caused a few irregular heartbeats in the American camp on that final day. Was the tide beginning to turn?

1955 Thunderbird Golf and Country Club, Palm Springs, California, US

The format for selecting the Great Britain and Ireland team was top of the agenda for the PGA. The mood in America for the continuance of the Ryder Cup was still lukewarm compared with the solid support on this side of the Atlantic. How could we ensure that our Ryder Cup players could actually challenge the supremacy of the Americans? A think tank of top professionals and the PGA came up with the idea that an Order of Merit was the way to achieve this. The first seven places would be filled over five tournaments in the calendar year. The remaining three spots would be at the discretion of a new PGA tournament sub-committee.

Mindful of the 1953 loss at Wentworth, the Ryder Cup team to play in California would not have Peter Alliss and Bernard Hunt in the line-up. This was a devastating blow for the two English professionals. Also part of this new selection procedure was the clause that Order of Merit points would be deducted if a player failed to qualify for the final thirty-six holes of a tourna-ment. A nice thought, or maybe not − what if a player didn't play in a tournament?

Is the Ryder Cup now redundant?

There was very good news from an Irish point of view. Although Fred Daly had made his last Ryder Cup appearance at Wentworth two years previously, Harry Bradshaw would be joined by fellow countryman, Christy O'Connor. Bradshaw lost both his four-somes and singles matches, while newcomer O'Connor lost the only match he played in, his singles encounter with Tommy Bolt.

It was to be yet another disappointing Ryder Cup result for the Great Britain and Ireland side. The Americans had a very convincing win by 8 points to 4. *Quo vadis?* Where do we go from here? Was the Ryder Cup now destined for the scrap heap? Was Sam Ryder's dream finally on its last legs? How much more humiliation was to be inflicted on the home team? Surely, enough was enough. The Americans were the dominant force in world golf. Why prolong the agony?

Despite all the negative factors, much would happen over the next few years to give The Ryder Cup the boost it so badly needed to change the face and future of this biennial event.

1957 LINDRICK GOLF CLUB, SHEFFIELD, YORKSHIRE, ENGLAND

In 1960 the Canada Cup, now the World Cup of Golf, was played in Portmarnock, which was when my interest in golf began. As a teenager and a member of Sutton Golf Club on Dublin's north side, the two main talking points in golfing circles were about the home side's 1957 Ryder Cup victory over the Americans at Lindrick and Ireland's 1958 Canada Cup triumph in Mexico. Ryder Cup victories over the Americans since the very beginning were rarities. The inaugural event referred to earlier was in 1927. Up to and including the 2004 event, thirty-five matches in all have taken place (there were no biennial matches from 1939 to 1945). The Americans have won twenty-four matches, lost nine and tied two. These statistics need to be teased out and explained.

Looking at the statistics from the home side, we won nine, lost twenty-four and tied two. However, the Ryder Cup from 1927 to 1939 was really a Great Britain team. Northern Ireland's Fred Daly was a Great Britain and Northern Ireland team member in 1947, 1949 and 1951. In 1953 the team was in effect the Great Britain and Ireland one, with Southern Ireland's Harry Bradshaw making his first of three appearances (1953, 1955 and 1957). 1977 was the last year of the Great Britain and Ireland team. From 1979 onwards, it would be called Europe.

The 1957 Ryder Cup took another turn for the worse at Lindrick. Two of the world's greatest players, Ben Hogan and Sam Snead, decided not to play. These negative vibes confirmed an imminent death knell for the continuance of the biennial matches. In addition, there was no sponsor for the event until late in the day. Sir Stuart Goodwin, a Yorkshire industrialist, agreed to finance the series of matches but insisted that his own home club of Lindrick would be the venue. The course was just over 6,500 yards – a rather short length, making the Americans clear favourites as they excelled in every department of the game, especially when it came to chipping and putting.

Why not a links course? The counter argument was that the Ryder Cup had been saved yet again. With a revised format for the selection procedure, the matches took place over the fourth and fifth of October. Despite the controversies and difficulties, Great Britain and Ireland beat the Americans 7½ to 4½. The occasion will be remembered for the controversial and humiliating defeat of Dow Finsterwald by Ireland's Christy O'Connor, Sr. (discussed in more depth in Chapter 9). The 1957 matches would mark Harry Bradshaw's final Ryder Cup appearance.

1959 ELDORADO COUNTRY CLUB, PALM SPRINGS, CALIFORNIA, US

Hopes were high for a victory over the Americans following the Great Britain and Ireland success at Lindrick. However, there was no Harry Bradshaw, as he had already made his Ryder Cup departure. Christy O'Connor, Sr. would make his third Ryder Cup appearance and was joined by newcomer Norman Drew from Northern Ireland.

Whether or not the decision to travel by sea to America had been prompted by the tragic 1958 Munich air disaster, the Great Britain and Ireland squad set sail on the *Queen Elizabeth*. Turbulent Atlantic seas caused much sea sickness amongst the golfing fraternity before finally docking at New York. From there, the players and officials flew in a small twin-engine plane destined for Palm Springs. What they didn't reckon on was more turbulence, this time air turbulence as a result of recent hurricane weather, and the plane had to return to New York. There was a huge sigh of collective relief when they touched down safely (see Chapter 9 for more on this).

Despite the weather shock by air and sea, the visiting team was in a buoyant mood. Their opponents had an unpleasant surprise in store for them when they beat the very good team led by Welshman Dai Rees by 8½ to 3½ points. Again, the old chestnut would raise its ugly head. How could the matches be more evenly balanced? The Americans were getting more disillusioned than ever. There was also a controversy of a different kind. Day one of the event had players playing off tees that were in line with the ladies' red tees. Apparently this was to satisfy television coverage in the hope of viewers seeing 'low scoring'.

Christy O'Connor, Sr., paired with his great friend Peter Alliss, defeated the American foursome partnership of Art Wall and Doug Ford in a convincing fashion. Regrettably, Christy was pulverised by 7 and 6 in the final day's singles by Art Wall. Norman Drew's Ryder Cup initiation was a pleasant one. Although he was omitted from the opening day's play, he managed a marvellous halved match in his singles encounter with America's Doug Ford.

A post-mortem would focus attention on a much-needed change in playing format for all future events. The first question to be seriously addressed was the feasibility of having thirty-six-hole matches. A second issue to be seriously considered was the possibility of extending the composition of the team to allow players from the Commonwealth to compete. This would, as some suggested, bring better talent to a team to face the acknowledged might of the Americans.

1961 ROYAL LYTHAM AND ST ANNE'S, LANCASHIRE, ENGLAND
'Festina Lente'

The US would win yet another Ryder Cup, this time at Royal Lytham and St Anne's Golf Club. This was the first Open Championship venue to stage a Ryder Cup match. The home side went down by 9½ to America's 14½ points. Calls for some changes in the playing format voiced after the 1959 matches were implemented at this event. It would still be over two days with four morning and four afternoon foursomes on day one. Day two would be devoted to singles, with eight in the morning and eight in the afternoon.

The American side still wanted to have fourball matches included on the playing agenda. The US players weren't as familiar with the foursome -'alternate' encounters, as they call them. In fact, they would really have liked the biennial matches to be extended to encompass three days. However, the small number of 1961 changes were implemented on a 'festina lente' (hasten slowly) basis.

Ireland's Christy O'Connor, Sr. was again paired with Peter Alliss, and this successful foursome partnership delighted the enthusiastic galleries with a resounding 4 and 3 win over Doug Ford and Gene Littler. However, they were narrowly defeated in the afternoon matches. Christy won one and lost one of the singles matches on the second day.

The 1963 matches would see additional welcome changes to the overall format of the event that would become one of the world's greatest sporting extravaganzas, next to the Olympics and soccer's World Cup.

1963 East Lake Country Club, Atlanta, Georgia, US

Despite more fundamental and far-reaching changes to the matches, Great Britain and Ireland suffered a humiliating defeat at the hands of playing captain Arnold Palmer's team. It was the old saga of American dominance and supremacy over the team that could boast of golf's origins being associated with their side of the globe. Palmer was very proud indeed with his players' magnificent performance in beating their opponents by 23 points to 9.

The Americans were especially happy when their requests for additional changes to the Ryder Cup format, aired at the 1961 matches, were not only listened to but implemented. Fourball matches were added to the event, which led to the biennial event being played over three days. The fact that additional points were on offer was supposed to favour the Great Britain and Ireland side, but the reverse turned out to be the case. With a legacy of defeats, they now had a high pain threshold which would, in fact, stand them in good stead over a considerable period of time to come. Their patience would be tested to the limit.

The O'Connor/Alliss solid pairing met with an unexpected morning foursome defeat on day one. The partnership was quickly dissolved, with Christy O'Connor being paired with Neil Coles over the morning and afternoon fourballs on the second day. They won one and lost the other. Peter Alliss had mixed fortune in his remaining games. He won a half point in one set of fourball matches and lost his other fourball clash. However, the Englishman took a rare scalp in the first series of singles, beating the legendary Arnold Palmer. In the second series he won a half point from 'Champagne' Tony Lema, who sadly lost his life three years later in an air crash.

1965 ROYAL BIRKDALE, SOUTHPORT, LANCASHIRE, ENGLAND

Former lumberjack turned professional golfer Harry Weetman captained the 1965 Great Britain and Ireland squad to face the Americans in the hope of turning the proverbial tides that had been mounting against the home side since the Cup began. The 1965 Ryder Cup might not have gone ahead were it not for the financial intervention and vision of a businessman called Brian Park. In fact, he was a former captain of Royal Birkdale, a former vice-chairman of the British PGA and would go on to become executive director of the same body. Brian Park wanted to raise the profile of Royal Birkdale. He provided the huge financial boost that was needed to ensure the staging of the event, otherwise the Ryder Cup would have become a thing of the past.

It was fortunate that Brian Park had a huge interest in golf. Even though the Ryder Cup was rescued on this as well as on other occasions in the past, the continuance of the event was under constant threat. Regular thrashings of the Great Britain and Ireland side by the Americans certainly didn't help the situation. Brian Park might well be regarded as a visionary in copper-fastening the successful future of Sam Ryder's dream.

Up to now the appeal associated with the Ryder Cup principally revolved around the players and those passionate about the game. Brian Park set about widening that appeal. He visited America, observing firsthand how tournaments there were organised. He was no doubt aware of the American PGA's own financial concerns in staging tournaments there, particularly in the staging of the Ryder Cup throughout its turbulent history. We have only to look at how today's Ryder Cup matches are staged and promoted to realise how far this biennial event has come since its humble beginnings.

Commercial sponsorship gradually came to grips with the enormous future potential that beckoned. Modern tournaments throughout the world encourage mass commercial and public appeal. Today's spectators are not only the purists of the game – they include those who have a social and allied interest in golf. Television has been a huge influence in promoting the sport and bringing live coverage of events into our living rooms. Golf is big business in the modern era, with massive prize funds available to players. In many cases players in the upper echelons of the sport earn arguably more from golf-associated activities like course design, sponsorship, endorsements and advertising than they would from playing the game professionally. In the past, demand from some players commanding huge appearance fees was a controversial issue.

Huge attendances are now recorded at golf events like the Open, the US Masters, the European Open and, of course, the Ryder Cup itself. Each successive year usually records increased attendances at the many tournaments across the globe. Tented villages are the norm at big events today. Those who have attended these international spectacles will see how sophisticated the entire operation has become. Restaurants, dining marquees, exhibitors' tents, mobile banks and post offices, tourist centres, giant screens with updates on the day's progress of play, elaborate media centres together with medical and police presence are some of the by-products associated with the modern game. These profound inno-vations were not a feature at Birkdale, but were arguably in their infancy stage in 1965.

Ireland's Jimmy Martin made his one and only Ryder Cup appearance at Royal Birkdale. It wasn't a happy outing for the man from Rush, on Dublin's north side. The Americans won by 19½ points to 12½. However, Christy O'Connor, Sr. and Peter Alliss had quite a successful innings at Birkdale. They were victorious in their foursomes clash with Ken Venturi and Don January, and like-wise in their foursomes encounter with Billy Casper and Gene Littler. Fortune still favoured the brave as they disposed of Arnold Palmer and Dave Marr in one of the fourball series. Playing against the same opposition in another fourball series, they went down by 6 and 4. However, the overall result again confirmed the Americans as the number one force in world golf. More disap-pointment would follow in 1967 before there was some light to be seen at the end of the tunnel.

1967 CHAMPIONS' GOLF CLUB, HOUSTON, TEXAS, US

Christy O'Connor, Sr. was joined by compatriot Hugh Boyle from Omeath, County Louth, just across the estuary from Warrenpoint, where Northern Ireland's former Ryder Cup player, Ronan Rafferty, came from. Unfortunately, Hugh lost all his matches. The same was true for Christy O'Connor. The Great Britain and Ireland team succumbed yet again to the unquestionable and unchallenged supremacy of the mighty Americans. The result was 23½ points to 3½ in favour of the US. Enough was enough.

The only partnership success involved England's Tony Jacklin and Welshman Dave Thomas. Huggett, Alliss and Coles had wins in the singles matches. Otherwise it was a bleak outcome. Ben Hogan, the American captain, played the mind game at the opening ceremony when he introduced his players as the world's best. This was in stark contrast to the Great Britain and Ireland address given by captain Dai Rees, who went on ad nauseam praising his own players. Hogan said it all using an economy of language and delivering the final and fateful blow to the visitors.

1969 ROYAL BIRKDALE, SOUTHPORT, LANCASHIRE, ENGLAND

For the first time in years, the result of the Ryder Cup matches played again at Royal Birkdale was very acceptable. The two teams tied this historic match, with 16 points apiece. For the first time in Ryder Cup history, each side was composed of twelve players, and also for the first time, all players would use the larger-sized American golf ball. It's important to understand the significance of the bigger picture of events over the three days to appreciate the enormity of this unforgettable occasion.

There had been a great deal of rancour between the two sides almost from the start. But sport and, on this occasion, golf was the ultimate winner. I will always cherish the moment when Jack Nicklaus and Tony Jacklin walked down the eighteenth hole all square in their match. The excitement and tension for spectators and television viewers were unbearable. Imagine what it was like for the players themselves! They had walked off the seventeenth green a few minutes earlier having halved the hole in unbelievable eagles. Their match was the final one, with the two teams tied at 15½ points each. The pressures on Jack Nicklaus and Tony Jacklin were enormous, to say the least. What was to follow was simply magnificent.

Both players made the green in two at the eighteenth. Nicklaus's eagle attempt went five few feet past the hole. Tony's eagle putt to win his match and the Ryder Cup stopped short of the hole by one to two feet. The 'Golden Bear' was next to putt, as he was further away. He holed the short, tricky five-foot putt to leave much shoulder pressure on the newly crowned British Open champion. While Tony was sizing up his own putt, obviously conscious of the enormity of the moment, Jack walked quietly over, picked up the ball and conceded the putt!

What were Jack's thoughts at the time? He felt that if Tony missed the putt, he would be forever criticised. Jack wasn't going to allow that to happen. Jack was also instinctively aware that his gesture would be hugely symbolic for golf and for sport.

That must be the greatest single sporting gesture of all times. He could certainly have missed. It was anything but easy and the pressure under which he found himself added to the difficulty. Sam Ryder would have been more than pleased to have witnessed this gesture of gestures, thus consolidating his philosophy of 'cordial, friendly and peaceful' Ryder Cup matches.

Many years later, I was interviewing Jack's son, Garry, at the European Open in the K Club, and I couldn't let the occasion pass without resurrecting the moment in 1969 when his father made that profound sporting gesture. Garry was very aware of the event. 'Many players and journalists have related the story to me. That would be my dad,' he said.

It was also said at the time that some of Jack Nicklaus's own team-mates were not at all happy with what he did. The same people felt Jacklin could have missed and America would have won another Ryder Cup. However, what Jack Nicklaus did actually sensitised his team-mates into recognising and appreciating the important and irrefutable finer points associated with the game of golf. It promoted friendship and goodwill, qualities that were associated with golf's traditional etiquette. Golf was the winner on that occasion. Both teams and their spectators shared in that holistic triumph.

Irish interest centred on Christy O'Connor, Sr. His contribution to the Ryder Cup result was significant. Playing in one of the morning's opening foursome matches with Peter Alliss, they notched up a half point in their tied match against Billy Casper and Frank Beard. Christy played with Peter Townsend in a four-ball match on day two and added another point to the team's total for day two. He played in both morning and afternoon singles on the final day, winning one match and losing the other.

Tony Jacklin and Peter Townsend were a powerful partnership in the 1969 Ryder Cup. They played against Dave Hill and Tommy Aaron in one of the morning foursomes, opening with three birdies. They played the par five seventeenth in superb fashion. Townsend hit a beautiful three wood with a high trajectory to finish only a few feet from the cup. British Open champion Tony Jacklin confidently holed out for a 3 and 1 team victory. Peter and Tony were seven under par when they closed the door on their opponents.

Sam Snead's boys hit back with venom, winning three of the second series of foursomes. Jacklin and Townsend continued their winning form and were the only pairing to gain points when they beat Billy Casper and Frank Beard by a single hole. The drama, particularly on day two, was magic. Seven of the eight matches went down the eighteenth. At the end of play on the second day, the two teams were level pegging with 8 points apiece.

This Ryder Cup was one of the best ever. It wasn't because one or other of the two teams won, but rather for the simple reason that it was a halved match. Even more importantly, it was one of the very best because of the manner in which the half was achieved. (Incidentally, how long was that famous putt that Jack conceded to Tony? The 'Golden Bear' figures it was between twenty inches and two feet. Given the pressure, it was most definitely missable.)

1971 OLD WARSON COUNTRY CLUB, ST LOUIS, MISSOURI, US

The weather in Missouri was unbearably hot during practice sessions, followed by torrential downpours which caused the cancellation of the traditional opening ceremony, the first time that had happened in the history of the Ryder Cup. When matches finally got underway, they were somewhat behind schedule, but this didn't deter the visitors from getting off to a flying start against a predominantly young American side. In fact, they won three of the four morning's opening foursomes. Hopes were high, but the US side eventually got their act together again and as was their wont, chalked up another victory.

Even though America won the spoils in Missouri, the Great Britain and Ireland team only lost by the credible margin of 18½ to 13½. The opening foursomes referred to on day one featured Ireland's Christy O'Connor, Sr. paired with the rock-steady Englishman, Neil Coles. They beat Billy Casper and Miller Barber 2 and 1.

The Americans recorded a whitewash result in the morning four-balls on the second day, and almost did the same in the afternoon.

They were in cruise control on the final day and won comfortably. The Great Britain and Ireland team's post-mortem resulted in much criticism being targeted at the captain, Eric Brown. Despite the superbly solid start, he was attacked for losing the plot by changing winning partnerships. He was never asked to captain another Ryder Cup side.

1973 MUIRFIELD, GULLANE, SCOTLAND
'QUESTIONING THE NEED TO CHANGE THE STATUS QUO'

As is often the case, the Great Britain and Ireland side started day one in buoyant form. They were convincingly ahead by 5½ points to 1½. Northern Ireland's Eddie Polland made his Ryder Cup debut. Eddie had always been regarded as a very good match player, but unfortunately lost the only two 1973 matches he played in. Christy O'Connor, Sr. would play in his final Ryder Cup, but in so doing he would make his exit in style. In the singles match on the final day, he managed a half point in his match with the reigning 1973 British Open champion, Tom Weiskopf.

In golfing circles, the same perennial post-mortems would raise their ugly heads again. At official level, the seriousness of the imbalance in abilities was again addressed ad nauseam. Surely it had dawned on everyone before now that some radical solution to a situation that had been festering for so long had to be found. There seemed to have been a stubborn reluctance to face a reality that could have so easily been resolved. Suggestions aired so many times in the past would invariably find favour amongst many. Would opening the Ryder Cup to Commonwealth players save the day, and more importantly, save the Ryder Cup? How about English-speaking European players on a Ryder Cup team? How about a European team, full stop?

INTERPRETING SAM RYDER'S DREAM

Of course, there were counter opinions. Some would say there was a dearth of European English-speaking professionals, or more to the point, there was a dearth of good European professional golfers. Did the traditionalists perhaps see a veiled threat? They would say Sam Ryder's dream and deeds of trust legally acknowledged the status quo, i.e. Great Britain and Ireland versus the US. Perhaps it was time to revisit Sam Ryder's dream and reinterpret it. Surely Sam himself would endorse the need for change. The issue was simple – change the system or face the harsh reality of the end of the Ryder Cup.

1975 LAUREL VALLEY, PENNSYLVANIA, US

Three Irish players travelled to America with the 1975 team. Gone was one Christy O'Connor, but on board was another. Christy O'Connor, Jr., a nephew of the great man himself, would make his debut at Laurel Valley. His two compatriots would join forces. Eamonn Darcy from Wicklow and Dublin's John O'Leary would each make Ryder Cup debuts. They weren't the only Ryder Cup newcomers – there were three other first timers: Norman Wood, Tommy Horton and Guy Hunt. This meant in overall terms that the Great Britain and Ireland team might be considered to be lacking in depth of experience.

As had happened when the matches were last played in America (Missouri, 1971), downpours were the order of the day before the official matches were due to begin. This meant exceptionally difficult playing conditions. Many fairways were flooded. For similar reasons, the greens were almost unplayable. The ground staff did Trojan work to ensure play was possible.

With the ongoing debate about the future of the Ryder Cup, it was no surprise to witness an American clean sweep in the morning foursomes on day one. The visiting team did well to have accumulated a total of 11 points when the biennial matches ended on 21 September. However, in beating the visitors, the favourites recorded almost double the points – the final result was Great Britain and Ireland 11, US 21. Profound changes in the Ryder Cup team structure were imminent.

1977 ROYAL LYTHAM AND ST ANNE'S, LANCASHIRE, ENGLAND

American dominance in the Ryder Cup continued unabated and, more importantly, unchallenged in 1977. Despite all the professional cries for changes in the basic structure of the Ryder Cup, there were a few half-hearted attempts to make changes that would turn out to be disastrous. Instead of tackling the root causes of the dilemma that faced them, the powers that be made the unwise decision of greatly reducing the number of matches to be played. The spin-off was to prove detrimental.

There were forty-five-minute intervals between games. This was to accommodate television coverage. The spectators were not considered to be a vital ingredient in the whole scheme of things. There wasn't enough golf to watch for them. There was no atmosphere. The whole affair was a damp squib. Day one was devoted to five morning foursomes with five fourballs in the afternoon. Day two had ten singles matches.

The result was another win for the Americans. They beat their opponents by 12½ to 7½ points. Wicklow man Eamonn Darcy won a half point in his opening foursomes duel with Tony Jacklin against the US pairing of Ed Sneed and Don January. Regrettably, he and Tony lost their afternoon fourball match. Regrettably again, Eamonn lost out in his singles clash with former Irish Open champion, Hubert Green. It was a very close contest, with the Irishman losing on the last hole.

After many turbulent years, the Ryder Cup would be subject to a profound change in the 1979 team composition, though the resulting benefits wouldn't be immediate. It would take time but would pay enormous dividends. *Tús maith leath na hoibre* – a good beginning is half the work, or as we more commonly say, a good beginning is half the battle.

CHAPTER 3

Modern Era

This was a momentous occasion. For the very first time in the history of the Ryder Cup, there would be a new team to play henceforth against America. It would be known as 'Europe'. In hindsight, this would prove to be the best, most far-reaching, profound change to take place in enabling the 'home side' to compete against US teams on a reasonably level playing pitch. This didn't happen overnight, and the benefits wouldn't be immediately obvious.

It cannot be stressed strongly enough how significant Jack Nicklaus's influence was in bringing about this new European structure. There was much resistance to considering ideas like having a world team versus America Ryder Cup, or even an English-speaking European team to play the Americans. There was even more reluctance to consider players from the Commonwealth taking part in the biennial matches. Matches could be played in France, South Africa or even Australia. Would British players find it harder to qualify for matches under these new proposals?

The event had never taken place in Wales since the inaugural matches in 1927. Scotland hosted the matches once, and that was in 1973. Having gone 'Europe', Spain would be the 1997 venue. Ireland never hosted the event, despite the legacy of players that made significant contributions down the years to the Ryder Cup. Fred Daly was on the Great Britain and Ireland team in 1947, and in 1953 Harry Bradshaw heralded a new era of Irish Ryder Cup players. This would change, however, when the matches would take place at the K Club in September 2006.

As mentioned earlier, Jack Nicklaus had contacted Lord Derby, stressing the urgent need for change. Meetings on the issue followed during the 1978 US Masters at Atlanta. All would change – as far as Europe was concerned. What about Asia and the Commonwealth countries? These issues would be addressed with the introduction of the President's Cup in 1994 when the rest of the world (players from all over the world with the exception of Great Britain, Ireland and mainland Europe) would play against America.

So it was that the new Ryder Cup structure came into being for the first time at the Greenbrier in West Virginia. John Jacobs, the man who brought the first advanced driving range to Ireland in the 1960s, would captain the new team. The format for the 1979 matches would incorporate four morning foursomes with four afternoon fourballs on day one. The reverse procedure would happen on day two, followed by twelve singles on the third and final day.

A rather disturbing matter within the European camp caused captain John Jacobs some concern from the word go. This was to be the first outing for a European showcase, but two new members of the squad, Ken Brown and Mark James, didn't help the situation by not being obviously part of the team. When the rest of their team-mates would turn up for various official functions at appointed times and wearing the side's dress code, the two 'rebels' decided to do their own thing. For instance, they wore their own casual attire, an outward sign of disassociating themselves from the traditional format expected on this formal occasion.

As expected, America beat Europe, 17 points to 11. Despite the problems that John Jacobs had to address concerning two English players in his camp, the matches at the Greenbrier were considered to be an outstanding success. (Incidentally, Ireland's Des Smyth made his Ryder Cup debut at this event.)

1981 WALTON HEATH, SURREY, ENGLAND

Europe was now in full swing. Things could only get better from here on in. However, there was an unhappy undercurrent experienced by the 1981 team captain, John Jacobs. Two of Europe's greatest players, Severiano Ballesteros and Tony Jacklin, were not on the team to play the Americans. The 1981 original venue chosen was the Belfry, which didn't meet with much approval. It was a relatively new parkland course and resembled American layouts. Some critics would say we were aping the Americans too much. However, the problem was promptly addressed, with Walton Heath as the chosen venue.

The 'Seve controversy' didn't go away. He was now based in the US and played most of his golf there. The US was where the money was and where players learned to cope with the most extreme pressures. The downside was that he had played too few tournaments at home to be considered for a place on the Ryder Cup team. Despite all this, many sponsors wanted him at their events and were willing to pay for the privilege to have him at their tournaments. He was an excellent player and very exciting to watch. Spectators were mad about him.

This overall view wasn't shared by golfing officialdom on this side of the Atlantic. Appearance money was out of the question and would never be condoned. The Walton Heath Ryder Cup captain, John Jacobs, was always opposed to appearance money being paid to players as long as it applied to both sides of the Atlantic. However, Tony Jacklin supported the notion. He felt the very good players deserved it. The authorities didn't relent, however, and chose Peter Oosterhuis and Mark James to complete their Ryder Cup line-out. Some felt it was ironic to have chosen American-based Oosterhuis over someone like Ballesteros or Jacklin. The same people would have questioned the advisability of having Mark James on the side, given what happened at the 1979 event during John Jacobs's watch, when Mark James and Ken Brown didn't seem to respect the importance of the traditional Ryder Cup protocol in relation to the official opening ceremonies.

That background scenario was very much alive when the matches got underway on 14 September. Des Smyth was on this team. It would mark his final appearance on a Ryder Cup team. However, Des would have a more successful outing this time around, with wins in both the foursomes and fourball matches on day one. He was unfortunate not to have recorded at least one win in the last three remaining matches that followed. The US beat the Europeans by 18½ points to 9½.

1983 PGA NATIONAL GOLF CLUB, PALM BEACH GARDENS, FLORIDA, US

The next best thing to Jack Nicklaus's intervention to save the Ryder Cup was to have Tony Jacklin at the helm of a team. Jacklin was approached to head the squad to Florida, but he had to consider the matter very carefully first. After all, the approach was made by the same officialdom that had omitted him from the team the last time. Some thought he would reject the invitation outright, but surprisingly, Tony accepted the challenge. He was full of uncompromising ideas that he alone could implement. The track record on this side of the Atlantic was absolutely dismal. It was a mammoth task to turn defeat around. Having nailed his colours to the mast, he prioritised his demands before any ball was struck.

As already stated, the American 'feel good' factor played an important part in boosting the US players' confidence. Jacklin knew instinctively what this meant. If you don't feel good, it will invariably have a negative effect on you. The European team would now be selected from an Order of Merit system. Jacklin insisted on having the right to nominate players of his own. He also demanded the very best for his side regarding travel and accommodation. There would be first-class travel for players, their wives and partners, and also their caddies. Officials would have had this in the past; now everyone would benefit. This would have a spin-off advantage – the psychological bonding would influence everyone, and not just the players themselves. They all travelled first class on Concorde.

Seve Ballesteros needed to be on the team. He was one of the world's best players and Tony had to address the issue of appearance money that had plagued the last Ryder Cup outing at Walton Heath. Without having been privy to a subsequent conversation between Tony and Seve, what emerged was a very welcome and pleasant outcome. The Spaniard agreed to come on board. He too shared deep passions about the Ryder Cup. Not only did the two of them know the Americans could be beaten, but they wanted to do it more than anything else.

When the European team arrived in the States, the heat was stifling. Thunderstorms threatened, but the European desire to win was uppermost in the players' minds. The European team captain had his own hotel suite as the HQ. It was there that all the plans and deliberations were put to good effect, thus ensuring the very best from every member of the team. The mood was positive. US captain, Jack Nicklaus, sensed the buoyant mood and optimism in the enemy camp. Some said it even unnerved him, and this became apparent throughout the progress of the matches.

It was a close contest. Although the American side won, they did so only narrowly. The result was the US 14½, Europe 13½. After the end of play on day one, the visitors were ahead by 4½ to 3½ points. Day two results were the complete reverse in favour of the Americans. The two groups were level pegging going into the singles on the final day, with the Americans emerging victorious, but only by a single point. Tony Jacklin had set out to beat the opposition and all but did that. He was a hero, a favourite with the Ryder Cup committee, a favourite with the players and spectators alike.

There was no Irish player on the team.

1985 The Belfry, Sutton Coldfield, West Midlands, England

Tony Jacklin was the flavour of the month. He would lead the European team for a second time at the Ryder Cup matches, this time at the Belfry. The same location had come in for much criticism in 1981 when it was considered a likely venue. Tony Jacklin was still somewhat unhappy, as the layout resembled an American one. In fairness to the Belfry, much course work had been carried out to make it more challenging and spectator and player friendly. There was now an on-course hotel which could accommodate the players and officials.

Jacklin had instilled into his players the absolute need for team spirit. Where this was abundantly evident, it would help to get the players focused and committed to the task at hand. They would exude confidence and this would negatively affect their opponents in an area they themselves once excelled in. The seed merchant Sam Ryder had planted a seed back in 1927 that would blossom in abundance at the Belfry.

Again, nine players would qualify for Ryder Cup matches from the European Order of Merit system. Tony Jacklin wanted to reserve the right to pick another three. The thinking behind his philosophy was to enable him to include the very best Europeans who didn't make the team because of their American commitments. Perhaps it was because Tony was once again at the helm that both Ballesteros and Langer (who won the US Masters earlier in the year) devoted more time than usual playing in European events.

Tony Jacklin led his team to victory at the Belfry, and it was a very convincing one at that. The European team won by 16½ points to 11½. A new era had dawned. After day one the home team was behind by 3½ to 4½ points, but rallied to lead after day two by an aggregate of 9 points to 7. They outplayed their American opponents in the singles encounter on day three by 7½ points to 4½. The home team had turned the tables, as the Americans had so often done in the past. For the second time in a row, there was no Irish player on the team.

1987 MUIRFIELD VILLAGE, COLUMBUS, OHIO, US

These matches would take place in Jack Nicklaus's own backyard – a cliff-hanger was in store. On this occasion, we would have an Irishman on side. Tony Jacklin would face his adversary from 1969 – Jack Nicklaus, who was the 1987 American captain. The Americans had to start favourites – the matches were in America and the 'Golden Bear' himself was the architect of Muirfield Village. He was familiar with every nook and cranny, as was witnessed in the Darcy/Crenshaw singles tussle going down the eighteenth on the last day.

There was huge media interest generated by the loss the Americans suffered at the 1985 Ryder Cup at the Belfry. ABC television transmitted the matches live. There was also worldwide interest in an event that had captured the imagination of golfers and non-golfers alike. The dress code for both teams assumed an importance that matched the formality of the occasion. The American team was proudly presented at the official opening ceremony amidst partisan music and fanfare of all types that conveyed a strong American bias. The Europeans were very much considered the underdogs. Captain Tony Jacklin had a surprise in store for them.

It would be two victories in a row for Tony Jacklin's European team. Europe accumulated 15 points against America's 13. After day one, Europe was ahead by 6 points to 2. At the end of play on day two, the visitors went further ahead with an aggregate of 10½ to 5½. This was a very welcome situation going into day three and the singles clash. They won the overall event with 15 points to 13. One of the exciting results involved Eamonn Darcy's magnificent win over America's Ben Crenshaw. (This match will be discussed in more detail in Chapter 10.)

1989 THE BELFRY, SUTTON COLDFIELD, WEST MIDLANDS, ENGLAND

Tony Jacklin would captain a Ryder Cup team for the last time. The event would turn out to be another tense and exciting one for golfing enthusiasts everywhere. Happily, there would be two Irish players on the team: Order of Merit winner Ronan Rafferty was one; the other was Christy O'Connor, Jr., who was a captain's pick. Again, the matches attracted huge galleries and media interest. It had now become a world-class event appealing to sports enthusiasts the world over.

After the morning foursomes on day one, the American visitors took the lead with 3 points to 1. Tony's squad hit back in the afternoon fourballs with a clean sweep and won all 4 points on offer. The two teams shared the spoils 2 points apiece in both the foursomes and fourballs on day two. It was on then to the singles clash on the third and final day. The Americans won 7 points and Europe 5 points, leaving the 1989 Ryder Cup result at 14 points to each team. Since Europe held the cup, they would continue to be the custodians following the tie at the Belfry.

Those who were at the event or watched the incredible drama unfold on television will remember Christy O'Connor, Jr.'s 200 yards plus two iron to the final hole in his match against Fred Couples. The two players were all square going down the eighteenth, but Christy's incredible second shot to within 'gimmie' range unsettled the American, who played the hole so badly he conceded the Irishman's own putt for a win and a point. The spoils were shared.

The Ryder Cup was now confirmed as the jewel in the golfing crown.

1991 KIAWAH ISLAND, SOUTH CAROLINA, US

This Ryder Cup match must surely go down in the annals as one of the most tense and dramatic in the game. Sam Ryder would have loved the event, apart from some of the unhappy undercurrents that were obvious between players from both teams. Poor gamesmanship and unfriendliness between some individual players did not lend themselves to an event of this calibre. Then there was the questionable situation coming down the eighteenth in the Langer/Irwin match. The American hit a very bad tee shot that was destined for jungle territory, but suddenly ended up in the middle of the fairway. Situations like these do not belong to Sam Ryder's dream.

From a high at the last event in England, when Christy O'Connor, Jr. rifled an arrow-straight two iron to within a few feet to beat Fred Couples and so retain the cup, the European team were brought down to earth and Langer literally down to his knees at Kiawah Island. Bernard Gallacher had taken over the captaincy from Tony Jacklin. It was David Feherty's one and only Ryder Cup appearance and he was very proud indeed to have beaten the late Payne Stewart in the singles. Feherty is now a golf commentator on American television.

An interesting event took place in advance of the matches at Kiawah Island. The Americans are renowned for their welcoming hospitality to their visiting teams. The European team was invited to a film on the history of the Ryder Cup. Of course, the same history will tell us about the indisputable supremacy and dominance of their players since the inaugural matches in 1927. Was this a subtle attempt at undermining the confidence of the visiting team and at the same time instilling passion into the American squad?

The 1991 matches got off to a good start for the visiting team. One of their strongest pairings, Ballesteros and Olazábal, registered a win from the first of the morning foursomes. However, at the end of day one they trailed 3½ points to 4½. The same points were reversed on day two in favour of the Europeans. The rest is history, but it is worthwhile recalling the final day's singles, when the visiting team was still there with a fighting chance. Mark Calcavecchia had been four up on Scotland's Colin Montgomerie with four holes left, only to lose every remaining hole. Each player got a half point.

Bernhard Langer and Hale Irwin were battling it out going down the eighteenth. Theirs was the last match out and they were all square. The Americans needed just a half point to win the Ryder Cup. Langer had been two down after fourteen holes, but fought back courageously to be level with one hole left. He made the fairway on eighteen. Irwin hooked viciously left into the crowd but miraculously found a perfect lie on the fairway for his second shot! Hale Irwin went on to make a bogey five on the last green. The German was on in two some thirty feet from the cup. His putt went about six feet beyond the hole. To hole a six footer would win the Ryder Cup and silence the understandably partisan American galleries, but more importantly, it would mean a Ryder Cup triumph for his team on American soil. The tension was unprecedented. Langer missed.

We spoke earlier about Ryder Cup pressure. The Bernhard Langer putt must be the greatest example of the ultimate pressure in top-class golf. Whenever Kiawah Island is mentioned in golfing circles, the whole world empathises with the German. The agony of that devastating moment in time must come back periodically to haunt him. I recall Bernhard saying in a subsequent interview, 'I did my best. That's all anyone can do.' He was nevertheless devastated. Colin Montgomerie, playing in his inaugural Ryder Cup event, remembers seeing the German in tears alongside Seve Ballesteros shortly afterwards. It was emotionally draining. Had Langer only sunk that putt – in effect two putting the final green – Europe and the US would have tied.

1993 THE BELFRY, SUTTON COLDFIELD, WEST MIDLANDS, ENGLAND

The biennial event would create its own drama at the 1993 event. The ever-popular Tom Watson would captain his side against the Europeans at the Belfry. Bernard Gallacher had been reluctant to take charge of a team for the second time, but under persistent, gentle persuasion, he agreed. When the event got underway, there were rumours that the undercurrents prevalent at Kiawah Island surfaced once again. Both Tom Watson and Bernard Gallacher would not condone such behaviour. Golfing tradition and good behaviour were opposite sides of the one coin.

Tom Watson took his captaincy very serious. As a psychologist he paid particular attention to the psychological aspects of winning. He went to the trouble of pacing and measuring the course, observing and noting where tee shots would land in all types of weather. His team was invited to the White House to receive official good luck wishes from President Bill Clinton.

The heretofore strong partnership of Ballesteros and Olazábal suffered a blow when they were beaten by Tom Kite and Davis Love in the morning foursomes on day one. However, at the end of the day's play, the Europeans led by 2½ points to 1½. The home side won the morning foursomes on day two by 3 points to 1, but the tables were turned, with the visitors winning the foursomes by exactly the same margin. Montgomerie and Faldo played solidly over the two days, winning 2½ points and dropping 1½.

The Europeans led by 8½ points to 7½ going into the final day's singles. Montgomerie ended up with an unbeaten record after the singles, but the European team could only manage 4½ points out of a total of 12 on offer. The Americans, with 7½ points, brought their aggregate to 15, beating the home side's total of 13 points. The Ryder Cup belonged to the American side.

1995 OAK HILL COUNTRY CLUB, ROCHESTER, NEW YORK, US

The rules would be changed again to allow the European captain two 'wild cards'. It would be Bernard Gallacher's last of three captaincies in a row and it proved to be third time lucky. After a brief absence, Ireland would be represented this time by

Dublin's Philip Walton. The word going around in American circles was that the Americans had regained their supremacy in the Ryder Cup. They were on home soil and they were going to drive the proverbial nail home to consolidate dominance in world golf.

Ian Woosnam and Nick Faldo were Bernard's two 'wild cards'. The US captain's choices were Curtis Strange and Fred Couples, players of great ability and track record. The morning foursomes on day one were shared, but the Americans won three of the afternoon fourballs. Day two opened with 3 points to 1 foursomes' win for Bernard's side. In the afternoon's fourballs, the Americans hit back in similar fashion, with a 3 points to 1 result.

Going into the final day's singles trailing by 7 points to 9, the Europeans faced an uphill battle. What was normally the preserve of the Americans – to excel in the singles on the final day – suddenly emanated from Bernard Gallacher's group. The Europeans chalked up 7½ points to the Americans' 4½. Europe won the overall matches by one point. They would be the proud custodians of Sam Ryder's precious chalice.

There was much drama that led to this great result. The Faldo/Strange clash was exciting, to say the least. The pair had been rivals over the years. Faldo would privately recall how Curtis beat him in a play-off for the 1998 US Open at Brookline. Their Ryder Cup match went to the last hole. Strange played the hole rather badly, carding a bogey, and opened the door for Faldo, who faced a six-foot pressure putt to register a point on the board for Bernard. He got it.

Another drama unfolded on the course involving Philip Walton. He was three up on the great Jay Haas with three to go. There was much tension and anxiety on the shoulders of both players. Haas was in the bunker at the sixteenth and went on to hit a bad shot out that hit the pin at speed and dropped in. There were two holes remaining. Haas won the seventeenth also. The drama heightened at the eighteenth, where both players played the hole rather indifferently. However, Walton played that bit better to have his short bogey putt conceded.

The Europeans had beaten their opponents in America, again! American supremacy was now under question.

1997 VALDERRAMA GOLF CLUB, SOTOGRANDE, SPAIN

Valderrama was the venue for the 1997 Ryder Cup matches. There was much debate and controversy generated about the event going to Spain. After all, Wales and Ireland had been part of the Ryder Cup tradition long before Spain. Why should Spain be conferred with the honour of a hosting? As far back as the 1970s, voices were being raised advocating change to redress the total imbalance in Ryder Cup matches. We will also recall how these pleas to widen the team structure met with a stubborn reluctance on the part of officialdom. It wasn't until 1979 that these calls for change were heeded and taken on board. Now the 'Seve factor' appeared to have influenced the authorities in his country hosting the 1997 matches.

With Spain hosting the event, Seve was the obvious choice for captain. As an individual he had the enthusiasm, the drive, the will and the passion to lead and motivate his team. Some might even say he had all of these qualities in abundance, but he all put played the shots for individuals. Many found his leadership style to be intrusive and overpowering. However, his team beat the Americans.

One of his main concerns was the team. He would have loved to have had three picks. He wanted the pedigree of Nick Faldo and the doggedness of Jesper Parnevik. But he also wanted his compatriot José Maria Olazábal on the team. He knew Olazábal inside out. They themselves were a strong foursomes and fourball partnership in many Ryder Cup battles. The Order of Merit table didn't allow him the freedom he wanted. His friend Ollie didn't make it through the normal channels of qualification.

However, his other compatriot, Miguel Angel Martin, made the team, but a wrist injury left him out of much competitive tournament play over a prolonged period. Seve was worried and demanded that Miguel Angel have a fitness inspection. He refused. He had officially qualified for the event. He believed rest would sort out his problem in time for the official Ryder Cup matches. Things got progressively nasty, but Seve stepped in and spoke at length with his compatriot. Reason would prevail at the end of the day. Martin would remain an official member of the 1997 Ryder Cup team but would not play owing to that injury.

Severiano Ballesteros got his way and his long-time friend, José Maria Olazábal, would replace Miguel Angel on the European team.

US captain Tom Kite, like his compatriot before him, did his homework extremely well. He was particularly interested in the weather patterns experienced in this region of Spain over the previous thirty years. This research confirmed little or no rain as a matter of course in Sotogrande. He familiarised himself with the intricacies of the course, paying special attention to the infamous seventeenth. In short, he was thorough and meticulous in his attitude and approach to everything.

The Americans were the favourites to win the cup. They could boast of six major champions on their team. Tiger Woods would make his first Ryder Cup appearance. Northern Ireland's Darren Clarke would also make his debut. The Spanish captain wanted to emulate Bernard Gallacher's winning performance the last time round.

Tom Kite got one hell of a shock on the opening day when heavy downpours caused a two-hour delay. In fact, there was a threat that play would be abandoned altogether. However, mammoth work from ground and green staff relieving the rain-soaked fairways and sodden greens enabled play to take place on a course that had excellent drainage.

The opening fourballs on day one were shared. The Europeans managed better than their opponents in the afternoon foursomes, winning by 4½ points to 3½. Day two saw the home squad take six of the 8 points on offer. Montgomerie paired with Clarke excelled, as did Woosnam and Björn. Olazábal and Rocca crucified Love and Couples in the afternoon foursomes. Tom Kite was thunderstruck. What had gone so disastrously wrong with his meticulous preparations?

He sought guru advice from former President George Bush, who was in attendance at Valderrama. After all, he had experienced many difficulties in his presidency. The advice seemed to work wonders, for there was much red to be seen on the score boards on the final day's play. The Americans managed twice the points the Europeans gathered, but it wasn't enough. They were shy by one point. The European team won the 1977 Ryder Cup matches by 14½ to 13½. The Americans would have to wait another two years for their matches at Brookline before they could avenge their shock defeat of 1997.

1999 BROOKLINE, BOSTON, MASSACHUSETTS, US

Mark James was the European captain of the 1999 Ryder Cup, with Ben Crenshaw leading the Americans. Unfortunately, Brookline may be remembered for all the wrong reasons.

The visitors got off to a magnificent start, accumulating 6 points out of a maximum of 8. They shared the spoils with the Americans on day two, and going into day three, Mark James was in a buoyant mood as his team led by 10 points to 6. The American side needed 8 points from the singles to tie and 8½ to win. The Europeans needed only 4½ points out of a possible 12 to win. The Americans got 8½. From absolutely nowhere, they avenged their recent defeat in Homeric style. Padraig Harrington, making his Ryder Cup debut, beat Mark O'Meara in the singles, Colin Montgomerie beat the late Payne Stewart and Paul Lawrie accounted for Jim Maggert. They were the only three winners from a European team of twelve.

Yet what happened at Brookline was a vexation to the spirit of golf. After Justin Leonard holed his unbelievable forty-five-foot putt on the seventeenth, his fellow players, wives and caddies raced across the green in boorish triumph. The partisan galleries and marshals were reluctant to stem the tide of chaos that emanated unchallenged. Olazábal maintained his dignified silence amidst the onslaught of partisan intrusion. He still had a twenty-five-foot putt. How he could maintain any kind of composure under those circumstances? He missed.

HISTORY MOVES WITH THE TRAMP OF EARTHQUAKE FEET

The 2001 Ryder Cup matches due to take place at the Belfry were postponed as a mark of respect to all those who tragically died in the terrorist attacks of 11 September 2001.

There was much debate at first about the matches going ahead or not. The Americans had other, more serious preoccupations to consider. 9/11 was uppermost in their minds. The Ryder Cup authorities wondered about the matches being cancelled out of sympathy for their colleagues, with a possible resumption of matches in 2003. Upon further reflection, though, there were other considerations. Would the team for the 2001 event be the same for 2003? Or would it perhaps be more advisable to postpone the matches for one year and keep the same team for 2002? This seemed to be the more appropriate course of action and is what was decided on. Future events would take place on even years.

2002 THE BELFRY, SUTTON COLDFIELD, WEST MIDLANDS, ENGLAND

Montgomerie played a blinder and justified his selection as a wild card. Padraig Harrington partnered him in the winning fourballs on the second day. Going into the twelve singles on the final day, the two teams were level pegging.

Sam Torrance galvanised his troops admirably to ensure overall victory. Ireland's Paul McGinley fought back from two down with six to play against Jim Furyk. Paul had a putt of some say six to ten feet to win the Ryder Cup. His caddie reminded him that it was exactly the same line he'd had a few years previously in the Benson & Hedges tournament. He heeded the advice, calmly lined it up and found the bottom of the cup. It was a dramatic end to a classic event. With the confirmation that Europe had won, a small number of enthusiastic supporters carried McGinley shoulder high and baptised him in the Belfry waters.

2004 OAKLAND HILLS COUNTRY CLUB, MICHIGAN, US

The Americans have been analysing why their dominance in Ryder Cup matches has plummeted in recent times. A criticism voiced after yet another defeat, and a devastating one at that, suggested that it was due to a lack of team commitment. Some American spectators suggested that they didn't gel, or that Hall Sutton didn't inspire his teams as other captains have done.

'He should have taken a leaf out of captain Bernhard Langer's book,' was another angry comment emanating from an unhappy fan. Langer was serene, quietly confident and inspired his team by gently igniting the passion that lay within. He knew how to trigger a deep-rooted desire to win. Honour, pride and glory were qualities he resurrected in everyone under his charge. These qualities were channelled and directed into meaningful competition.

Europe won by 18½ points to 9½ on American soil. This wasn't the first time this happened, but when repeated, it damaged the opposition's self-esteem and confidence. The Americans were getting a taste of their own medicine that they had for so long inflicted on others. After day one, Europe had a convincing lead of 6½ points to 1½. This was stretched to a lead of 11 points to 5 after day two. Day three turned out to be a formality, with Langer's team in cruise control en route to another classic performance.

Montgomerie amassed points in three matches out of four. Clarke managed points from four out of his five matches, McGinley accumulated points in the three games he played and Harrington, like Clarke, managed points from four of his five outings.

The next Ryder Cup event will take place in September 2006 at the K Club in Ireland. The one advantage for the visiting American team is that the course resembles one of their own. They have to be careful, however, as a new legacy of Ryder Cup supremacy is now firmly in the grip of the new stars, the Europeans.

SECTION 2

Ireland
Hosts
the
2006
Ryder Cup

CHAPTER 4

The Bids

There were two official bids from two Irish clubs to have the 2006 Ryder Cup staged at their venues: Portmarnock and Druids Glen. Mount Juliet didn't formally make a bid, but there was much speculation in the golfing world at the time that it might have been interested in hosting the biennial event. This chapter evaluates the three clubs' credentials as potential host locations.

PORTMARNOCK'S 1993 BID

Ireland won the Canada Cup in 1958 in Mexico. Two years later, this prestigious team event would be hosted in Ireland. There was never any question as to where the event would be staged. Ireland is proud to be home to one-third of the golf links in the world. Two of these, Royal Portrush and Royal County Down, are in Northern Ireland, and another two, Ballybunion and Portmarnock, are in the Republic. These same four links layouts figured in the top dozen or so best links in the world in the late 1950s and early 1960s. Little has changed since. Some new magnificent links courses have emerged in recent times, and these are very high-calibre layouts indeed. Waterville links in Kerry, Carne links in Mayo and the European Club in Wicklow are three such courses.

However, tradition would still single out the original four being top of the pile. Of the chosen four, Portmarnock arguably had a slight edge on the others, and it was this venue that would accommodate the Canada Cup.

There were naturally many excellent parkland courses at the time of staging the Canada Cup in Ireland, with others like Druids Glen and Mount Juliet coming on stream much later on, but given the fact that our traditions were by and large associated with links, it was wisely decided to adhere to our golfing heritage by scheduling the event at this famous links on Dublin's north side. The course was truly challenging – 7,000 yards plus with the golfing emphasis being on sandy soil, deep bunkers and sand dunes. Apart from a few drains and small natural ponds, water did not really feature. The only water was the surrounding Irish Sea bordering the course. This is in stark contrast to modern-day courses, mainly parkland, where the new emphasis on hazards is placed on huge artificial lakes and long, vast expanses of flat sand traps that are more inviting to play from than the traditional rough.

The world-renowned links at Portmarnock should have hosted a Ryder Cup. Much to the dismay of many golf enthusiasts, it didn't. Padraig Slattery was the 2005 captain of this national asset, and no one was more disillusioned than he when Spain managed to host the Ryder Cup before Ireland. Padraig was a member of a small group under the chairmanship of Tom Cuddihy charged with bringing the Ryder Cup to Portmarnock. They were serious contenders and were very hopeful of the event being staged at their venue in 1993. Nobody from the golfing world would have questioned Portmarnock's proud legacy and rich pedigree when it came to hosting a world-class event; they have an envious track record in that regard.

The inaugural Irish Open Championship was held there in 1927, the same year Sam Ryder's biennial matches began. Abe Mitchell, whose figurine adorns the Ryder Cup trophy, won the 1929 Irish Open at Portmarnock. Countless Irish Open Championships have taken place there since. The last Irish winner of this coveted title was former Ryder Cup player John O'Leary, who shot an aggregate winning score of 287 at Portmarnock in 1982.

The Ladies' Championship was staged here in 1901, 1930 and 1954, and the 1954 British Ladies' Amateur Championship was also held at Portmarnock. In 1949, the club staged the Amateur Championship. This was followed by the famous 1959 Dunlop Masters Tournament where the maestro, Christy O'Connor, came from behind with a scintillating last-round 66 to snatch the title that was so tightly in the grasp of Ireland's legendary amateur, Joe Carr.

As already briefly stated, this magnificent venue staged the hugely successful 1960 Canada Cup. Those who attended this event will remember the week-long June heat wave that graced the fairways and enticed over 60,000 spectators to follow the golfing stars. It was a rare occasion to witness burnt fairways at Portmarnock, but South Africa's Gary Player took full advantage of the exceptional conditions and the extra run on the ball by shooting a course record 65.

A year later, Portmarnock was chosen as the venue for the 1970 International Alcan Tournament, won by Australian Bruce Devlin. Again the public thronged the fairways to sample the atmosphere of a world-class event at a world-class venue.

Praise has been lavished upon this famous links track over the years. The late Sir Henry Cotton regarded Portmarnock as one of the very best courses in the world. He went on to single out the par 4 fourteenth hole as the best he had seen anywhere. Five times British Open champion, Tom Watson, said Portmarnock was as fine a links as any he had encountered playing his many Open Championship venues. Mark O'Meara was another famous name that is known to have sung the praises of this famous links so many times. Four-time Ryder Cup captain, Tony Jacklin, was equally vocal in promoting this legendary venue being worthy of a Ryder Cup hosting. Another former British Open champion, Tom Weiskopf, went a stage further by saying, 'The Open Championship should be played at Portmarnock!' Although Severiano Ballesteros extolled the virtues of this northside links as an ideal Ryder Cup venue, he didn't hide his own understandable partisan feelings, for he hoped his country might get the positive nod for the 1993 event to be staged at Club de Campo in Madrid. Finally, you can get no better a recommendation than the one that has been put forward by a former Ryder Cup player and BBC Television golf commentator, Peter Alliss. Ireland, he reminds us, has some of the finest links courses in the world and he believes Portmarnock is world class. If a major event like the Ryder Cup is to be staged in Ireland, the undisputed pedigree that Portmarnock enshrines speaks volumes. There is little or no evidence of artificiality about the course. It is one of the most natural links in the world.

The reverse opinion would focus on the modern interpretation of staging Ryder Cup matches, wherein politics would play a significant and deciding role. The former executive director of the European Tour, Ken Schofield, made no apologies when he said his organisation was there to serve the needs of his players. Politics, business and investment all play a part in deciding where the biennial matches are to take place. This philosophy is by no means an attempt to downgrade or undermine the K Club as the venue for the 2006 event. The K Club has created and generated its own pedigree in a relatively short space of time. They have already hosted the European Open for quite a number of years and have committed themselves to this undertaking up to and including 2015. The course, designed by Arnold Palmer, is no doubt a quality course and will prove to be a challenging venue.

In addition, Dr Smurfit's club has hosted two PGA Cups and the Junior Ryder Cup. He has a proven record and commitment. These undisputed facts were taken on board by the European Tour and the Ryder Cup Committee before a final decision on a venue was reached.

I interviewed Padraig Slattery, the 2005 captain of Portmarnock, about these issues, because he, too, along with his colleagues, was of the firm conviction that the necessary financial commitment and investment referred to above could be generated by having Portmarnock as the 1993 venue for the biennial matches. They believed that Portmarnock should be chosen on merit.

'THE BRAD' AND PORTMARNOCK

Padraig and I spoke about his club's famous professional, 'The Brad'. 'Our famous links and Harry are inextricably linked,' he said. 'He was one of our greatest ambassadors, in fact, one of Ireland's foremost ambassadors to have left a mark all over the world. He was the consummate professional who went about his daily routine with dedication and commitment. Harry was at his post from early in the morning until late in the evening and this work ethic embraced weekends. I had the honour of playing with him on a number of occasions in the early 1970s, when he was past his best. Still, he was almost impossible to beat in his heyday. He would size his opponents up, give them six, seven or eight holes of an advantage and invariably beat them. I myself fell victim to his skills. But the experience of playing with Harry, a former Ryder Cup player, was invaluable.'

What kind of person was Harry Bradshaw? Padraig elaborated: 'He was a perfect gentleman who went about his business with a quiet passion. His very pleasant demeanour was one of his outstanding attributes that touched all who came into contact with him. He was also a great storyteller. He would sit with anyone who loved golf as he did, tell stories about his glorious past. He was particularly proud and passionate about his Ryder Cup days and about the unforgettable occasion when he and his friend Christy O'Connor won the 1958 Canada Cup for Ireland in Mexico. He had a remarkably relaxed manner in the way he would bring great memories of days past very much back to life. He is sadly missed.'

Padraig Slattery joined Portmarnock in 1974. He was no stranger to a links course, as he hailed from Lahinch, another area associated with one of Ireland's magnificent links. When the possibility of the 1993 Ryder Cup coming to Ireland became a reality, Portmarnock was a serious contender. The club formed a powerful sub-committee to make their official presentation to the Ryder Cup Committee. They wanted to convince the experts why their links should host the prestigious Ryder Cup matches. Portmarnock's serious campaign culminated in a formal presentation to the PGA on 14 March 1990. Additional bids, some say, emerged from other interested parties, such as Royal Birkdale, Ballybunion and the K Club, which hadn't even been built at the time. Spain also threw its hat into the ring.

Portmarnock's presentation highlighted the proud tradition Ireland had in its Ryder Cup players. It also drew attention to the significant contributions made by our country's players throughout Ryder Cup history. Players like O'Connor, Sr. and Bradshaw were specifically mentioned. It also focused on the modern era that would acknowledge the great winning performances of Irish players like Philip Walton, Christy O'Connor, Jr. and Eamonn Darcy.

Portmarnock was beyond a shadow of a doubt a prime links venue and must have been a frontrunner to host the 1993 biennial event. Purists of the game would have wholeheartedly agreed with the sentiments aired by the majority of professional golfers who regarded Portmarnock as the number one choice for the Republic of Ireland. Frank Fahey, TD and Minister for Sport at the time, confirmed his government's backing and support for the matches to be played on this world-renowned links course. Similar sentiments about having the matches at Portmarnock were aired by two former Ryder Cup players, Peter Oosterhuis and Peter Townsend, when I spoke with them during one of the Irish Open Championships held at Denis Kane's Druids Glen in the late 1990s. They recognised that there were great parkland courses that could successfully stage a Ryder Cup, but many pros, they felt, would like to see the event on a course that reflected our traditions, i.e. on a links. 'Perhaps it will come to Portmarnock one day,' said Peter Oosterhuis.

THE PRESENTATION COMMITTEE

The members of the official presentation committee were Tom Cuddihy, the-then captain of the club; David Keane, club honorary secretary; Peter Townsend, Portmarnock professional at the time; Con Haugh, Cospóir; Bord Fáilte's Simon Tormey; and Padraig Slattery (Portmarnock). The PGA and European Tour officials would make a thorough evaluation of Portmarnock's proposal. The PGA's Ryder Cup Committee included the Earl of Derby, PGA president; John Lindsey, PGA executive director; Neil Coles, PGA chairman; Ken Schofield, executive director of the European Tour; George O'Grady, assistant to the executive director; with Philip Weaver and Jim Stevens from the PGA.

These overseas alumni were to be invited to attend an Irish Open at Portmarnock and observe how this famous links could accommodate an event of the magnitude of a Ryder Cup. Tony Jacklin, Bernard Gallacher and Neil Coles would have had first-hand experience of the links, having played there on numerous occasions during their professional careers. Part of Portmarnock's presentation dealt with meeting infrastructural needs. On-site luxury hotel accommodation, an upgraded and restyled clubhouse, a landscaped tarmac parking facility for players and officials, a helicopter pad, the erection of temporary office/administration buildings and the utilisation of the 200-acre Baldoyle Racecourse site for public parking with a shuttle bus service to the course were some of the priority accommodating changes planned for the 1993 Ryder Cup. In addition, the course would have the advantage of being ideally located to air and sea ports. An excellent bus and train service would complement these facilities.

Natural spectator-friendly amphitheatres abound at the links, with enormous space to allow for a tented village on a grand scale. This 'village' would be adjacent to the ninth and eighteenth greens, incorporating centres to cater for a multiplicity of needs, such as media, restaurants, a post office, travel (bus, air and sea service), tourist information, shops, gardaí, medical, news and progress updates and corporate hospitality.

One of the main criticisms voiced against Portmarnock's staging of the 1993 Ryder Cup was its poor parking facilities. That problem would be seriously addressed in 1990 by the timely intervention of the late Minister of Defence, Mr Brian Lenihan, TD. He would arrange for Bailey bridges to be built from Baldoyle Racecourse over the estuary to Portmarnock. As mentioned, public car parking was to be confined to the racecourse, with a shuttle bus service being laid on to convey spectators across the estuary and on to the course proper.

All in all, there was a huge amount of goodwill towards Portmarnock hosting the event. However, the final decision would come from the Ryder Cup Committee. It was said that this committee was split in their deliberations, leaving the casting vote to its chairman, the late Lord Derby, who exercised it in favour of conferring the Ryder Cup hosting on the Belfry. Despite their flawless presentation, Portmarnock's club captain, Tom Cuddihy, received the news shortly afterwards informing them of their unsuccessful bid. Neither would it be chosen to host the 2006 series.

DRUIDS GLEN

Director-chief executive, Denis Kane, spoke to me earlier this year about Druids Glen's bid to have the 2006 Ryder Cup staged at this now-famous parkland venue.

In 1990, a consortium of Irish businessmen purchased the property and grounds at the Woodstock Estate near Kilquade in Wicklow. Within five years the creation we have come to know so well emerged. Druids Glen, often referred to as the 'Augusta of Europe', has in the interim become one of Ireland's greatest parkland courses. One year after its official opening, Druids Glen hosted the first of four consecutive Irish Opens (1996–99). The course is situated some twenty miles from Dublin in Ireland's sunny south-east. Golf architects Pat Ruddy and the late former Irish golf international Tom Craddock recognised the gem that would be created against the beautiful scenic background of soft rolling hills, purple glens and silvery streams.

Ireland's mystic past is resurrected at the picturesque par three twelfth, which is adjacent to an ancient druids' altar. This is followed by the signature par four thirteenth hole, which is both intimidating and challenging for the finest exponents of golf. The drive is from an elevated tee to a dog leg hole. Your goal is to make the rather narrow fairway off the tee, avoiding the meandering snake-like silvery stream that eats into and runs parallel to the fairway. The 'risk and reward' approach shot still poses a threat, with the wide-yawning pond there to welcome an errant shot. Having negotiated this formidable challenge, you have to conquer the intricacies of a long, undulating green with water on one side and hazardous rough on the other side. The hole is reminiscent in difficulty with the thirteenth in Mount Juliet.

Druids Glen won the 2000–01 Golf Course of the Year – the Hertz International Travel Award. It also hosted the 2002 Seve Trophy, a biennial Ryder Cup-type event between leading tour players from Great Britain and Ireland and Continental Europe. More recently, a second championship course came on stream. This 2003 layout is called Druids Heath and boasts natural rock quarries, lakes and gorse.

In 1997, Druids Glen tendered its own bid to host the 2005 biennial event (because of 9/11, the event was rescheduled for 2006). Their official presentation committee consisted of directors Joe Cowhie, Donal Flinn and Denis Kane. Their asset was short listed as a potential host for the 2006 Ryder Cup. As a club, it has supported all the promotional events for the Ryder Cup in Ireland at all the major European golf events. Their envious track record was part of the presentation: their vast experience achieved with Irish Opens, and in the knowledge of gaining further experience with additional Irish Opens and the Seve Trophy planned for 2002. The success of these events were based on infrastructure, space, the natural amphitheatre, beauty and design for the vast number of spectators, phenomenal golfing challenge, and an Irish design by Pat Ruddy and the late Tom Craddock. All of these qualities proved that their ability to host a Ryder Cup event were beyond question.

Before the official announcement regarding the 2005 (now 2006) hosting was made at Valderrama in 1997, Ken Schofield, the-then director of the European Tour, informed Druids Glen that the K Club had been awarded the Ryder Cup for 2005. He thanked the members of the presentation committee for all their efforts and support. Denis Kane, who was in northern Europe at the time, was naturally disappointed that Druids Glen wasn't successful in its bid, but he was extremely magnanimous in expressing delight at this great sporting spectacle coming to Ireland. Denis Kane sees the main benefits accruing will be in the future, 2007, 2008 and onwards.

The hosting of a Ryder Cup begs the serious question: What are the criteria, in rank order, for determining where the venue should be? Naturally, there would be a combination of factors that would govern a final decision: the quality of the course, the regional infrastructure and the financial support provided to both the event and the European Tour in general. However, many people in golfing circles nowadays would say that the main criterion appears to be financial. This financial consideration comes down to an individual club's viability. How does this augur for the future?

MOUNT JULIET

Contrary to what many people think, Mount Juliet did not make a formal presentation bid to host the Ryder Cup matches. This course, designed by Jack Nicklaus, enshrines all the qualities one would attribute to and expect of a high-class venue, a venue that could proudly play host to golf's most prestigious event. The beautiful parkland layout hosted three Irish Opens in 1993, 1994 and

1995. Dr Tim Mahony, the inspiration behind Mount Juliet, spoke to me earlier this year about the course and the situation regarding Mount Juliet's view of hosting the Ryder Cup.

In the early 1990s, when the possibility of Ireland hosting the Ryder Cup event was a talking point in golf and tourism circles, Mount Juliet was no different to other quality courses being suggested as a possible host venue. Naturally, if the Ryder Cup authorities were to approach Killeen Investments (Tim Mahony's investment vehicle) to have one of the world's most important sporting spectacles take place at Mount Juliet, they would have been interested.

Who decides on a Ryder Cup venue and what are the criteria applied? The venues for the next six Ryder Cups have already been confirmed, but for the 2018 event onwards, the PGA European Tour, as managing partner on this side of the Atlantic, has the final decision on selecting the host nation and venue after consultation with the founding partner on behalf of the Tour membership. Mount Juliet has had a very healthy relationship with the PGA European Tour over the years. As already stated, it has staged three Irish Opens, as well as a Seniors' Irish Open. Their credentials for staging the Ryder Cup were impeccable and there was no question about the regional infrastructure not living up to the Tour's expectations.

Initial informal conversations about a possible Ryder Cup hosting at Mount Juliet did take place with the club. During one of those Irish Opens at Mount Juliet, the-then executive director of the PGA European Tour, Ken Schofield, was asked what it might take to host the biennial matches there. Ken's reply would have been the same as the criteria listed above. Nothing more emanated from the informal enquiries; there was no presentation and no bid, though Ken Schofield did have the courtesy to inform Mount Juliet in advance of the public announcement of their choice of the K Club as the 2006 venue.

Seven years on, the International Federation of PGA Tours, which is responsible for the annual staging of the WGC–American Express Championship, honoured Mount Juliet by choosing it as the championship venue for 2002 and 2004. Their philosophy was to alternate between an American and a European location. It had already been to Spain earlier and the general feedback from there was somewhat disappointing, as the spectator numbers were poor. The International Federation of PGA Tours believed it should go to northern Europe next time there was to be a European staging of the event, and so Mount Juliet was invited to stage the championship. This proved to be an inspired choice, as the Championship attracted a record 125,000 people in its first staging, and the decision was quickly made to stage the event at Mount Juliet again in 2004.

The 2002 championship saw America's Tiger Woods take the coveted title, while South African Ernie Els captured first prize in 2004.

So did Mount Juliet throw their hat into the ring for Ryder Cup consideration? In a vague way, they did. Did they pursue the matter actively? Most certainly not. Did they make a bid and an official presentation? No.

CHAPTER 5

The K Club is the Venue

IRELAND GETS TO HOST THE RYDER CUP

Padraig O hUiginn was chairman of Bord Fáilte (now Fáilte Ireland) from 1993 to 1996. He was a member of the same organisation for a further five years. In Charles Haughey's government, Padraig was Secretary-General of the Taoiseach's Department and negotiated the Programme for National Recovery. Years ago, agriculture was Ireland's number one rural industry, but that role has been taken on in more recent times by tourism. Padraig and I met in July 2005 to talk about the Ryder Cup coming to Ireland.

Padraig O hUiginn was under no illusion that golf and tourism were opposite sides of the same coin, and he was well aware that this product needed to be positively exploited for Ireland's benefit.

THE RYDER CUP COMMITTEE WAS WELL DISPOSED TO HOSTING THE EVENT IN IRELAND

The Irish Tourist Board brought golf marketing to a new level. Top-class amateur and professional events took place in Ireland, including the Irish Seniors Open, the Irish Ladies' Open, the

American Express World Championship, the Walker Cup, the Curtis Cup, the Irish Open and the European Open.

Ireland made a positive impression on Ken Schofield. That was the 'Irish card' Bord Fáilte played to entice the Ryder Cup matches to Ireland. They did their homework carefully and diligently, and in time they would be rewarded handsomely.

The European Tour looked very favourably on Ireland as a country that could successfully stage a Ryder Cup. Ireland's playing legacy in this prestigious event spans fifty-seven years. On top of that, our significant winning contributions have earned the respect and praise of those throughout the golfing world. The Ryder Cup Committee is acutely aware of our record, and Ireland will become the second European country outside Great Britain to host the event (Spain was the first in 1997). This was somewhat upsetting for Ireland at the time, as Wales and Ireland, despite their acknowledged track records in these biennial matches, would take a back seat to Spain when it hosted the Ryder Cup at Valderrama in 1997.

There was a belief in the early 1990s that Portmarnock would get the Ryder Cup if it ever came to Ireland (see Chapter 4). One thing was certain, though, and that was that the event would visit our shores. However, in the late 1990s, the emphasis was on the costs associated with bringing it here.

Bord Fáilte wasn't in a position to come up trumps on that count. This wasn't simply a matter of sponsoring a regular European event, but rather, the prestigious Ryder Cup, the jewel in the golfing crown, something then on a much larger scale. For tourism reasons, Padraig O hUiginn felt the golfing road was the one to go down. He met with the European Tour officials and with one man in particular, Scotsman Ken Schofield. Ken was a tough negotiator who wanted the best for his tour players. Padraig was also a very experienced individual who knew the Scotsman would recognise harsh realities. The Irishman discussed the matter at some length with the then Minister for Sport and Tourism, Dr Jim McDaid. Both agreed that the government was unable to meet the huge financial demands associated with hosting the matches in Ireland. The exact figure the European Tour wanted is not known, but it was believed to be somewhere well in excess of IR£8 million.

What we do know is that as advisor to the Minister, Padraig O hUiginn suggested bringing commercial sponsorship on board, which would go a long way in bringing the greatest golfing spectacle to Ireland. Imagine the tourist benefits it would generate. Kildare man and Minister of Finance at the time was Charlie McCreevy, in whose constituency Michael Smurfit's K Club was. Padraig approached him asking for IR£4 million towards the costs of funding the Ryder Cup in Ireland, with the balance coming from a joint sponsorship interest. The Minister agreed.

The Bord Fáilte guru went into conclave with three companies, the Smurfit Group, Tony O'Reilly's Waterford Crystal and Aer Lingus, Ireland's official airline. He asked each to contribute IR£1.2 million over a period of six to seven years. They agreed, and this IR£3.6 million together with the government's IR£4 million should consolidate Ireland's financial bid in attracting the Ryder Cup here. The six- to seven-year period was important. Bord Fáilte and the other three companies would have hospitality rights and signage exposure at all the Ryder Cup qualifying events in the interim, which would be every second year, as the Ryder Cup was a biennial event. Part of the overall deal would see Aer Lingus being designated as the official Ryder Cup carrier.

Padraig went to Minister McDaid, informing him of the financial commitments he had arranged. He conveyed his own belief to the minister that a IR£7.5 million package from a tourism point of view was worth it, a package he was convinced would pay handsome dividends over time.

Padraig O hUiginn had done his bit by marrying the interests of the government and the commercial bodies. The total financial investment figure of IR£7.5 million on offer was as much as Ireland was prepared to give. Padraig put Minister McDaid and Ken Schofield on the telephone with one another, when they discussed the matter at some length, with the focus on IR£7.5 million. They reached an agreement on that figure. Schofield was a hard negotiator, but he equally recognised the reality that was being conveyed to him. Padraig knew IR£7.5 million was a huge amount, but he also knew it was worth it.

Ireland's offer was accepted. It would be officially announced at the conclusion of the 1997 biennial event that the Ryder Cup would come to Ireland in 2005. (Owing to 9/11, however, the biennial event would be postponed until 2006.) The promised financial investment by the government and three business concerns would be passed on to Bord Fáilte for them to manage the payments according to the terms of reference.

However, there were a number of unforeseen circumstances which had to be addressed before everything was finalised. Firstly, there were changes in the commercial sponsorship. The Smurfit Group withdrew from the arrangement. They decided they wanted to throw their hat into the ring in the hope of hosting the event. If they were successful, it would involve them in additional expenditure to that already agreed as one of the joint sponsors. This was a reasonable situation they found themselves in. They were about to embark on serious negotiations regarding the hosting of the Ryder Cup, and as an interested party, it didn't make sense to have to pay another IR£1.2 million. This was seen to be a minor hiccup, as Allied Irish Banks (AIB) agreed to take Smurfit's place.

Another problem would emerge at a later stage. In the early 1990s, Aer Lingus was in deep financial difficulties and as such they abandoned all sponsorship involvement, including the Ryder Cup. This was an unexpected turn of events. Padraig hUiginn could arrange for them to remain on board with their part of the Ryder Cup deal being honoured when their finances recovered. On principle, however, they couldn't avail of this generous offer. In their recovery plan, they adopted a hard line approach and in their wisdom they decided to cease the sponsorship deal. Bord Bia would take their place. Everything was again in full swing.

During our July 2005 conversation, Padraig O hUiginn was passionate about the significance of golf and our tourism industry. Golf, he enthused, is 'one of our great tourist products'. Padraig continued, 'We have one-third of the golf links of the world here in Ireland. We have four outstanding links courses on the island of Ireland: Ballybunion, Portmarnock, Royal County Down and Royal Portrush. These four figure in any list of the best ten to twelve courses in the world. Golf is extremely important to us, bringing in about €200 million annually. We have a product which I regarded on assuming the chairmanship of Bord Fáilte as being very precious indeed. My commitment from the beginning was to invite more and more tournaments to our country. I realised the huge significance of tournament golf vis-à-vis tourism promotion. You get unparalleled potential and opportunities to publicise your product through the powerful medium of television.'

CONSTANT TV EXPOSURE – GREAT PUBLICITY ON AMERICAN TELEVISION

At this stage, Padraig drew my attention to the US Masters at Augusta National. 'Look at the marvellous TV coverage of this prestigious event. Long hours of exposure are beamed into every golfer's home. As a result, everyone wants to play the venue. It's exactly the same for us here in Ireland. When our golf courses came on TV, every avid golf tourist around the world wanted to play here. The numbers of golf tourists coming to our shores have risen dramatically in recent years. The 1997 Programme for National Recovery spearheaded a plan to bring more and more tourists here. The numbers of golf tourists increased over a short period, from 80,000 to 90,000 annually to 250,000!' Padraig cites an example of this marvellous upturn: 'Denis Kane, Druids Glen director-chief executive, told me some time ago that an Irish Open played at his venue was shown eight times on the Golf Channel in America. As a result, they were inundated with American visitors.'

'We cannot stress enough the absolute power of television,' Padraig said. 'Golfers see their idols on screen and they follow every shot from tee to green, taking in the beautiful natural surroundings, and deep down they want to trace their idols' foot-steps.' Padraig also added, 'We are most fortunate in this country, having golf played twelve months in the year. Our mild climate lends itself very much to this reality. People don't want to play in thirty-eight to forty degree Celsius temperatures. Some courses in the States are too cold and snowed under. Take Augusta, for instance. It was built so that when courses in the northern parts of the United States were closed because of severe winters, Augusta can facilitate the investment bankers of New York who were eager to come and play golf here.'

'During this period,' Padraig went on, 'there were a number of golf tournaments taking place: the Irish Open, the European Open and then the Irish Ladies' Championship, the Irish Seniors' and the Challenge Tour event – all of which showed we had a worthy product to promote. There is no use in having a good product – which we know we have – unless you advertise it. We had another advantage which resulted in private clubs like Ballybunion opening its doors to tourists. After all, Ballybunion was a tourist resort. They were pioneers in this field. We also had the benefit of commercial golf courses in recent years. Courses like Mount Juliet, the K Club and Druids Glen came on board and opened their venues to tourists. The Bord Fáilte tourist programme provided grants to those businesspeople who wanted to build new golf courses and open them to tourists.' Padraig's idea had been successfully launched and was now bearing fruit.

Bord Fáilte won a number of awards recently for promoting golf as a tourist attraction. One was in the early 2000s, when Ireland won the award for the best golf destination in Europe, beating Scotland in the process. Denis Kane's Druids Heath won the award for the best new golf course to come on stream in recent years. Scotland admittedly has some magnificent courses, but most of them are private members' clubs and as such don't encourage tourists. Ours, on the other hand, and particularly the spectacular ones, are open to the tourist golfer. The new range of commercial courses, like our traditional links, is promoting the good name of Ireland at home and abroad. The tour operators are delighted to promote this sport in Ireland to golf customers who are enamoured with what we as a small nation have to offer the keen golfer.

I drew Padraig O hUiginn's attention to an earlier remark he made about our classic links courses. I reiterated what he said about the island of Ireland having one-third of the golf links in the world. He had singled out four, two from the North and two from the South, saying that they ranked among the world's top dozen or so. The obvious question to Padraig was why had the K Club, in his opinion, been chosen as the venue for the 2006 Ryder Cup matches given the fact that Ireland was proud of its links heritage and boasted of the fact that it had four of the best links courses in the world, one of which was Portmarnock? Why couldn't the Ryder Cup matches be played there, for instance?

The simple answer was, 'I don't really know.' He acknowledged that the K Club was obviously a very fine course and worthy of a

Ryder Cup hosting. 'The government – the Ministers for Finance and Sport – and we in Bord Fáilte were interested in only bringing the event to Ireland. This is what happened. We didn't want to become involved or take sides when it came to choosing a venue. This should be left in the domain of the professionals. It would be a matter for the Ryder Cup Committee to enter into negotiations with whatever club that would prove to be the successful venue at the end of the day. It's not our place to impose our views in that respect. The professionals would choose the venue they deemed to be the most suitable. We weren't aware of the financial terms that needed to be teased out to confirm the location. Naturally, I would have heard of names like the K Club and Mount Juliet being aired at the time. There was also talk about Druids Glen and Ballybunion being interested. The bottom line for us was we had a clear policy which precluded us from entering the fray.'

Padraig O hUiginn, along with Bord Fáilte colleagues Mark Mortell and Matt McNulty, brought the Ryder Cup here. Now they can look forward to September 2006, when they can enjoy the fruits of their combined wisdom and efforts. It will be without doubt one of the most spectacular sporting occasions ever to visit our shores. Padraig, who is an honorary vice-president of the European Tour, is looking forward to the biennial matches at the K Club in September 2006.

Padraig O hUiginn loves the game. He is an honorary member of Ballybunion Golf Club, where they have a family house close by. He is also a member of Druids Glen in Wicklow, the Grange in Rathfarnham, where he lives, and of Mount Juliet in Kilkenny.

For his ongoing commitment and dedication to golf in Ireland, and particularly for his indulgent passion in bringing the Ryder Cup to our country, Padraig was the 2005 recipient of the Distinguished Services to Golf award, presented by the O_2 Irish Golf Writers' Association. It is a well-deserved accolade.

THE K CLUB GETS THE NOD – THE FOCUS WAS THERE FROM THE BEGINNING

There was an ongoing relationship between the European Tour and the K Club. The K Club had done their homework from the word go. As far back as April 1991, three months before the Club was officially opened, they actually made an official presentation to the Ryder Cup Committee to have the biennial matches staged at their club for 1997. Although they didn't succeed on that occasion, they showed how serious they were in their endeavours and would prove a force to be reckoned with as time passed by. The PGA and Ryder Cup Committee were both very impressed with the K Club's excellent marketing plan, which confirmed that they had a leading edge on their principal competitors. Their track record spoke for itself. They staged two PGA Cups, the 2001 Junior Ryder Cup, two Irish Professional Championships and ten European Opens with a further commitment to stage the latter up to and including 2015. They also staged a Challenge Tour event. This was a very impressive and envious pedigree. Who could compete with this legacy? Portmarnock? As far as the European Tour was concerned, they met all the criteria; the Ryder Cup Committee was obviously of a similar view. The K Club's credentials were impeccable.

The K Club was successful in their bid for the 2006 Ryder Cup matches. What remains for Dr Smurfit now is to ensure that his location will be deemed worthy of selection. There is little doubt but this 7,300-yard course, designed by Arnold Palmer, will prove a challenging test for both sides when the matches get underway.

The two on-site hotels will provide welcome accommodation for the two teams, their families and officials. The magnificent clubhouse will also be at their disposal for the week.

Cork man John McHenry must be proud. He joined the Smurfit team in 2002 as director of golf, and now he is head professional at the prestigious K Club, the venue for the 2006 Ryder Cup. The last time I saw John was in 1998 at Druids Glen, where he was at one stage joint leader of the Irish Open. I was one of the enthusiastic fans fully behind him, hoping he would emulate John O'Leary's Irish Open win in 1982. No Irish player had lifted this trophy in the intervening period. An unfortunate blip early on in the final round was responsible for John plummeting down a few rungs of the ladder. He recovered soon afterwards, finishing birdie par par for a final round of 72 to finish joint third in the event. I spoke with him in April 2006 at the K Club.

John had a very rewarding amateur career which augured well for the future professional ranks. He was a winning team member of two international amateur events: the Europe Youths' Championship and the Europe Seniors Championship. The pinnacle of his amateur career was when he was honoured with a Walker Cup place on the team that faced the Americans at Sunningdale at the end of the 1980s. Scotsman Colin Montgomerie was on the same team. 'I would have loved to have gone on to have achieved the equivalent at professional level by becoming a Ryder Cup player; it wasn't to be,' said John. He was on tour until 1999, but decided to take two years out for family reasons.

'Things always have a habit of working themselves out. I feel very honoured and proud to have been selected to become a significant member of Dr Michael Smurfit's winning team.'

It is marvellous that Ireland has been conferred with the hosting of the Ryder Cup matches. It's a great tribute to the involvement of the Irish government in bringing the biennial event here. It is also a true recognition of the remarkable vision and insight of Bord Fáilte's former chairman, Padraig O hUiginn, who worked tirelessly in bringing the event here.

DR MICHAEL SMURFIT AND THE RYDER CUP

What were John McHenry's feelings about this prestigious event visiting the Kildare and Country Club? 'A tremendous honour! It is a justified accolade and a vote of enormous confidence in Dr Smurfit's visionary zeal over a long period of time. Dr Smurfit has enjoyed a close relationship with the European Tour for many years. He worked hard indeed in bringing the Ryder Cup to Ireland and especially to the K Club. On merit alone, the Kildare and Country Club won out. It was long overdue.'

Would it not have been more appropriate were the biennial matches staged on a traditional links like Portmarnock? After all, one-third of the world's links courses are in Ireland. John was particularly vocal in repudiating this contention. 'There are many who have a fascination with links courses. Many Americans have it. The best parkland courses can match the best links tracks. I'm not against links. I love them. However, when it comes to the K Club staging the 2006 matches, it is important to realise that not only do we have a quality layout – in fact, we have two top-class courses designed by the Arnold Palmer Group – but our 550-acre infrastructure can accommodate all of the requirements that are peculiar to an event of this magnitude. Not all layouts can boast of this. The K Club is familiar with hosting international events like the European Open and the PGA Cup. The scale of preparation required for an international event of this size is huge.'

STAGING THE RYDER CUP – A MAMMOTH OPERATION

Staging a Ryder Cup involves multiplying the scale of preparation for a European Open by ten to fifteen times, so one can appreciate how important this massive 550-acre site is in accommodating a large-scale tented village capable of housing corporate hospitality units, a members' pavilion, an enormous media centre, restaurants, merchandise outlets, a television compound and security, to name but a few. There is a top-class on-site hotel for the Ryder Cup players, their families and the PGA officialdom from both sides of the Atlantic. Everything is on the one complex. There are no commuting or traffic problems to contend with.

Will the K Club be able to cope with the unprecedented amount of traffic? John McHenry said, 'On road infrastructure we are delighted with progress so far. All the planed trunk road improvements and main road widening schemes will be completed by June 2006. Some 40,000 to 50,000 people will be at the K Club each day throughout Ryder Cup week, and so our roads will be of the highest standards.'

THE COURSE

The course for the Ryder Cup will be long, challenging and will demand great skills.

John added, 'Like the roads, our venue, the Arnold Palmer course stretching to some 7,300 yards, will be of the highest quality imaginable. Our greens are exceptional and this is thanks to the head green keeper/agronomist, Gerry Byrne. He and his staff have put in Trojan work over a long period to ensure a quality layout which we will all be proud of.'

THE CAPTAINS

Does the European team captain have any say in the course layout for the September matches? John responded, 'Very definitely! Ian has already been busy by adding a few of his own priority changes. The Woosnam Strategy meant adding a few well-placed trees at a number of the challenging dog legs to compound the existing difficulties at these holes.'

Will the US captain be a playing captain? Arnold Palmer is on record as saying, 'Why not?' Arnold himself was a playing captain in the past. US 2006 captain, Tom Lehman, is close to automatic team selection, and given his fine progress this year on tour, he may well just clinch that place. Does the K Club's head professional think the American will captain his side if he is a team member? John feels Tom Lehman will step down as captain, leaving the role for another to take on. There would be too many demands on him if he played. It would end up being a mind game for the American, resulting in Tom not being in a position to devote his all to both commitments. If he is playing, Tom would be wondering how his guys are performing. He wouldn't always be in a position to follow team members to support them if he were engaged in his own match. There is the situation that Tom might lose his own match if he played. Would he blame the added mental pressure that he arguably didn't need to have subjected himself to? Tom Lehman's preference at the end of the day would be, John thought, to play rather than to captain.

As already noted, Arnold Palmer designed the course. He is honoured by the Ryder Cup being hosted here in September. Will he be with us on what will be a truly momentous occasion? John confirmed that an invitation has already been sent to 'The King', as he is still affectionately called.

What were John McHenry's thoughts about which team would win the thirty-sixth Ryder Cup? 'I believe Europe will win,' he said. He gave three principal reasons. 'The Europeans have experience at the K Club – they play it all the time. The temperatures are cooler in September and our guys are more at home in these conditions, and of course the Europeans are more at home with the greens,' he added.

'We are really looking forward to September,' John continued. 'I have been to a few Ryder Cups and the atmosphere is just fantastic. The countdown has begun!'

GERRY BYRNE AND THE 'MIDAS TOUCH'

Arnold Palmer designed both courses at the K Club, the Smurfit and the Arnold Palmer layouts. They are 'uniquely different', according to Gerry Byrne, resort superintendent at the K Club. Peculiar to the Palmer course, the venue for the 2006 Ryder Cup, will be the poa annua grass-growing greens. These greens are to be seen on most American courses and will be a noticeable feature at Winged Foot for the US Open in June 2006.

When Gerry joined the K Club in 1996, creeping bent grass was the norm, a grass that proved to be totally unsuitable for the Ryder Cup venue. The Palmer course rejected it instinctively. Making it his top priority from the beginning, Gerry converted the Palmer course to being positively receptive to poa annua. It was like somebody being allergic to penicillin and not being allergic to another tablet. Strangely enough, whatever soil composition the Smurfit course had, it welcomed this grass with open arms. After Gerry nurtured and manicured the Palmer layout over some four years, the operation yielded fruit a hundredfold. The standard of greens at the K Club has advanced from strength to strength and is now comparable with the world's best.

The European Tour has put it on record saying that the Palmer course can be rightly proud of their magnificent quality of greens – they are the envy of many.

Gerry's father was a green keeper in both Elm Park and the Hermitage. Jim Byrne left his own proud legacy for Gerry to build on. Such was his dad's success in this delicate and skilful area that he received nationwide acclaim. Jim Byrne was made life honorary member at both the Hermitage and the European Club. In fact, son Gerry subsequently donned the mantle and went on to emulate his father's talent, bringing agronomy to a new level at the K Club.

What does Gerry think of the K Club being honoured with the 2006 hosting of the prestigious Ryder Cup? 'I am absolutely thrilled. To be honest, it is the pinnacle of my career! The enormity of the occasion has finally sunk in.' How much work was involved in bringing the Ryder Cup venue up to this envious standard? 'Over the last three to four years, we peaked and once recognised, we bottled that ingredient and have continued to maintain that high standard ever since. We are so well prepared we could have the Ryder Cup here today. We have no worries and no issues. The Palmer course is in prime condition.' What staff does Gerry Byrne have to carry out the many demands that lie ahead between now and September? 'I have a full-time staff of twenty-two and that will rise to thirty-eight over the summer period.'

What significant changes will face the two Ryder Cup teams in the autumn? 'Over the years, 1.3 million trees have been planted on the Palmer course. Most of these would be mature nursery trees with heights of up to forty feet. The huge emphasis will be on strategically placed bunkers – extra bunkers will also surprise many. European Ryder Cup captain, Ian Woosnam, visited us during the early summer of 2005 with the result that we had thirteen extra trees planted at sensitive areas. Darren Clarke's record of 60 some years ago will be under no threat,' Gerry added. He continued, 'Ian also had a number of swales around certain greens, which will test the best in September.'

Was Dr Smurfit visionary in demanding that a high-class venue like this would host the biennial Ryder Cup? Gerry Byrne was very vocal in his response. 'If it were not for Dr Smurfit, Ireland would not have had a Ryder Cup. We have the quality venue par excellence and the land mass to support the necessary infrastructure to stage the event.' Is there any hope the architect of this exquisite 7,300-yard course will be present for the September matches? Gerry was very optimistic about this eventuality.

Did Gerry ever meet Arnold Palmer? 'Not only did I meet him, but I played with Mr Palmer. It was about three or four years ago. I was playing with "The King" on the Palmer course. There were three of us. I was playing off six, 'Spider' Miller was off two and there was Mr Palmer. He was a perfect gentleman and such a fine golfer who lived very much up to his reputation. I will always remember his comment on the sixth tee – he said it was time for a big mahoo, which in our parlance was to give it a lash! He nailed it, out-driving Spider and myself by miles. Then at the eight (which will be the seventeenth at the Ryder Cup in September),

I drove into water, Spider finished too far right but Mr Palmer split the fairway and followed up with an arrow-straight perfectly hit three wood landing no more than a couple of feet from the pin for his birdie.'

Gerry elaborated on Mr Palmer being a gentleman. 'He reminds me very much of the late golf architect Eddie Hackett. He too was a gentleman very much in the mould of Arnold Palmer. I was very much impressed with both. When Spider and I played with Mr Palmer, he would always insist in teeing off last. He had a wonderful philosophy. He didn't want to embarrass us by hitting a huge drive off the tee and risk upsetting and unnerving us when it came to our turn.'

Gerry went on to relate yet another great story about the legendary Arnold Palmer. 'When Mr Palmer last visited us, we took him down to Courtney's pub in Lucan to sample a little Irish pub hospitality. The pub had their own golf society with members from a mainly working-class family background. You can imagine the look on their faces when they realised that it was the real Arnold Palmer that had paid a visit to their haunt. They were totally in awe of the man. Mr Palmer stayed the best part of four hours chatting with the lads, exchanging stories and most importantly signing autographs for everybody. Normally music and singing were not allowed in these licensed premises, but with The King being present, ceili dancing, singing and merriment were the order of the evening. What Arnold Palmer did on that one evening is still remembered and spoken about. They all remember Arnie as a thorough gentleman who had a lot of time for them.'

CHAPTER 6

September 2006 –
Ryder Cup Week

This chapter will profile Ian Woosnam and Tom Lehman, the
Europe and US captains, respectively. The system explaining
how players from both sides of the Atlantic qualify for this prestigious event will be analysed, providing a full and comprehensive
guide as to how the two twelve-man teams are selected. The associated activities that take place during Ryder Cup week will also
be examined. These will include the official ceremonies, the
massive marshalling operation, the garda operation and the Ryder
Cup's own environmentally friendly policy – four principal ingredients in ensuring the success of an international event of this
magnitude.

RYDER CUP WEEK

Although the actual matches take place over three days – Friday,
Saturday and Sunday – there is much pomp and splendour for the
spectator throughout the early part of the week. Tuesday and

Wednesday are devoted to official practice, which is usually the best opportunity for ardent fans to follow games at close quarters and see the players in action. Usually, each team plays a few four-ball and foursome matches amongst themselves to give their captain a final insight as to who might be paired with whom when the official matches get underway. Golf enthusiasts should take full advantage of these opportunities, as they most certainly will be few and far between in the midst of the real encounter. Again, early in the week, fans can stay for hours on end by the practice range and putting green to learn from the experts.

DRESS CODE

Although Ryder Cup matches officially take place over three days, there is much happening throughout the entire week. There is the official opening ceremony with welcoming speeches from officials representing both the visiting and home teams. The general tone of these speeches echoes Sam Ryder's aspirations of having the matches played in a spirit of goodwill and friendship. The closing ceremony also echoes these principles.

Those who have already attended Ryder Cup events will recall the marvellous atmosphere there is during the opening and closing ceremonies. Each side wears its own team uniform. To avoid a clash of colours, the captains choose the Ryder Cup apparel for the week after consultations with each other. All players are supplied with a full range of attire, which includes trousers, shoes, polo necks, jumpers, waterproofs, hats, bags and umbrellas. Traditionally, the captain of the home side is given first choice of colour scheme. Again, tradition stipulates that team members are informed of their colours on the Tuesday of Ryder Cup week.

Even though the event has yet to take place at the time of writing, there is already a huge buzz about the forthcoming series, much of it being generated by golfing fans and the general public in Ireland and abroad. The players who are safely in and those who are still contending for an automatic slot don't seem to initiate discussion about the Ryder Cup, as they are too engrossed in either their quest for automatic selection or just excluding it from their minds while they focus on the tournament scene they are currently engaged in. Either way, interest is generated to a great extent by the media. Invariably, journalists broach the topic at the many interviews with players that take place during the progress of the remaining qualifying events between now and the time the final team selections are made. They evoke discussion and comment on the topic and hone in on headline-making stories, like the story that has created much interest and concern for Irishman Paul McGinley regarding his fitness for the September matches.

The thirty-nine-year-old had to retire from the Nissan Irish Open at Carton House in May. He had been having left knee problems for some time and matters came to a head after thirteen holes into his first round. After consulting with his medics, he felt there was no option but to have immediate minor surgery to remove a piece of broken bone floating in his knee. Perhaps what came to a head at Carton House was a blessing in disguise. The follow-up rest period after surgery would give the former Ryder Cup player a chance to fully recover and recharge his batteries well in time for the September event at the K Club. Naturally, Paul wants to consolidate and no doubt improve on his position in the interim. In May 2006, he was lying in seventh position on the European points list. His main focus continues to be on consolidating his place. A fine performance at the European Open has helped significantly. All going well, he should accomplish his goal.

PARK AND RIDE SCHEME

It is estimated that 40,000 spectators will attend the Ryder Cup matches each day this September. Chief Superintendent Michael Byrnes of Naas Garda Station is in charge of Ryder Cup Planning with Garda Tim Burke, of the Ryder Cup Planning Office, Naas Garda Station, co-ordinating and implementing the programme at ground level. A 'park and ride' system will be operational for those attending the Ryder Cup event at the K Club. Vehicle access around Straffan and the K Club is not permitted. Roads within an approximate 2 kilometre stretch north and south of the K Club are out of bounds for the commuter. This restriction applies to all private and commercial vehicle users, including private bus transport and taxis. There will be no discretion and where motorists arrive at the traffic cordons they will be directed away.

Clockwise from top: Sam Ryder (centre) with Walter Hagen (left) and George Duncan (right) at a Ryder Cup banquet, 1929. Ireland's only British Open Champion and first Ryder Cup player, Fred Daly. Former Ryder Cup player Harry Bradshaw at impact.

Ireland's Christy O'Connor, Sr with his famous follow through as Welshman Dave Thomas and Englishman Bernard Hunt look on.

Eye on the ball: Christy O'Connor, Jr playing in the 1975 Ryder Cup.

In the heat of battle: Johnny Miller follows the trajectory of his tee shot looked on by fellow players Tom Weiskopf, John O'Leary and Christy O'Connor, Jr in the 1975 Ryder Cup.

Eamonn Darcy is congratulated by Jack Nicklaus after beating American Ben Crenshaw to win the Ryder Cup for Europe for the first time on American soil in 1987.

Christy O'Connor, Jr after hitting a narrow straight two-iron shot to the eighteenth hole at the Belfry to defeat American Fred Couples in 1989.

Philip Walton celebrates his win against American Jay Haas in 1995.

Brookline, 1999 Ryder Cup: Tiger Woods hits a shot.

Three-time Ryder Cup player
Padraig Harrington plays an
iron shot.

Ryder Cup teamwork: Ireland's
Padraig Harrington and
Scotland's Colm Montgomerie
examine the line of the putt.

Darren Clarke punches an iron shot.

Paul McGinley proudly holding the tricolour
after Ryder Cup victory.

Inset: Victory is sweet: Bernhard Langer kisses
the Ryder Cup in 2004

There will be two park and ride schemes in operation. (1) The North Park and Ride Scheme operates regularly from Weston Aerodrome in Lucan, just off the N4, with commuters coming primarily from the Dublin Region, the North and West. (2) The South Park and Ride Scheme operates regularly from Palmerstown at Johnstown (near Kill), Co. Kildare, just off the N7. These Ryder Cup ticket holders are from the South and East and will be accommodated on this route. Ryder Cup shuttle buses will transport everyone from the two locations to the bus terminals at the K Club.

There will be directional signage erected at all approach roads informing drivers where the park and ride facilities are. Ticket holders can then avail of the free shuttle bus service direct to the K Club. The reverse procedure will operate when commuters are leaving the grounds.

It is planned to use 110 double-decker coaches as part of the park and ride scheme. Some 10,000 people are expected to park at the Weston Aerodrome which is linked to the Leixlip–Celbridge roads and they will then be transported to the North Bus Terminal at the K Club site.

Tim Burke believes that 20,000 commuters will be parking at Palmerstown, Johnstown, Co. Kildare on the N7 south of the K Club and will then be transported to the South Bus Terminal at the K Club site.

All tickets holders will know in advance which park and ride they should go to. All persons travelling to the Ryder Cup should plan their travel routes in advance to ensure that they will arrive in time to the correct park and ride facility. Arriving early and at the correct location will aid everybody's comfort in getting to/from the K Club.

Intending spectators will also be supplied with a Comprehensive Spectators' Guide with their tickets on the 2006 Ryder Cup event. The guide will detail travel routes and other information.

There is also a dedicated regular train service operating from Connolly train station, Dublin to Louisa Bridge (Leixlip) train station from 19 to 24 September. Spectators will then be taken by bus from Louisa Bridge train station direct to the bus terminal at the K Club where they can access the course. Tickets and

information for this service are available on www.irishrail.ie.
Advance tickets must be purchased for this service. Spectators will
be returned to the train station by bus after the event.

The gardaí will update the general public regarding further
traffic flow arrangements nearer the Ryder Cup event. The public
can get traffic information updates from www.garda.ie,
www.europeantour.com, www.aaroadwatch.ie, www.sdublin-
coco.ie and www.kildare.ie.

Tented village

John McHenry, the senior resident professional at the K Club,
spoke in Chapter 5 about the importance of infrastructure at the
K Club. Their 550-acre layout can, he said, accommodate all the
necessary requirements associated with a prestigious event of this
magnitude. Those who have been at a major tournament like the
European Open will recall the tented village area. The Ryder Cup
tented village and its environs will be massive by comparison.
There will be 195 mobile offices/toilets located around the
course. 2,700 metres of perimeter fencing will be erected. There
will be twenty grandstands with 15,000 seats. In addition, there
will be seven Jumbotron screens around the course to provide
spectators with live progress of matches. The 2,000 square metre
merchandise area will be located by the main tented village.

There will be catering and hospitality units, with 8,000 meals
served per day. Some 350,000 gallons of fresh drinking water will
be consumed throughout the week. In all, there will be over 10,000
people working in various areas, such as catering, first aid, policing,
medical services, media, parking and corporate hospitality.

Environmentally friendly 'race against waste'

Since the Ryder Cup biennial matches at Valderrama in 1997,
there has been a concerted effort to put 'best environmental practice' into place at this and all future events. At a press gathering in
Dublin's Merrion Square Gardens last May, the Minister for the
Environment, Heritage and Local Government, Dick Roche, TD,
paid tribute to the Ryder Cup authorities for being associated
with one of the most environmentally friendly golf events ever

staged in Ireland. The Minister was delighted to put on record his support for 'the Race against Waste Team, who have been working closely with the European Tour organisers on the Ryder Cup to ensure that waste produced at the 2006 biennial event be reduced, reused and recycled, in keeping with Irish national waste policy and the European Tour's commitment to better environmental standards at all their events.'

I spoke with Ryder Cup director Richard Hills, who reiterated his organisation's commitment to the race against waste initiative. 'This commitment began at our Ryder Cup matches in Spain, when Jaime Patino, the patron of the 1997 event at Valderrama, introduced a number of ecological procedures. We adopted many of these and have been "green" ever since, with a gradual integration of best practice measures. We will be encouraging maximum recycling and minimum waste at the K Club. Our tour players are very environmentally conscious and, in fact, many of them are interested in golf course design and building and are therefore cognisant of prevailing legislation as to what is and is not best practice. September's event will include a wide range of best practice environmental measures to promote maximum recycling and minimum waste.'

He continued, 'This year we will be concentrating on raising spectator awareness of environmental issues. An environment brochure is being produced for the thirty-sixth Ryder Cup to inform people of the environmental activities associated with the tournament and to encourage people to play their part. Alongside the recycling information, we will provide other wildlife and landscape information for spectators as they move around the course.'

Elizabeth Arnett is the technical director of Race against Waste and she is enthusiastic about facing the enormous challenge that lies ahead. 'We have been working with a lot of sectors over the last few years in this area and more recently we have concentrated our efforts on golf clubs. We have organised a series of seminars for these clubs around the country, helping them to reduce, reuse and recycle. We have carried our activities further by working alongside the Ryder Cup key personnel at the K Club for September 2006. After all, this is the biggest golfing event on the planet! We know the K Club is very advanced in their thinking about environmental issues. We will support them in their efforts at waste management. The Ryder Cup will attract up to 45,000 people daily, so it makes sense to encourage all to be environmentally conscious throughout Ryder Cup week,' she said.

Visitors to Straffan will see extensive recycling activities in the tented village, where they can separate their plastic, aluminium and paper waste. There will be a poster campaign on buses bringing people to the course. They will have constant reminders on ways they can manage their waste properly and efficiently. Apart from targeting the 45,000 daily visitors expected, Elizabeth Arnett will also be singling out the catering personnel and suppliers working on site to promote the ecological message.

Five years ago, Elizabeth admitted, it would have been extremely difficult to do what is being done at the K Club today. As a nation, we have come a long way in a relatively short space of time in terms of our race against waste. The natural progression of their endeavours leads them to the Kildare and Country Club at Straffan. 'We are confident that the event will significantly help to minimise a large-scale generation of waste but will, rather, promote a committed partnership of golfing and environmental bodies working as a unit to encourage environmental sustainability in European golf,' she enthused.

The K Club's resident superintendent, Gerry Byrne, is particularly proud of Dr Smurfit's track record on environmental issues. The club has already signed an international commitment to the Green Foundation. Along with Joe Bedford of the Golfing Union of Ireland (GUI), the two men are adamant that green keepers are custodians of our environment. These green keepers ensure that golf courses are kept practically free from pesticides with the least use of fertilizer possible. The K Club is no exception. Their philosophy is quite simple. What is wanted is for nature to do its own thing. The K Club's lake edges are free from any pesticides; the authorities let grow what is naturally wild. All of these measures encourage fish life at the K Club, where trout and other fish are stocked in the lakes. Gerry Byrne confirmed that their management plan would have conservation of key habitats and landscape features on the site as top priorities. These areas would be free from machinery and any crowd movement.

Joe Bedford reiterated the GUI's commitment to environmental issues. 'Our union represents 413 golf clubs in Ireland. The

280,000 male members would play on 50,000 acres in total. Along with that, the Irish Ladies' Golfing Union, a separate body, caters for 55,000 ladies who also play the length and breadth of our country. Another golfing sector needs to be taken into account when these environmental issues are being addressed – this sector embraces the 80,000 non-registered male and female players who, although not affiliated to any particular club, play the casual game or two, or more. All of these players are anxious to adhere to what best practice is in the field of ecological issues.'

Paddy Holohan is president of the Golf Course Superintendents Association of Ireland (GCSAI). He comes from Baltray country in County Louth, and along with Gerry Byrne and Joe Bedford, he, too, is committed to promoting a sound environment that is commensurate with raising spectator and player awareness in this all-important area.

Consider these statistics: fourteen twenty-ton compactors for rubbish collecting will be strategically located at the K Club. There will be 500 wire bins around the course itself, 280 x 240-litre wheelie bins, 100 x 1,100-litre Eurobins, fifty dumpmasters, fifty tons per day of dry waste, 30,000 gallons of wet waste for the entire week and 9,600 toilet rolls.

This complementary partnership of golfing and environmental bodies is a key ingredient in ensuring ecological sustainability in European golf. The Ryder Cup is teeing off by example.

THE 2006 MARSHAL PLAN

David O'Hora is the Chief Marshal for the Ryder Cup 2006. I spoke with him about the honour bestowed on him for September.

Q. Are you looking forward to the Ryder Cup?
A. Very much so! I think that it is a great honour for Ireland and my home county of Kildare to stage such a prestigious event. We have planned meticulously for the occasion and have assembled the best team of marshals that you could hope for. I can't wait for it to start.

Q. To be a Chief Marshal, you must have a lot of experience behind you.
A. For the last three years I have been Chief Marshal at the Smurfit European Open. Prior to that, my experience in marshalling was gained through working as a volunteer marshal. I was also fortunate enough to work in a variety of different roles at the Belfry in 2002. More importantly, though, I have built a very good team around me. Our team at the European Open consists of 240 marshals, many of whom have been marshalling for much longer than I have. We got a good feel for how the K Club can handle large volumes of spectators the day after Darren Clarke's scintillating record-breaking round of 60 in the 1999 event. There were, in fact, 29,000 spectators on that final day – the biggest one-day total ever.

Q. How do you think that will compare with the Ryder Cup galleries?
A. Forty thousand are expected each day. To manage that, we will have a team of 800 marshals on duty. Not all of the spectators will be on the golf course, however, as the grandstands will accommodate 15,500 and there will be another 5,000 or so enjoying the corporate hospitality.

Q. Where do the marshals come from?
A. The core group are those that have marshalled at the European Open for the past twelve years, and essentially they are members of local clubs in addition to three clubs from Northern Ireland – Holywood, Lurgan and a group from Letterkenny Golf Club. I am lucky that I have also been able to draw on other groups from England, Scotland and Wales that have marshalled at past Ryder Cups, including the Chief Marshal from the Belfry. Others come from as far away as Australia, Canada, the US and the Bahamas. The remainder are from Croatia, France, Spain, Portugal, Germany, Belgium, Holland, Denmark, Italy and Sweden. All have two things in common: their dedication and commitment to helping out at the matches and their love of the game of golf.

Q. You were an observer at the 2004 Ryder Cup in Oakland Hills. Do they do things differently there?
A. They certainly do. Firstly, they had a pool of 3,500 marshals and

each marshal only had to work four half-day shifts. Our marshals will be working all six days of the biennial event. Our marshals will be directly involved with the golf, whereas in the States they take on many more ancillary duties. Another significant difference in the States is that marshals pay for the privilege of becoming marshals and the money raised goes to local charities.

Q. What did you gain from the 2004 experience?

A. My deputy and good friend Ciaran Moore and I arrived on the Monday of Ryder Cup week and we met with my brother Donal, who had travelled independently. However, our journey was cut short, as our father died on the Tuesday and we returned home for the funeral. After the funeral we made our way back to America for the Saturday matches – Dad would have wanted this. It was a long journey from Ireland, necessitating visits to a number of airports en route trying to make connecting flights to reach our final destination. Ultimately, however, the long journey was worth it, as I got to meet the various principals involved in running the marshalling operation at Oakland Hills, all of whom were tremendously supportive and passed on some very good advice. In addition, it was nice to witness the greatest European win on American soil. A moment of happiness in what was otherwise a sad week.

Q. What will your schedule be for September 2006?

A. My management team, each of whom has shown an extraordinary enthusiasm for their respective roles, have had their briefing sessions and are now in the final stages of planning the allocation of resources. I have just finished a volunteer's newsletter, which contains information relating to registration, training, timings and other general information and is being mailed to all marshals. The next stage in the process is to finalise our training programme to ensure that the marshalling operation will be the finest on tour. We will have our final review at the end of August once the infrastructure is in place at the K Club. I will be on site with my administration team for the week prior to the event. We will have to set up our offices, check our equipment and package all the uniforms and accreditation.

Registration for all marshals will take place on the weekend before the matches and then, hopefully, as the event gets underway, the two years of planning will come to fruition to allow us all to enjoy the experience. We will have a big party for all the marshals on the Sunday evening after the closing ceremony. I will probably take the Monday off, maybe get to play golf and then back to work on Tuesday.

Q. Do women feature in marshalling?
A. Absolutely! One hundred and forty of the team will be women and many of them will be playing key roles. They are a very dedicated and committed bunch.

Q. Your experience at the K Club is really coming into its own now.
A. Most definitely! Twelve years ago I was there when the K Club opened and played in the inaugural pro-am with former Ryder Cup captain, Brian Hugget. I have played the course many times since, so I know it intimately. Twelve years ago I started as a marshal at the Smurfit European Open and I progressed through the ranks with much help and encouragement from my predecessor, David O'Neill, the then Chief Marshal. He was Chief Marshal for nine years and I learned a lot from him. Over those twelve years I have learned where the potential problems may arise and have planned to ensure that those problems don't arise during Ryder Cup week.

Q. Can you highlight some of the activities your marshals will be involved in?
A. Out of the 800 marshals previously mentioned, 440 will be static marshals, i.e. they will marshal tee boxes, greens, crossing points on the fairways and ball spotting duties. They will also be conveniently located at intermittent points along the fairways when players play their second shots to par fours or in some cases their third shots to par fives.

One hundred and twenty marshals will manage the twenty-five grandstands located around the course. One hundred marshals will be assigned to scoring duties, forty marshals will be assigned to player care. We will also have a team looking after the needs of the world's media and photographers to ensure they get unhindered passage around the golf course. There will also be a team of travelling marshals to assist in any other unforeseen eventuality. And, of course, my administration team, which will look after all our daily administration requirements, but more importantly will also be available to assist with disabled spectators.

Q. What do static marshals do?
A. Essentially, the role of these marshals is to ensure that players get the best possible conditions in which to play their shots. They also ensure that the players and entourage can travel unhindered around the golf course. Spectators will be outside the ropes, but marshals will also do their utmost to ensure maximum spectator comfort in following matches. Finally, marshals will play a very important role in the event of any emergency.

Q. What do the player care marshals do?
A. Player care marshals will be on duty from dawn to dusk and will transport and escort the players to and from the hotel, the club-house, the practice facilities, the media centre for interviews and be available to transport players from the course wherever the matches finish. Their role is also to ensure that the players are not unduly hindered by autograph hunters and well wishers.

Q. What about vigilance when matches are finished for the day and when the final day's play is over? Do some of the fans look to take home some keepsake memories like flags or signage?
A. This is the not-so-glamorous role for the marshals. The course opens for the spectators at 7 a.m. and closes at 7.30 p.m. There will be a team of 70 marshals on duty for out-of-duty match-time to ensure that the integrity of the course (greens, tee boxes and grandstands, for instance) is maintained. Their role is to ensure that spectators arriving and leaving the course use the crossings and don't wander needlessly over the playing surface. They will also act as important information officers.

Each and every marshal will have to do one of these graveyard shifts over the course of the week. In relation to memorabilia, Ryder Cup organisers will have a team following the final matches each day collecting tee markers and flags.

Q. Are the marshals easily identifiable?

A. Marshals have their own distinctive uniform, which has been chosen with Irish September weather in mind. In addition to the normal polo shirts, sweaters and caps which will have the 2006 Ryder Cup logo, marshals this year will have waterproof weather gear made with the exclusive colours of the Irish Ryder Cup tartan. This is a new initiative and it is hoped that it will continue in Wales in 2010 and Scotland in 2014. Other than that, marshals will also be easily recognised by their Ryder Cup armband.

THE 2006 CAPTAINS

CAPTAIN IAN WOOSNAM

Ian Woosnam is still playing the regular tour, but is just two years away from being eligible for the Seniors' Tour. He will lead the Europe team to face the Americans in the Ryder Cup at the K Club in September 2006. As a captain, he is very different to the 2002 captain, Bernhard Langer, but without question he possesses all the necessary ingredients to achieve what the German did – to lead Europe to victory at the Kildare and Country Club.

What essential characteristics does the Welshman have in equal abundance to Langer? First and foremost, he is a very experienced and seasoned professional. He joined the professional ranks in 1976 at the age of eighteen and went on to become an accomplished player, winning tournaments all over the world. He won the European Tour Order of Merit in 1987 and 1990. In 1991, at the age of thirty-three, he donned the green jacket after winning the US Masters title at Augusta National.

He has made eight Ryder Cup appearances and has been a member of both losing and winning teams. He knows what Ryder Cup pressure is all about. Topping all these prerequisites is another hugely important attribute – his burning desire and passion to beat the visitors, who haven't tasted victory since 1999. Ian Woosnam is acutely aware of the hurt felt by the Americans and knows how the American adrenalin will flow at the K Club. The once-dominant force in world golf will be very finely tuned indeed and intent on bringing back what they believe is rightfully theirs, Samuel Ryder's trophy.

The American Ryder Cup captain is very aware of the quality and depth of talent of the European team. Much of that superb talent is obvious on the world tour, which of course takes in the American circuit. He actually said on one of his visits to the K Club that 'the US team tended to play with a little more apprehension, a little more pressure, self-inflicted pressure, a little more fear of failure, maybe.' Gone are the days when the US players felt that all they had to do was turn up to win. Tom Lehman also acknowledged the fact that 'the Americans would come to Ireland as underdogs', but be that as it may, they will, individually and collectively as a group, rise to the challenge with a rejuvenated team spirit.

Ian has already been to the K Club a few times over the last while to help fine tune the course to compound the already existing difficulties to be experienced by the world's great players. The European Ryder Cup captain is keeping a sharp eye on events throughout the globe. He will be observing which individuals might be paired with others in foursomes and fourballs. His vice-captains will be doing likewise and reporting back to him. One thing Woosie is grateful for, is his own experience at having worked under Sam Torrance, the 2002 Ryder Cup captain. As Sam's vice-captain, he helped guide the European team to victory over the Americans at the Belfry. The experience was invaluable. Ian is looking forward to the 2006 matches and is confident it will be one of the most exciting Ryder Cup spectacles ever.

CAPTAIN TOM LEHMAN

Tom Lehman is not only playing the American circuit this year, but he is also a strong contender for gaining automatic qualification as a member of the 2006 US Ryder Cup team. There are obvious ramifications should he qualify and play. However, his compatriot, Arnold Palmer, is on record as saying why shouldn't he play? Palmer had a very good reason for saying this, for he was playing captain in 1963. 'The King' played in all matches on that occasion at Atlanta, Georgia, winning a total of 4 points out of a possible 5. Arnold's only defeat came at the hands of England's Peter Alliss in the singles, when he lost out by a mere one hole. Thus there is a very good precedent for having a playing captain on the team. The counter argument focuses on the great changes that have taken place in more recent years in the Ryder Cup. Today's captains have too much to do relative to earlier times. The pressure is arguably more intense. In the modern era, a captain doesn't need the distraction of playing his own matches. He can't be playing and looking after his team at the same time.

To look at the situation objectively, it can be said that in Arnold Palmer's time the Americans won the biennial series time and time again. They did so when there was no real opposition. There was a huge imbalance of abilities between the US and the Great Britain and Ireland teams. However, when the decision was made for the Great Britain and Ireland team to go 'European', things changed quite dramatically. Recent Ryder Cup victories were no longer exclusively American ones. The balance of power has shifted. Europe is now a dominant force and it makes sense that a captain's lot should be a happy one. This would rule out a playing role for him. There again, he might make history by becoming his own captain's pick should he not qualify automatically.

Tom Lehman was born in 1959, the year South African Gary Player won the Open Championship. Tom turned pro in 1982 and had to wait twelve years before he broke his non-winning mould by taking the 1994 Memorial Tournament. Two years later, he captured the Tour Championship at Tulsa, resulting in him being voted US PGA Player of the Year and propelling him to second in the world rankings. The same year saw Tom Lehman finish in a tie for second place with Davis Love III in the US Open. The following month he captured the 1996 Open Championship at Lytham. He has been in the winners' circle many times since capturing the Memorial Tournament. Team-wise, he represented his country three times in the President's Cup, in 1994, 1996 and 2000; he was on the 1996 World Cup, the Alfred Dunhill Cup in 1999 and 2000 and, of course, he played in three consecutive Ryder Cups in 1995, 1997 and 1999.

Like Ian Woosnam, he is excited about the imminent Ryder Cup matches at the K Club.

TEAM QUALIFICATION FOR THE THIRTY-SIXTH RYDER CUP
EUROPE TEAM

Selection for the European team is based on the Ryder Cup World
Points List and the European Points List.

The Ryder Cup World Points List

This list is comprised of official World Golf Ranking Points won
by a European Tour member from each tournament in which he
participates between 1 September 2005 and 3 September 2006.

For the final week of qualifying only, World Ranking Points
will be awarded solely for the BMW International Open on the
European Tour international schedule. World Ranking Points are
allocated to all officially sanctioned tournaments (on any federated
tour) and are allocated according to the event rating of the tournament.

The Ryder Cup European Points List

This list is comprised of points (1 euro = 1 point) earned by a
European Tour member from all officially sanctioned events
counting towards the European Tour Order of Merit between 1
September 2005 and 3 September 2006.

The final team will comprise:
- The leading five players on the Ryder Cup World Points List (1)
  as of Sunday, 3 September 2006. In the event of a tie (equal
  number of points accumulated), placings will be decided by the
  player with the higher ranking on the Official World Golf
  Rankings as of Monday, 28 August 2006.
- The leading five players not otherwise qualified (having selected
  the five players from the Ryder Cup World Points List above)
  from the Ryder Cup European Points List as of Sunday, 3
  September 2006. In the event of a tie (equal number of points
  accumulated), placings will be decided by the player with the
  higher ranking on the 2006 European Tour Order of Merit as
  of Sunday, 3 September 2006.
- In addition, two further selections will be made by the 2006
  European team captain, Ian Woosnam.

THE UNITED STATES TEAM

Selection for the United States team is based on points earned on the US PGA Tour from 22 August 2004 through to the US PGA Championship on 20 August 2006. The top ten in the US Team Standings at the time automatically qualify and a further two selections are then made by the 2006 US team captain, Tom Lehman.

Points are awarded for top ten finishes at US PGA Tour co-sponsored events as follows:

2004 Regular Events
75, 45, 40, 35, 30, 25, 20, 15, 10, 5.

2005 Regular Events
75, 45, 40, 35, 30, 25, 20, 15, 10, 5.

2005 Majors
450, 225, 200, 175, 150, 125, 100, 75, 50, 25.

2006 Regular Events
375, 180, 160, 140, 120, 100, 80, 60, 40, 20.

2006 Majors
675, 360, 320, 280, 240, 200, 160, 120, 80, 40.

The European team is selected over a one-year period, while the United States team is selected over a two-year period.

The regular tour events for US team selection in year one attract fewer points than they would in year two. Majors in year one for US team selection attract considerably more points than regular events, but in year two the points in the majors attract more than in year one. Although Ryder Cup points for US team selection are over a two-year period, the bulk is accumulated in year two.

THE RYDER CUP COMMITTEE IN EUROPE

What is the composition of this inner sanctum? How is it selected? What is its term of office? Steve Franklin, press officer at the European Tour headquarters, answered these questions.

There are two structures in place and its members are nominated by the shareholders, who also decide on the term of office.

The Ryder Cup board
Ken Brown (European Tour)
Jim Christine (PGA)
Donato Di Ponciano (PGA of Europe)
Heinz Fehring (PGA of Europe)
Mark James (European Tour)
Miguel Angel Jiménez (European Tour)
Bernhard Langer (European Tour)
Colin Montgomerie (European Tour)
Jan Van de Velde (European Tour)
Phil Weaver (PGA)

The composition of this board mirrors the shareholding of each party: 60%–20%–20%.

Administration board
Richard Hills (Ryder Cup director and head of player relations, European Tour)
Sandy Jones (chief executive of the PGA)
George O'Grady (executive director, European Tour)
Jonathan Orr (financial director, European Tour)
Mikael Sorling (PGA of Europe)
John Yapp (PGA)

CHAPTER 7

The Journalists

I spoke to eight golf journalists who have covered Ryder Cup events over the years, six of whom are print journalists. Tim Barter is a golf instructor and commentator with Sky Sports. Greg Allen is a sports journalist with RTÉ Radio. Dermot Gilleece is golf correspondent with *The Sunday Independent*. John Hopkins is golf correspondent for *The Times*. Charlie Mulqueen is golf correspondent with the *Irish Examiner*. Pat Ruddy worked with *The Evening Herald* and is now the proprietor of the European Club in Wicklow. Colm Smith was golf correspondent with the *Irish Independent*. Seamus Smith is general secretary of the GUI and is a former golf correspondent with *The Irish Press*.

TIM BARTER IS A GOLF INSTRUCTOR AND COMMENTATOR WITH SKY SPORTS

I met with Tim Barter during the 2005 European Open at the K Club. What did he think of the Ryder Cup coming to Ireland?

'The event will be absolutely huge and it is long overdue. I say this given the massive input that Irish players have had in the Ryder Cup over the years. I myself have been very much involved with the golfing scene over the last fifteen to twenty years and it strikes me that somehow, somewhere there has always been an

Irish player who has holed the winning putt, hit the crucial shot or who has made a significant contribution to this marvellous event. It is high time the biennial matches came to your shores.'

What were Tim's views on the K Club as a venue?

'Ireland is very fortunate in having so many wonderful courses, the K Club included. The K Club is a splendid course and an excellent venue to host the Ryder Cup. So much work has gone into making the course the magnificent layout it undoubtedly is. Every Ryder Cup player who will make the 2006 team will be delighted with this very high-class Arnold Palmer-designed layout. I know Arnie himself is delighted at his course being selected.'

He continued 'You have also an incredible infrastructure here at the K Club. There will be between 30,000 to 40,000 spectators each day looking forward to golf's biggest spectacle. Your road and rail network will be able to cope with the enormous crowds expected for Ryder Cup week. The air and sea facilities are ideal. Your wonderful capital city of Dublin is at everyone's doorstep. Many of the golf fans from overseas who will be attending the event in September next will be anxious to take in a golfing holiday while they are here. Ireland is fortunate in having so many high-standard golf courses and these golf enthusiasts will want to play them while they are here.'

I put it to Tim that golf purists wanted the Ryder Cup on a links rather than on an inland course.

'Of course, Ireland has a plethora of links creations that have hosted many golf championships in the past. Portmarnock, Ballybunion and Baltray are magnificent layouts. There are also other considerations that have to be accommodated when an event as huge as the Ryder Cup is played here. I mentioned some of them already. In addition, there are commercial and business concerns. There is also the issue of spectators being able to follow individual matches in comfort. The K Club can satisfy all of these requirements. Let's not forget the tented village. This will be a miniature village that needs ample space to accommodate eating areas, banks, post offices, media centres, merchandise outlets, corporate hospitality centres, hotel accommodation for players and officials, garda offices, tourist information and medical centres. The entire operation is massive. The K Club is an ideal location in all of those respects.'

Tim had already alluded to the great legacy that Irish players have in relation to Ryder Cup history. What Irish players stand out in his memory?

'I will never forget the marvellous contribution Eamonn Darcy made at the 1987 Ryder Cup at Muirfield Village in the States. Just think of it. He beat a US Masters champion on American soil. Crenshaw had broken his putter leaving the sixth green and he had to improvise with his other clubs for the remainder of the game. That incredibly difficult putt that Eamonn sank on the final green was a devastating blow not only to Ben, but to the entire American team. It was the first time we beat the opposition in America. Some Americans looked at Eamonn's technique during the match and were confident they would easily take care of "the Irishman". Obviously they didn't know Eamonn Darcy very well. He is a feisty character and an incredibly good player, as he showed on that occasion.'

Tim was on-course commentator for Philip Walton's 1995 Ryder Cup singles against Jay Haas – was it exciting?

'This was just a fantastic Ryder Cup. Imagine the tense scenario! Walton was three up with three to go. Haas holed out of the bunker on the sixteenth, leaving him two behind, and played another incredible shot to the penultimate hole and winning it also. One down with one to go! Both Walton and Haas found themselves in trouble going down the final hole and it actually came down to who could hold his nerve. The pressure was enormous. It was an advantage to the Irishman on the one hand, as he was one up with one hole to go, but he had just lost two holes on the trot which unsettled Philip psychologically. Viewed from another perspective, it inflated Haas's self-esteem hugely. Bernard Gallacher was in his third captaincy. What Bernard would have given for a win! He knew on paper the Americans were favourites – we were nothing like as strong as they were. Walton held his nerve and closed the door on Haas. We won the Ryder Cup.'

Would Tim agree Philip Walton has gone off the boil in recent years?

'It is sad to see he has lost form since his glory days. None of us likes to see any player struggling. Philip is having a really wicked year of it and if he is not able to make the cuts, then this becomes a big problem. What happens is that it becomes an issue in a player's mind. The pressure of making the cut becomes the problem. We all feel for him, but he's a quality player. I'm sure he'll come back and be able to put in some more quality performances.'

What of the new breeds – Clarke, Harrington and McGinley?

'They have played massive parts in the Ryder Cup. Darren has played in four Ryder Cups. In 1997 he was on a winning Ryder Cup team in Spain. He and Monty beat Couples and Love on the Saturday, but unfortunately Darren lost out to Mickelson in the singles. In 1999 he had mixed fortunes at Brookline when the US beat us by one point. In Europe's win in 2002 Darren took points in three out of his five matches. He and Thomas Björn had a great win on the opening day against Woods and Azinger. He was again on the winning side in 2004 at Oakland Hills, having played in five matches and taking points in four of them. When Darren is on form he provides huge momentum to his team-mates. This is crucial in the Ryder Cup. He welcomes pressure and revels in it.'

Tim continued, 'Padraig Harrington is a great player. He has already played in three matches and we know he is in the top ten players in the world. As a rookie in 1999 he took points out of two of his three matches. In 2002 he managed to get points from two of his four outings and in the 2004 series Padraig played in five matches and got points in four of them. He is an incredibly disciplined golfer, somebody who absolutely puts 120 per cent into everything he does, and even today he is out here at the European Open and having missed the cut he is on the range hitting balls. Padraig is a guy who deserves every ounce of success he gets, and he is having a lot. The level of dedication that he's got is exemplary. Obviously the Open Championship is not far away. He is capable of winning it and he wants to make sure that he is absolutely ready. He'll be a contender, I'm sure.' (Owing to the death of his father in July 2005, Padraig Harrington withdrew from the British Open Championship, which was held at St Andrew's.)

What does the Sky Sports commentator think of the Ryder Cup legacies of the two Christy O'Connors?

'Actually, I was never fortunate enough to see Senior playing in his hey day – everyone who did says that he was one of the greatest ball strikers they had ever seen. I did see him in later life when he was way into his sixties and won the British Seniors. He impressed the socks off me! He was still hitting drivers off the fairway – things that other players dream of. So I'm sad I didn't get to see Christy in his prime.'

What memories does Tim have of Christy Junior?

'I was asked by Sky Sports on one occasion to go to the Belfry and recreate Christy Junior's two iron shot into the eighteenth green. I don't possess Christy's talent, I can tell you. It was on a cold, wet October afternoon and the wind was against me – I stood at the plaque on the eighteenth fairway where Christy had hit the shot from. The plaque was inscribed with the details, the distance, the club he used, etc. I just stood there, looked at the shot that would have confronted Christy Junior on that memorable September afternoon in 1989. I thought of Christy, Freddie Couples, the crowd and the match, as tight as it was. That two iron shot to the green was an incredible shot and will live in everyone's memory forever,' he enthused.

'I remember interviewing another one of Ireland's great Ryder Cup players, Paul McGinley. It was immediately after he sank the winning putt at the Belfry in 2002. I trotted across the green with people shouting and roaring. I managed to seek him out and asked the question: What does it feel like to hole the winning putt in the Ryder Cup? He went through his emotions there and then and spoke not about the putt but rather his second shot to the eighteenth. "My tee shot on eighteen finished a yard from Christy's plaque – I'm looking at the plaque and said to myself, 'No, Christy, not now!'" Paul's thoughts had gone momentarily back to that September afternoon in 1989 and realised the enormous pressure Junior was under and Paul was in exactly the same spot and he had to deliver the goods! And of course the pressure mounted until McGinley finally made that winning putt. That was a precious moment in time.'

How long was the winning putt? Eight feet, ten or maybe fourteen?

'I'm going to split it. I would say around nine feet. That's a pretty good estimate. I said at the time six feet, but I was away with the fairies anyway. But it was downhill, left to right, it was horrid. Paul said his caddie had reminded him that he had holed exactly the same putt in the Benson & Hedges Tournament a few years before. The caddie repeated his advice to Paul: "Exactly the same putt – you know exactly what it does, hole it!" And hole it Paul did.'

GREG ALLEN IS A SPORTS JOURNALIST WITH RTÉ RADIO

In his early days, Greg Allen's reporting interests revolved around soccer and rugby, but in his subsequent twenty-two years with RTÉ, Greg concentrated on his two loves, athletics and golf. Those regular sports listeners to our national radio station will get insights from Greg's reports into his enthusiasm and passion for athletics and golf. How did they differ from a coverage standpoint?

'Athletics reporting is easier. It all takes place in a stadium, where you have a complete overview of all that is happening, and happening live in front of you. Golf is by its nature very different. You can be out reporting on one match and two holes away it might be all happening. I love to spend a lot of time out on the course because it's there where the atmosphere is,' he enthused.

During our interview at his home club at Blainroe in Wicklow, the conversation invariably led to September's 2006 Ryder Cup matches at the K Club. What were his thoughts about this imminent occasion?

'The spectacle will be one of Ireland's greatest ever sporting events. It's a great honour for us to stage the Ryder Cup given Ireland's own legacy down the years.'

Should the choice of venue not have been a links course, like Portmarnock? Greg Allen was emphatic in his reply.

'When you consider that Ireland has approximately a third of the world's links, you can understand why the purists say we should be playing on a links, which would reflect our traditional strengths. I can empathise very much with those traditional sentiments. That aside, however, make no mistake about it but the K Club will be a fine course and will live up to expectations. I have played the course on a number of occasions and I know it will be an appropriate challenge come September.'

Will Portmarnock ever be able to stage a Ryder Cup in the future?

'I believe this world-renowned links had its golden opportunity in 1993. It almost happened back then, but as we know, the Ryder Cup powers that be ended up with a split decision regarding the venue. This resulted in the chairman exercising his right to use his casting vote in favour of the event going to the Belfry. Then there was Valderrama in 1997. Spain was the first

European host country outside Great Britain to host the Ryder Cup. A new era had dawned. Bolivian businessman Jaime Patino was the financial wizard that put the Ryder Cup on a commercial course for the future.'

The RTÉ journalist has attended six Ryder Cups in all, covering a twelve-year period. They have all been hugely exciting encounters. There were some classic Ryder Cup battles. Greg singled out a few memories.

'Paul McGinley's memorable nine-foot putt for a half point in his match against Jim Furyk was a great occasion. That must be seen against the backdrop of the match immediately ahead of McGinley's, where Niclas Fasth was one up on Paul Azinger going down the eighteenth. Everybody remembers how the American holed out from the bunker to snatch a half. Paul McGinley was down the eighteenth fairway ready to play his second shot amidst the thunderous roars ahead. What pressure for Paul – and to do what he did. Fantastic stuff!'

Oak Hill tops the list of Ryder Cup moments in time for him. It was his first time reporting on the biennial event on American soil. The Europeans would be playing on one of the toughest American courses, if not *the* toughest. The fact they were playing on American soil meant that the Americans were the clear favourites to win. It was fair to say there was an unusual air of pessimism palpable within European ranks. The long-standing formidable partnership of Ballesteros and Olazábal was now confined to the archives. The cloudy, rainy opening day arguably matched the mood of some European players.

The Friday morning fourballs were shared 2 points apiece. The afternoon foursomes were a different matter, as the firm favourites accumulated 3 points from a possible 4 to lead 5 points to 3 at the end of day one. There was silver lining for Bernard Gallacher's squad in Saturday's morning foursomes, which they won 3 points to 1. This reversed their trouncing of the previous afternoon. The highlight of Saturday morning's encounters was the crushing blow Sam Torrance and Costantino Rocca inflicted on Jeff Maggert and Davis Love III. The matches were now evenly poised at 6 points each.

Then there was the electrifying atmosphere on the Saturday afternoon. The cheers audible all over the course were naturally

American. These cheers were magnified ten times over when US Open champion Corey Pavin chipped in from some twenty feet to give himself and Loren Roberts that crucial one-hole win over Woosnam and Walton. The Americans now led 9 to 7 going into the final day. Laddy Wadkins was in buoyant mood. Bernard Gallacher was down hearted and didn't relish the thought of captaining three consecutive unsuccessful European teams.

Tom Lehman kept American adrenalin pumping on the final day when he disposed of Seve Ballesteros by the convincing margin of 4 and 3. The proverbial writing was on the wall. The visitors were in a defiant mood, however, and had a surprise in store for their opponents. Woosnam would halve with Couples, while Englishman Mark James would dispose of Jeff Maggert. Inspired by an earlier hole-in-one, Howard Clarke put an end to Peter Jacobsen's challenge by beating him one up. These performances gave encouragement and impetus for the other Europeans to build on. David Gilford and Colin Montgomerie would also come up trumps. The pressure and tension of it all were enormous. There were huge expectations from the American galleries – they in their own way put additional pressure on their squad.

Meanwhile, Nick Faldo was one down with two to play against Curtis Strange. It was the former US Open champion who succumbed to the enormity of the occasion by finishing bogey, bogey to lose out to his old rival, Faldo, by one hole. Bernhard Langer beat Corey Pavin 3 and 2. Finally, Ireland's Philip Walton would have his own mettle put to the test. His true grit and tenacity won out when he closed the door on Jay Haas. We did what seemed to be the impossible. We came from 9-7 points down going into the last day's singles and we achieved what was normally the preserve of the Americans – to come from behind to win Sunday's singles and the Ryder Cup.

Greg also remembers the 2004 Ryder Cup at Oakland Hills for a special reason. Not only did the European team win, but the result – 18½ to 9½ – was the most convincing trouncing of a US side on home soil. The last time that result was recorded was in 1981 at Walton Heath in Surrey, when the US team beat the home side by the same margin. Greg also recalls the McGinley/ Harrington tussle with the formidable Woods/Love partnership. The Irish pair was two down after two holes and Padraig

Harrington seemed a little down. It was Paul McGinley who got his compatriot back on track and into focus and the all-Irish pairing went on to beat their opponents 4 and 3.

What did Greg think of the great Irish record of ten Ryder Cup caps achieved by Christy O'Connor, Sr.? 'I didn't really see Christy in his Ryder Cup prime, but if you consider that when he played his last Ryder Cup in 1973 he was in his late forties – that is some achievement. Given the competitive nature of Ryder Cup matches nowadays, his record is under little or no threat. It is unlikely to be broken. He was truly a great player. I saw some of his greatness about ten years ago when I was playing in a links (pro-am) outing at Baltray. I think Christy was seventy-one at the time and he shot 71! He was playing immediately behind me and I couldn't help looking back occasionally at the great man himself and I was so impressed with his swing fluidity late in his life. I can only imagine and marvel at Christy's ball striking in his prime.'

How come he never won a major? Again, Greg gave a very definitive and insightful reply. 'The only major Christy played in was in the Open Championship. The other three are in America and when you consider he never played in them, his only annual opportunity to compete in a major was confined to the Open. Those players who take part in all majors and who are in regular contention create more opportunities to win. Christy was not in that league. However, we must not diminish his wonderful track record for a non-winner of the Open.'

Finally, we spoke about the possible outcome of the 2006 Ryder Cup event. Greg believed the odds as to who would win were evenly distributed. He also added that the European team would bond better when Ryder Cup week gets underway. The Americans, Greg maintains, generally don't regard being Ryder Cup team members as pinnacles of their careers. They would prefer to win individual tournaments. This doesn't mean they aren't proud to be on the team. Making the Ryder team is certainly a goal for the US players, but once achieved, the Ryder Cup 'thing' dissipates as the months go by, he said.

Will Tom Lehman be a playing captain if he qualifies for the team? 'I don't believe he will play. I have been at six Ryder Cups already and I am convinced a captain is under enough organisational and team pressure without adding to it. How can he select his team properly if he is out on the course playing? Imagine if the matches come down to the wire at the K Club and the Americans lose by a tiny margin. Imagine the consequent remorse.' However, I reminded Greg of Arnold Palmer's playing captaincy of 1963 when he won 4 out of a possible 6 points. Arnie is on record as saying, 'Why shouldn't Tom Lehman be a playing captain if he qualifies?' Greg disagrees.

'Times were different in 1963. The Americans could have fielded two, three or more teams and have won. Look at the recent Ryder Cup matches with many actually going down to the final hole. It is no longer a one-sided affair. The pressures associated with modern Ryder Cups are enormous. Tom will not be a playing captain,' said Greg.

DERMOT GILLEECE IS GOLF CORRESPONDENT WITH *THE SUNDAY INDEPENDENT*

One of Dermot Gilleece's cherished Ryder Cup memories goes back to 1995 at Oak Hill. Dermot was already out on the course looking at other matches when Ireland's Philip Walton was three up with three to go and in command in his encounter with 'Mr Consistency', Jay Haas. The then *Irish Times* golf journalist joined the gallery following his fellow Irishman. The American had already clawed back one hole after holing out from the bunker for an unexpected winning birdie at the sixteenth. Dermot merged into the gallery circling the seventeenth green as the Malahide player was lining up his 3½ footer hoping to close the door on Haas. Would he miss? Of course not, he'll rattle it into the back of the cup; Dermot was wishing the putt into the hole. Alas, Philip missed. Dermot heard a voice nearby saying 'a pity'. It was the voice of England's Prince Andrew, who was one of the ardent spectators following the Walton/Haas tussle.

After reducing the deficit from three holes to a mere one hole, the infectious buzz of excitement spread around the course. The eager gallery swelled and surrounded the eighteenth tee. Dermot felt a sudden surge of patriotic adrenalin as Philip Walton addressed his final tee shot with the intention of propelling it down the eighteenth fairway. It ended up in the rough on the right. Dermot Gilleece remained loyal to Philip, following him at close quarters and encouraging his compatriot to carry out his mission. Ian Woosnam, who was Walton's foursomes partner on day two, was in the gallery hoping his Ryder Cup colleague would use his five wood, the perfect club selection, to reach his target. Philip's Liverpool caddie, Brian McLachlan, was in ribbons. The occasion was making him and his man more tense and anxious by the second. The Irishman left his five wood short for two but pitched on for his third. Jay Haas, also feeling the almost unbearable pressure, had pulled his drive into trouble on the left and was unable to make the green in two. Being one down, he had to win the hole to prevent Walton winning the match and so his overstrong pitch overran the green for three. Philip left his first putt eighteen inches from the hole. The American at best could hole his rather lengthy putt for five, but he was obliged to concede his opponent's winning bogey putt. The one-hole victory clinched Ryder Cup victory for the European team.

Dermot Gilleece was caught up in the huge excitement and noticed how Philip went over to Seve, who was in the crowd supporting him, and said out of the blue, 'Seve, there is nothing wrong with your swing – just hit the ball, all you need is confidence!' Seve was heard to say, 'It's a great day for Philip and a great day for Ireland!' Europe had won the Ryder Cup!

According to what Philip told Dermot, Prince Andrew actually travelled back on Concorde with the team, and when the plane landed at Dublin Airport, the prince prevailed upon the Malahide man to emerge with the Cup. Philip had originally resisted all pleas to do so. It was a proud moment for Philip and Ireland!

The Darcy/Crenshaw duel was another memorable experience for Dermot Gilleece. That was at Muirfield Village, when Ireland's Eamonn Darcy got the better of 'Gentleman Ben'. That was the occasion when the American 'broke' his putter after three putting the sixth to lose the hole to Darcy. The pièce de resistance for Dermot came on the eighteenth, when Dermot felt proud to be Irish as Darcy stood over that five footer to win the Ryder Cup for the first time on American soil. It was no ordinary putt. It was a slippery downhill left to right putt that needed to be stroked with a delicate authority, otherwise it would miss its target, leaving an equally difficult return. Dermot, still touched by his adrenalin-pumping moments earlier on the seventeenth, felt Eamonn could well miss this one. It was the final green and Eamonn's last chance for a bite of the cherry. And hole it he did! The relief Dermot Gilleece felt must have been palpable to all around that final green, except for Ben Crenshaw, his American team and fans.

Who does Dermot Gilleece believe was Ireland's greatest golfer? He was very definite with his response.

'What do we mean by great and greatest?' he asked. 'Christy O'Connor, Sr. had the best Ryder Cup innings of them all. He was a most gifted player who possessed all the skills – nobody had that level before or since. He had complete control over all clubs with one exception, his putter. But was he the greatest Irish player of all time? That's another matter.' Dermot recalled the 1976 Irish Open at Portmarnock, when Gary Player was asked a similar question. Gary had no difficulty whatsoever in saying Fred Daly was the greatest Irish golfer. Gary knew Christy had more Ryder Cup caps, but what he didn't have to his credit was a major. Daly won the 1947 Open Championship and that put him ahead of Christy O'Connor. Yet Player had the utmost respect for Christy Senior's fine ball-striking qualities. Christy also influenced the South African. Christy's animal grace, prowl-like approach and disciplined mind endeared him to the great South African player, according to Dermot.

If a player is in contention often enough, he should win a major. O'Connor was in that position often enough but didn't finish it off, so Dermot agreed with the South African's interpretation of what 'greatest' means. 'Daly was Ireland's best,' Dermot acknowledged, 'and this is in no way diminishing the magnificent achievements of Christy.'

What were Dermot's feelings about the greatest golfing spectacle coming to our shores? 'It's absolutely marvellous but long overdue. The Irish were hard done by over the years, not only in not having the Ryder Cup staged here but also in not having an Irish Ryder Cup captain at some stage over the years. We had the calibre in players like Fred Daly, Harry Bradshaw and Christy O'Connor. We didn't get due recognition in that regard.'

Now that it is to be staged here, what does Dermot think about the outcry of golf's purists, that it should be staged on one of our traditional links, such as Portmarnock? 'Of course, Portmarnock would have been an ideal venue back in the early 1990s. Things have changed dramatically in the interim. We are living in an age of "unashamed commercialism", as former executive director of the European Tour, Ken Schofield, maintains. Ken's statement echoes associated comments at the official announcement of the K Club location in January 1999, when he said that "the days of Muirfield [the 1973 hosts] are gone. It is no longer practicable for a members' club to stage the Ryder Cup."'

Is Dermot looking forward to the event at the K Club? 'Absolutely! It will be a fantastic occasion for golf, for Ireland. It will be a spectacle that will put our country on the world map.'

JOHN HOPKINS IS GOLF CORRESPONDENT FOR *THE TIMES*

I interviewed John last summer at the European Open at the K Club. What did he think of the Ryder Cup coming to our shores?

'The Ryder Cup has a missionary duty,' he said. 'I know that sounds rather patronising, but to explain, it has a duty to be moved around Europe. It went to Valderrama in 1997. Goodness knows the Irish have supported the event down the years, arguably better than the Spaniards, who themselves supported it well. Some would say Ireland should have staged it before Spain, but it was one of those things. Internal politics are well known. Ireland has lost ten years in the process, but it doesn't really matter because with your shrewd marketing in these intervening years you have shown the rest of the world how to market a Ryder Cup destination.'

What were his thoughts about the K Club as a venue?

'If I had one complaint, and it would be a very minor one, I wish it were a more natural and very non-American-looking golf course. Don't misunderstand me – the venue is an excellent and challenging course and as a venue it will be superb, I am sure. But there are great traditional Irish courses – links.'

Did John have any thoughts on Ireland's contributions to Ryder Cup matches over the years? He began by highlighting the Ryder Cup career of Christy O'Connor, Sr.

'I arrived on the scene to marvel at this man's great expertise as a world-class player. It was towards the end of his Ryder Cup appearances. He was a magnificent ball striker. I will always remember Muirfield Village when Eamonn Darcy beat Ben Crenshaw on the last green. It was a great occasion. You will remember Ben three putted the sixth green. He broke the putter afterwards and was obliged to putt for the remainder of the singles with a combination of different clubs. Still, the American fans were very confident their Ben would take care of Eamonn, whose swing they felt was suspect, to say the least. Obviously, they didn't know Eamonn Darcy. The fact that Crenshaw had to putt without his putter didn't matter and it should not be interpreted that this diminished Eamonn's victory in any way. What the Irishman had to do in the end was to hole a slippery five footer across a glassy green with his team-mates all around and knowing that the destiny of the Ryder Cup probably depended on that putt! And quite rightly he'll be remembered forever for that.'

Did any other Irish players impress John Hopkins?

'Although I never met Harry Bradshaw, I spoke with him on the phone. I am very aware of his expertise and I remember his great but unfortunate 1949 Open Championship. I remember seeing the piece on tape. It was the beer bottle incident – one of the most famous incidents in Open history. He had to hit a shot with the bottle to contend with and tied the Championship only to be beaten by Bobby Locke in a play-off for the title. Harry was really unfortunate then. Today he would get relief.'

If John had to single out one Irish golfer above all others – and this is by no means taking away from players like Darcy, O'Connor, Jr., Clarke, Harrington, McGinley and others – it would have to be 'Himself', as *The Times* golf correspondent referred to O'Connor, Sr. John felt O'Connor, Sr. was a very natural and gifted golfer and that's why he lasted so long at the top.

However, the Englishman's observation would not find favour with the Royal Dublin maestro. Christy rejects the notion completely out of hand that he is a gifted and natural player. His graceful, rhythmic swing as seen and admired by others was anything but natural. He is adamant that it is the product of long, arduous hours of practice.

Is John looking forward to the 2006 matches?

'Very much so! It will be a great occasion and one which Ireland will really be proud of. I am looking forward to the opening ceremonies and the razzmatazz that goes along with the event.'

On the topic of dress code, John feels very strongly about this tradition being carried too far. 'The wives of the players are there to support their husbands and they should refrain from dressing up in similar colours to their husbands and partners. It's overdone. It can give rise to inevitable comparisons. One year you can look at the Americans and say they all look stunning and by comparison the Europeans don't. Next time round it might be the reverse. Let's get on with the golf – let's get the players' wives and partners out on the course, smartly dressed to support their team.'

CHARLIE MULQUEEN IS GOLF CORRESPONDENT WITH THE *IRISH EXAMINER*

Charlie began his career at the *Limerick Leader*, a provincial newspaper. He became sports editor with the same publication and then moved on to be appointed golf correspondent of the *Cork Examiner*, now the *Irish Examiner*, in 1981. Anyone who has read his columns will realise that his passion for the game is unrivalled. As far back as 1966 – the year O'Connor, Sr. won the Carroll's International Tournament at Royal Dublin, finishing eagle-birdie-eagle – the Limerick man covered golf tournaments all over Ireland for RTÉ Radio. It wasn't long before he added major championships to his reporting repertoire.

He went on to cover Ryder Cup matches. Charlie recalls his first match vividly. It was at Royal Lytham and St Anne's in 1961, the same year the Berlin Wall was erected. Life was tough in those early days.

'I was an impecunious eighteen-year-old who hitch-hiked my way from Limerick to St Anne's with hardly the price of a good meal in my pocket, let alone a spare penny for an admission ticket,' Charlie confessed.

His zealous passion knew no bounds, and before long he gained access to the course having sourced a gap in the fence by the twelfth green. Once in, Charlie merged with the spectators, being acutely conscious that he might well be noticed for his blatant disregard for protocol, and he was afraid he might be unceremoniously evicted to the far side of the divide. 'But I loved every minute of it. There was even a touch of adrenalin from knowing I was somehow getting away with my little piece of subterfuge,' he said.

His inbuilt antenna guided him to where his idol, Christy, was. Charlie was bowled over at the magnificent ball-striking skills of the maestro and his ability to extricate himself from the most unlikely of difficult situations. It was a wish come true for Charlie later in his career to partner 'Himself' to victory in a Canary Islands pro-am.

Charlie Mulqueen followed the solid partnership of Christy O'Connor, Sr. and Peter Alliss when they 'walloped Gene Littler and Doug Ford by 4 and 3 in the first match on the first day of the 1961 Ryder Cup matches.' Charlie continued, 'They lost on the eighteenth in the afternoon as a typically powerful US team took control. I'll never forget the sight of Billy Casper carrying that large stomach of his around the Lytham links with the ease of a slim-line college kid, and Mike Souchak was another big man who lives in the memory.'

Charlie continued, 'The American who stood out for just about everybody was Arnold Palmer, a swashbuckling figure on the links if ever there was one. He and Casper were a powerful combination and Arnie also took 1½ points from his two singles. The man to hold him was Alliss, a beautiful swinger of a golf club and a man blessed with a lovely touch around the greens. Alliss distinguished himself later as the BBC television voice of golf. Palmer, a golfing legend and one of sport's most popular and successful exponents, went on to become a renowned course architect. Just as one was in awe of Christy O'Connor, Sr. in one's younger days and later got to know the man fairly well, it was my pleasure to meet up with Palmer and be accorded a one-on-one interview with the legend for RTÉ Radio during one of his visits to Tralee, where he designed the lovely links at Barrow. Jack Nicklaus was terrific when we met up with him on his many visits to Mount Juliet during the construction of that magnificent course.'

Charlie added, 'That's one of the beauties of our job, to have the opportunity to meet our boyhood heroes in privileged circumstances, to talk to them, to sometimes get to know them. As for the modern era, a lot of people might regard them either as prima donnas or just too full of their own importance, but that's not really the case. They say you can't have a one-on-one inter-view with Tiger Woods, but I managed it in 2000 when he came to Limerick Golf Club for the J.P. McManus pro-am. Mind you, J.P. had more than a little to do with that!'

Charlie Mulqueen also interviewed Montgomerie. 'Last April, I met up with Colin Montgomerie during the Spanish Open and he gave me a half an hour of his time and couldn't have been more interesting, articulate and charming. Not his public persona at all, I suppose.'

What about the Irish players? How facilitating were they? Charlie was very complimentary to them.

'Here in Ireland, we are blessed with Padraig Harrington, Darren Clarke and Paul McGinley. We regard them as friends as much as anything else and very much the same applies to Graeme McDowell and the other guys on tour. In the majority of cases, professional golfers are courteous and friendly and also co-operative within reason.'

What about the Nicklaus era? Charlie went on to resurrect a sporting memory from the 1969 Ryder Cup. 'Who will ever be allowed to forget the half he handed Tony Jacklin so the teams could finish on even terms at Birkdale? And yet it was Jack who ten years later successfully advocated that Britain and Ireland should change to Europe as a whole because the matches were just too one sided. One American, Tom Weiskopf, had been so turned off the whole idea that he turned down the opportunity to take part and went hunting instead!'

Charlie continued, 'The 1979 match is remembered for all the wrong reasons, especially here in Ireland. Des Smyth and Eamonn Darcy were members of the first European team. Unfortunately, the word "team" is a misnomer in this case. Ken Brown and Mark James could be safely described as the young rebels of the time and Brown's partnership with Smyth was a bit of a disaster. They were thrashed 7 and 6 by Hale Irwin and Tom Kite with even the Americans unimpressed with the Scotsman's behaviour. How times change, with Brown now one of the game's leading broadcasters and James a Ryder Cup captain of the recent past.'

How did Europe as a team meet up with Jack Nicklaus's hopes for future biennial matches?

'The idea that Europe would present the Americans with a more meaningful contest proved misguided for the first few meetings of the sides. One match that stands out was at Walton Heath in 1981. Smyth and Darcy were there again, but this was probably the greatest of all American sides: Nicklaus, Watson, Trevino, Kite,

Miller and Floyd, all at their scintillating best in beating Europe. The US squad accumulated 18½ points to Europe's 9½ points. Humiliation, yes, but at last the corner was about to be turned. It required a sensational shot by Lanny Wadkins on the final green to see the US home by a single match at the 1983 Ryder Cup at Palm Beach Gardens. The Ryder Cup would never again be a cake walk for the Americans. Instead, a European side without a single Irishman raced home at the Belfry in 1985 and Eamonn Darcy's heroics helped to clinch a first-ever win on American soil two years later. By now, Seve, José Maria, Nick, Bernhard and Sandy were in their prime. How proud we all felt when Christy Junior unleashed the majestic two iron that shattered Freddie Couples at the Belfry in 1989 and played a key part in the retention of the trophy. I well recall how he and Anne cried tears of joy behind the eighteenth green and how he so wanted to answer some damning remarks in one of England's so-called quality newspapers that had been widely circulated in the hotel that morning. Wiser counsel prevailed, as we reminded him the best response should have come from his clubs, and that was just what had taken place!'

Does Charlie recall Hale Irwin's 'wayward drive' at the eighteenth in his match against Bernhard Langer at Kiawah Island in 1991? Indeed he does.

'That was when the German missed his fateful putt on the final green. Hale Irwin snatched a half and so the Americans won. I have always wondered how Irwin's drive wound up in the middle of the fairway when in flight it looked to be hooking into jungle country miles to the left. That was the year of "the war on the shore" and the Americans, in a high state of jingoism at the time of the Gulf War, would have done anything to win the trophy back.'

And then there was Malahide man, Philip Walton, in his tussle with Jay Haas. That was a marvellous occasion for Charlie. 'Just like Darcy in 1987 and O'Connor, Jr. in 1989, Irish hearts burst out of their chests with pride when Philip Walton provided the winning point at Oak Hill in 1995, and that was to be the first of four wins in five matches for Europe. By now the Irish had arrived in force. McGinley sank another match winner at the Belfry in 2002. Oh, such blessed memories! And yet, there are so many more, like that idyllic Saturday afternoon at Oakland Hills outside Detroit when Harrington and McGinley fell two behind early on against Tiger Woods and Davis Love III and wound up winners by 4 and 3,' Charlie recalled.

'Irish flags abounded, "Olé, Olé, Olé" rang out. And that was nothing to the excitement twenty-four hours later, when the two Dubliners and Clarke again contributed handsomely to a runaway European triumph.'

What does the staging of the Ryder Cup mean for Ireland?

'The Ryder Cup is one of the world's greatest sporting events, perhaps ranked in prestige and interest behind only the Olympics and football's World Cup. Accordingly, the eyes of much of the planet are on us for one golden week and on the nation as a whole, it's an opportunity to capitalise in countless diverse areas, some of them with nothing at all to do with golf.' Does this mean that Charlie Mulqueen is sounding a note of caution in much the same way as Des Smyth, a 2006 Ryder Cup vice-captain, is doing? Former Ryder Cup player Smyth is on record as saying Ireland has invested much in bringing the event here and it would be a pity to damage the country's *céad míle fáilte* reputation if certain sectors were to negatively exploit the event. Charlie was quite vocal on this point.

'The ardent hope is that all this effort won't be jeopardised in any way. Sadly, that seems a forlorn cause. Many hotels have seen a killing coming their way for a long time and have duly swooped. Some of the hotels are charging €282 a night – without breakfast. Many other indigenous and international companies have come on board. Wouldn't it be a shame if it all blew up in our faces because of the actions of a greedy minority? And as a consequence, the American presence in the press tent will be lower than usual. The newspaper industry is struggling over there and there isn't as much money as there used to be to send golf reporters across the Atlantic. Those journalists forced to stay at home have already been telling their readers why, and those who are still coming won't be slow to raise the subject on arrival. It could all be so counter productive,' he warned.

'Fáilte Ireland has used government money wisely and courageously to promote the many delights of Ireland as a golfing destination since the Ryder Cup was first allocated to this country in 1997. For its part, the government did a fantastic job in bringing this world-class event to Ireland. To the best of my knowledge, though, the government did not have or want to have a say in choosing the venue except to favour the idea of a links venue if it were possible. It wasn't found to be practicable from a financial point of view, and they accepted that. Various sports ministers initially, and more importantly, Bernard Allen of Fine Gael and Jim McDaid of Fianna Fáil, were centrally involved in winning the Ryder Cup for our country.'

Finally, Charlie addressed another topical issue. Should Ireland have staged the event at one of Ireland's more traditional locations, a links course like Portmarnock, for instance? Once again, he was emphatic in his reply.

'Just as with the ramifications of the match coming to Ireland, the answer to this one is also self-evident. Money, money, money, as Abba might have said. Quite naturally, we all wanted to play it on a links, with Portmarnock just about everybody's first choice. But reality quickly dawned. The north Dublin club may boast some of the wealthiest and most influential gentlemen on this island, but that's just what it is − a club. They didn't have the wherewithal or indeed the inclination to go and find the kind of filthy lucre that would have clinched the deal in their favour.In any case, they were already well behind in the race. Dr Michael Smurfit down at the K Club had rescued the ailing European Open in 1995 and poured massive sums into the event while providing a magnificent location for one of the European Tour's flagship events. He promised to continue doing so long after the Ryder Cup had left our shores and he has kept his word. Combine that with all the other extras available at Straffan and really it was a no-brainer as far as the Tour was concerned. Those who still call it a shame that the match is not being staged on one of our many great links are not living in the real world, no matter how well and sincerely they may make their case. And in a recent general interview I conducted with the European number one and many-times Ryder Cup hero, Colin Montgomerie, he put the case for parkland links very succinctly when he said, "It is a shame in some ways that the Irish and Scottish Opens are played on parkland courses. On top of that, the next three Ryder Cups in Britain and Ireland are not going to links golf courses. Ireland and Scotland have some superb links and Wales has a few as well. It is a shame that we're inland on every one and all designed by so-called American designers, from Tom Weiskopf to Arnold Palmer to

Robert Trent Jones. You'd love to have the Ryder Cup at St Andrew's or Muirfield or Turnberry. Can you imagine the Ryder Cup being decided on the eighteenth at St Andrew's? To finish the Ryder Cup in that amphitheatre? Fantastic! Playing the seventeenth as a match play hole – amazing!"'

Charlie continued, 'Nowadays, as we all know, it's the mighty dollar that's talking. All that said, I think the K Club will be a great venue. We all can't wait for the Irish Ryder Cup to see what happens there. Talk about an electric atmosphere. The whole of Ireland will come to a halt, nobody will go to work on the Friday. The same Ryder Cup might not come back to our shores in our lifetime, so let's enjoy it while we can.'

PAT RUDDY IS A FORMER GOLF CORRESPONDENT AND NOW A GOLF COURSE ARCHITECT

From 1962 to 1968, Pat Ruddy was a freelance golf writer with *The Evening Herald* and a staff member from 1968 to 1973. He spent a further six years writing his own golf column with the *Irish Independent*. In more recent times he has devoted his considerable energies to another associated passion, golf course design. One of his greatest creations is Druids Glen. Along with the late former amateur international Tom Craddock, Pat was responsible for this challenging championship layout in Wicklow.

The jewel in his crown, however, is the European Club at Brittas Bay in Wicklow. He is the sole designer of this exquisite links, which has been rated in the top 100 courses in the world by the US *Golf* magazine (both in the 2003 and 2005 polls) and second amongst Ireland's greatest courses by *Golf Digest* (2005).

Along with Mark O'Meara and David Duval, Tiger Woods visited the European Club in 2002. Tiger shot a course record 67 off the tips. He liked it a lot. Pat Ruddy had a very close look at Tiger's record score on a links he had never played before. Pat promptly created some new tees to bring the links up to a massive 7,368 yards and added over thirty new bunkers for good measure. The Tiger-trap is reset!

Ruddy was offered a record price of £22.5 million for the European Club in the early 2000s. He declined on the basis that he didn't need the money. Were he to sell, he would have to buy another. Pat wanted to go on enjoying this little piece of heaven with his family and his ninety-eight members, who enjoy one of the most exclusive, if not *the* most exclusive, golfing experiences in the world at annual dues just above €1,100.

What does Pat think of the Ryder Cup, and more particularly of this spectacular sporting event coming to our shores? 'Marvellous – about time!'

One of his fondest Ryder Cup memories was when he was present for the 1975 matches in Laurel Valley, Pennsylvania. There were three Irish players on the team: Eamonn Darcy, Christy O'Connor, Jr. and John O'Leary. It was Arnold Palmer country. There were no ropes to contend with in those days; you strolled the fairways to your heart's content and brushed up against the world's greats. There was no need for crowd control, as is the feature of modern events. The fact that Great Britain and Ireland were trounced on that occasion (US 21, Great Britain and Ireland 11) was of little consequence to Pat. Being there and being part of the atmosphere was what mattered.

The 1969 Ryder Cup holds another fond memory for Pat. Great Britain and Ireland tied with the US 16 points apiece at Royal Birkdale. Pat remarked on the amazing gesture of sportsmanship shown by Jack Nicklaus to his opponent, Tony Jacklin. He conceded Tony's very missable putt, with the overall result being a gracious draw. Another Ryder Cup event was the 1987 tussle between Ireland's Eamonn Darcy and America's Ben Crenshaw, held in Jack Nicklaus's own backyard, Muirfield Village.

Darcy's golf swing came in for much criticism at the time. Some referred to his swing as being 'agricultural', with 'too many moving parts'. This was in direct contrast to Crenshaw's classic, free-flowing swing. However, Ben Crenshaw had a frustrating experience during his match with Darcy when he missed a rather short putt on the sixth green. He snapped the shaft of his Wilson putter. 'Gentleman Ben', as he was affectionately known, now had to improvise for the remainder of this great singles encounter. It was resolved on the eighteenth green when Eamonn smoothly rolled in a tricky, twisting downhill putt for a vital winning point, crushing the gentle spirit of his disconsolate opponent. The match result was Europe 15, US 13. This was the first home defeat on the US in six decades of Ryder Cup history. It was Eamonn Darcy's final putt that ensured victory.

COLM SMITH WAS GOLF CORRESPONDENT WITH THE IRISH INDEPENDENT

Colm Smith was golf correspondent with the *Irish Independent* for more than thirty years, starting in 1970. In recent years he decided on early retirement, more semi–retirement, actually.

Colm went into overdrive talking about his passion for the Ryder Cup. The first Ryder Cup he attended was at Muirfield in 1973. This was the first time in the history of the event that the matches were played in Scotland. There were two Irishmen on the team, Eddie Polland from Northern Ireland and Christy O'Connor, Sr. from Southern Ireland. This Cup was to mark O'Connor's exit from Ryder Cup appearances, having played on ten occasions. It would be an Irish record for Christy Senior. Colm recalls the wonderful singles Christy Senior had on the final day against the then reigning Open champion, Tom Weiskopf. They halved their match. It was also to be a last appearance for 'The King' himself, Arnold Palmer.

Colm was delighted to have been at Muirfield and to have seen Maurice Bembridge and Brian Huggett beat Arnie and Nicklaus by 3 and 1 in the afternoon fourballs on day one. It was an occasion to see the other greats in the game, Trevino, Casper and Brewer.

Colm has a great sense of Ryder Cup history and he drew attention to the Ryder Cup player from Northern Ireland, Fred Daly, who played on the team in 1947, 1949, 1951 and 1953. He was a fantastic player to have had on the Ryder Cup squad. Harry Bradshaw played in three Ryder Cups, but Colm said he was good enough to have played in more. 'The Brad' actually tied for the 1949 Open Championship and wasn't considered for a Ryder Cup place. The British PGA ruled on the situation, saying that Harry was not a fully fledged member of their association. He was an overseas member and therefore didn't qualify for Ryder Cup selection. Eventually, the situation would be rectified and Harry would go on to play in the Ryder Cup on three occasions.

The former golf correspondent recalls one 'marvellous Ryder Cup event'. This was when the European team faced the opposition on American soil in 1987. It involved Wicklow's Eamonn Darcy. 'I was at the eighteenth green when Eamonn was faced with that famous putt to beat Ben Crenshaw. Jack Nicklaus was there with a few of his players while Darcy lined up his pressure putt. One of Nicklaus's partisan players actually said Darcy would make his putt. The "Golden Bear" said, "Don't worry, guys, this is three putt territory. I should know, I built the green!" Darcy, as we all know, holed the winning putt. It's a great memory.'

The other great golfing memory involved Christy O'Connor, Jr.'s outstanding two iron second shot to the eighteenth hole at the Belfry in 1989 to beat Fred Couples. O'Connor actually prevented the Americans from bringing the Ryder Cup to the States. This two iron shot must surely be one of the greatest shots ever in Ryder Cup history.

Colm is very proud of Ireland's Ryder Cup legacy. He is certain the 2006 event will be a tremendous success and he is delighted to see Des Symth as one of Woosnam's vice-captains. After all, Dessie played on two Ryder Cup matches, the first of which was when he played on the first European team.

SEAMUS SMITH IS GENERAL SECRETARY OF THE GUI

Seamus Smith has been general secretary of the Golfing Union of Ireland (GUI) since 1996. On taking up office, there were 386 affiliated golf clubs under his wing. Ten years later, this figure has risen to a highly commendable 417.

Seamus and I met at the European Club in April last when we resurrected all those nostalgic occasions that seem to have happened only weeks ago. Avid golfers of the 1960s will remember reading Seamus's golf articles. He was golf correspondent of the *Evening Press* from 1962 to 1987 and was subsequently sports editor of *The Irish Press* from 1987 to 1995.

The year 1965 was when the great Christy O'Connor, Sr. finished joint second to Australian Peter Thomson in the Open Championship at Birkdale. Later that year, Seamus Smith and his friend, Eamonn Cheevers, travelled to England to Birkdale to follow 'Himself', as Christy O'Connor, Sr. was affectionately known.

'The galleries in those days were around 5,000, nothing like the massive numbers we have today. There were no ropes to contend with in 1965, you could almost rub shoulders with the players. The atmosphere was marvellous, the tension electrifying and the golf fantastic. We spent most of the time following our hero, Christy O'Connor. That was the year Christy and his great friend and playing partner, Peter Alliss from Parkstone, had a very successful innings in their Ryder Cup matches. They were paired together in four matches against the Americans and won three of them. The only real blip for Christy was in his singles against the 1964 Open champion 'Champagne' Tony Lema, who beat the maestro 6 and 4. Sadly, the occasion would turn out to be Lema's last competitive appearance in Britain, as he was tragically killed in an air crash early in 1966,' Seamus remembered.

What were the general secretary's views about the 2006 Ryder Cup?

'It will be a huge occasion. It should have been staged here long before now. It's long overdue. It will turn out to be one of Ireland's greatest sporting occasions. Everybody is looking forward to it. I hope it will be as exciting as the 2002 event at the Belfry. I was there and it was really fantastic. Paul McGinley did us all proud. I'm certain 2006 will be just as good.'

Who was Ireland's greatest Ryder Cup player? Without hesitation, Seamus emphatically said, 'Christy Senior.' I reminded Seamus about a great tribute paid to Ireland's maestro by Sutton professional, Nicky Lynch. Nicky said the Dublin man could hit a driver off a carpet. 'With backspin,' added Seamus, who was a good friend of Christy's and would have played numerous rounds of golf with him. Seamus also had the special privilege of compiling the great man's biography some years ago and holds the Royal Dublin ace in high esteem, regarding him as one of the best, if not *the* best, golfers Ireland has ever produced.

Was O'Connor a natural? 'Absolutely not,' said Seamus. 'Christy hates to think that people might regard him as a natural player. He worked very hard at his game and that was over a long period of time.' Did he have a reputation of being a bad putter? Seamus was very quick to defend his friend and mentor. 'One thing about the maestro is when he had a winning putt to hole he would have invariably holed it,' Seamus said.

Did Seamus have any other outstanding memory of the Royal Dublin professional who holds the Irish Ryder Cup record of ten appearances?

'Most definitely! It was the 1965 Dunlop Masters at Portmarnock. He was playing with his great friend, Peter Alliss, in the first round. The weather was atrocious, with heavy pelting rain accompanied by gale force-like winds, and Christy shot a 73! That even included one three putt. Peter Alliss said it was one of the greatest rounds of golf he had ever witnessed. Peter had an 81 and that put Christy's 73 into perspective. The weather conditions were so bad, play had to be abandoned and Christy O'Connor's superb round was cancelled. When play resumed the following day, Christy didn't regain his earlier momentum and Englishman Bernard Hunt went on to win the event. That was a memory for the archives,' said Seamus.

SECTION 3

*Profiles
of
Irish
Players*

THE SEVENTEEN IRISH RYDER CUP PLAYERS

1. Harry Bradshaw
2. Hugh Boyle
3. Darren Clarke
4. Fred Daly
5. Eamonn Darcy
6. Norman Drew
7. David Feherty
8. Padraig Harrington
9. Jimmy Martin
10. Paul McGinley
11. Christy O'Connor, Jr.
12. Christy O'Connor, Sr.
13. John O'Leary
14. Eddie Polland
15. Ronan Rafferty
16. Des Smyth
17. Philip Walton

CHAPTER 8

From Daly to the Emergence of O'Connor

FRED DALY

Fred Daly played in the Ryder Cup on four occasions: 1947, 1949, 1951 and 1953.

Geoff Bleakley is a professional golfer at Balmoral Golf Club in Belfast, Northern Ireland. Together with Terry Graham, the club's chief executive officer, they made me feel very welcome to the late Fred Daly's parkland course situated on the Lisburn Road in the leafy suburbs of south Belfast. Fred won the Open Championship in 1947. He was runner-up the following year, was joint third in 1950 and third in 1952. Fred Daly made four consecutive appearances in the Ryder Cup: 1947, 1949, 1951 and 1953. He was the first Irishman, or to be more precise, the first Northern Ireland player, to be a member of the Great Britain and Northern Ireland team to face the Americans in 1947.

1947 Portland Golf Club, Oregon, US

Following the Second World War, there was a hiatus of Ryder Cup play from 1939 to 1945. Matches resumed in 1947 at Portland,

Oregon, the same year Fred made his Ryder Cup debut. Apart from winning the Claret Jug that year at Hoylake, he had one of his most successful twelve months on the circuit, culminating with a win in the PGA Match Play Championship. Despite his *annus mirabilis* he certainly had a Ryder Cup baptism of fire. He and Charlie Ward faced huge opposition in the second of the morning foursomes when they were annihilated by Sam Snead and Lloyd Mangrum by a margin of 6 and 5. US captain Ben Hogan had his fingers on the pulse when he paired legendary Snead with Mangrum, a man who was decorated for his part in the D-Day landings.

The home pair never recovered after trailing by six down after the morning round. Fred Daly's misery was compounded by another defeat, this time at the hands of Dutch Harrison. Dutch beat Fred in the opening singles of the 1947 Ryder Cup by 5 and 4. For the record, the Americans won by 7 points to 1. Better times would beckon for the Open champion in his second Ryder Cup appearance.

1949 Ganton Golf Club, Scarborough, England

The 1949 Cup augured well, with an opening morning foursomes win for the solid pairing of Daly and newcomer Ken Bousfield. They were two holes to the good at lunch and went on to beat the opposition of Skip Alexander and Bob Hamilton by the very convincing margin of 4 and 2. However, Fred's old adversary of two years previously, Lloyd Mangrum, put an end to the Irishman's winning streak by beating him 4 and 2 in the singles, and this despite the fact that Fred was one up at lunch. Nobody could have stopped Mangrum's genius over the second eighteen holes. To use an old terminology, he was 'four under fours' from the eleventh to the fifteenth to close the door on Fred.

1951 Pinehurst Country Club, North Carolina, US

The record books confirmed the dominance of the Americans yet again, who won by 7 points to 5. More disappointment was to follow in the 1951 matches, when the British team suffered another humiliating defeat. They were totally outclassed by the superb performance of the home side at Pinehurst, North Carolina. Fred Daly was the only player in the singles encounters who managed to put a score on the board, albeit a half point when he halved with Clayton Heafner. This was a highly commendable fight back by the 1947 Open champion, as he was dormie three down to his opponent. The gloss was taken off the near whitewash victory by the Americans, who beat the visitors by 9½ to 2½ points.

1953 Wentworth Golf Club, Surrey, England

Fred Daly got a psychological boost when his friend from Southern Ireland, Harry Bradshaw, joined the Ryder Cup squad in 1953. It was no longer the British team. For the very first time, it was to be the Great Britain and Ireland team. The welcome news was that both players had a 100 per cent record at the matches in Wentworth. Daly and Bradshaw were an obvious pairing for captain Henry Cotton in the opening four-somes. They beat the stiff opposition of Walter Berkemo and Cary Middlecoff, taking the spoils on the final hole. Daly's clash with America's Ted Kroll in the singles showed how great a player the man from Portrush was. He disposed of his opponent by 9 and 7.

Although the Great Britain and Ireland team didn't achieve a victory at Wentworth, they made the opposition really fight and dig deep into their reserves to come out on top by 6½ points to 5½. A mere point separated the two sides. This would be Fred Daly's last Ryder Cup appearance, but this 'Fuzzy Zoeller'-type character continued to play his usual relaxed game, whistling his way down the fairways of his much-loved Balmoral parkland course. He certainly exited from the Ryder Cup scene on a high note. He did Ireland proud.

HARRY BRADSHAW

Harry Bradshaw played in three Ryder Cup matches: 1953, 1955 and 1957.

I spent a pleasant afternoon with two members of the late Harry Bradshaw's family in the summer of 2005. Over afternoon tea in Harry Junior's house, he, his sister Breda and I talked about their famous dad. Harry Junior isn't really a golfer, although his golfer son is the proud owner of his granddad's Ryder Cup bag.

Breda, though, is a keen golfer and is extremely proud in extolling the virtues of their dad: 'You know our dad was the only player from the Republic of Ireland to have tied for first place in the Open Championship.' She showed me a cherished family possession that her late dad was particularly proud of. It was the 1953 silver salver that players received after winning the British Masters at Sunningdale. The salver was unique, for it contained in script the names of all previous winners of the title, including Harry's. Harry actually won this coveted title on two occasions; the second time was in 1955.

During the 1940s and 1950s, Harry Bradshaw was a household name in Ireland. He monopolised the Irish Professional Championship, winning it ten times between 1941 and 1957. He also won the Irish Open in 1947 and 1949 and almost added the British Open to his 1949 collection. Breda and Harry took me down memory lane.

Harry was born in 1913, the youngest of six children. The family originally lived in Killincarrig, quite close to the hilly course of Delgany, where his father was professional and where young Harry spent a lot of his spare time as a caddie. The father's love for the game rubbed off on his son. Soon Harry's own love for golf would be evidenced by his constant desire to play and practise. He wasn't a good putter in those early days until another avid golfer, Fr Gleeson from the parish of Bray, took him in tow. Endless hours on the putting green reaped huge rewards over time.

Harry took over from Eddie Hackett as professional of Portmarnock Golf Club in 1950. Within a few years, Harry would win two British Masters titles (it might have been three, had Bobby Locke not prevented him from a third) and would go on to team up with Christy O'Connor, Sr. to win the Canada Cup for Ireland in Mexico in 1958.

Harry all but won the 1949 Open Championship. In fact, it was only through a twist of fate that he was unfairly denied the Claret Jug due to the famous 'bottle incident' at Royal St George's at Sandwich, Kent.

Harry's opening round was a commendable 68, one behind the leader, Jimmy Adams, but, more importantly, one ahead of favourite Bobby Locke's 69. It was in the second round at the fifth hole where the greatest single tragedy in the history of the British Open unfolded. Harry hit a reasonably good tee shot to the 422 yards par four, but it just tapered off to the left a little. There was no cause for concern until he got up to the ball. The tee shot found itself resting by a broken beer bottle! Harry was thunderstruck. After much reflection on and concern and respect for the existing rules of the day, Harry took out a nine iron and with his eyes firmly closed for safety reasons, relied on 'memory swing' to dislodge the ball. This he did, but only managed to move the ball forward by about twenty yards. On finally reaching the green in four, he two putted for a double bogey six. 'The Brad' finished his round in 77 and was surprised to find that both he and his great rival were level on 145, five shots behind the leader, Sam King, with two rounds to go. The Irishman and South African carded third rounds of 68 apiece, still leaving them level pegging. Harry went out in 33 in the final round, but came back in a disappointing 37 for a final score of 70. Locke likewise finished with a 70, leaving the two tied at 283, the lowest aggregate from all the competitors.

Northern Ireland's Fred Daly had won this coveted trophy two years previously. Now, despite the 'bottle incident', Southern Ireland's Harry Bradshaw had the prospect of bringing the historic Claret Jug to the Emerald Isle. But it wasn't to be, as Harry lost out to Bobby Locke in the thirty-six-hole play-off. For the record, Locke scored 135 (67, 68), while Bradshaw scored 147 (74, 73). True to his nature, Harry was magnanimous in defeat.

Long-standing members at Portmarnock are unanimous about Harry Bradshaw's work ethic. He believed in an early start, and after a long, arduous day was invariably late going home. Apart from a long day, his working week extended to Sunday. A game of golf at this famous links would take anything up to five or more hours on average. Many Portmarnock players will recall seeing Harry practising his short game as they teed off for a game and, upon finishing, seeing him still immersed in practice. In his devotion to the short game practice, Harry Bradshaw would use both wedges and a nine iron. He would rarely practise with any other iron except, perhaps, with his 'Texas wedge', the putter. The intense commitment he gave to this department of the game was astounding and exemplary.

Although he ran a very successful pro shop, his love and preoccupation would be with playing and, to be more precise, with practice. The great Bobby Locke was known to have marvelled at Harry's short game from about 100 yards out. He went so far as to believe the Irishman was one of, if not the best of, the finest exponents of this department in the world. Harry himself felt chipping and putting were probably the most important components of the game. That's where the pressure is. Master this area, and you'll beat the world.

One of Harry's great moments came when he beat Billy Casper in a televised match in Portmarnock in 1966. Casper was the reigning US Open champion at the time, but 'The Brad' beat the 'King of the Castle' by three shots. Off the tee, Harry wasn't particularly long. He often preferred a brassie (a two wood) to a driver. He wasn't short by any means, either. One thing is for sure, though – he was rifle-straight. He himself put this down to his unorthodox grip.

Early in his career, he discovered something by accident. His right hand was too dominant in his swing and, more to the point, at impact. This would cause the shot to go left all the time. By sheer coincidence he began changing his grip in practice, and on one occasion decided to overlap three fingers of the right hand on top of the left. This was completely different from the traditional grip, but it turned out to be a very useful experiment indeed. Instead of his previous hooks, he was now hitting arrow-straight drives down the middle. He continued to indulge in this newfound experience by putting in long hours of practice so that the grip and swing would become second nature to him over time. Despite this successful grip change, Harry's swing came in for some criticism throughout his golfing career. Swing purists would say it wasn't graceful; there was a pronounced sway evident, and to compound matters, he had a loop, considered to be a mortal sin in golf. It didn't concern Harry Bradshaw, though. It worked for him, as another unusual swing would for another Wicklow player years after him – Eamonn Darcy.

One admirable characteristic about Harry Bradshaw was his briskness of play. He was remarkably quick at sizing up a situation. After hitting a tee shot, he would pick up his tee and be walking down the fairway while his ball was still in flight. Once he got to the green, the same disciplined approach would follow. This struck me quite forcibly when, if memory serves, I saw Harry on the par three twelfth hole at Portmarnock during the 1970 Alcan Tournament. He had a putt of some twenty feet. He swiftly studied it, put the blade in front of the ball, then behind, and gave it an authoritative hit. With his head absolutely still, he waited for the ball to drop.

I have never seen Harry Bradshaw get down to study a putt. His study method was to view a putt from above, where arguably a player would get a better and more concise view of things. There was no 'plumbobbing' for Harry, a method favoured more by the Americans, whereby the player would hold the putter virtually upright while sizing up a putt from wherever the ball lay on the green. The player would close one eye and carefully move the shaft of the club in slow pendulum-like fashion to determine the line for the putt. Theoretically, a player would see all the undulations that had to be taken into account, holding the club shaft in a vertically still position before the putt was struck. This was a method that had no appeal for Harry. He would certainly not be a candidate for incurring penalty strokes for slow play in today's game.

The 1949 and 1951 Ryder Cup matches – ineligibility clause

Harry Bradshaw wasn't in any of the matches in 1949 and 1951. He most certainly should have been, given his status in the game at the time. His daughter, Breda, feels very strongly about this. The whole matter of the British PGA and its attitude to 'the ineligibility clause' defies logic in this respect. Harry was declared ineligible to play in the 1949 and 1951 matches because of his category of membership. As resident of the Republic of Ireland, Harry was an overseas member of the British PGA and as such was deemed ineligible. Yet he was a member of the British PGA team that was invited by the South African PGA to play a series of matches there that would last a number of months taking in the end of 1950 and the beginning of 1951. Justice would finally prevail in 1953.

1953 Wentworth Golf Club, Surrey, England

This was Harry Bradshaw's first Ryder Cup appearance. It also marked the first appearance of Peter Alliss, who was the youngest golfer ever to make the team. Fred Daly was also on the team, and both he and his professional colleague from the South would emerge with 100 per cent records from the event. However, their splendid performances did not prevent Lloyd Mangrum's US team from winning the 1953 biennial series, albeit by the tiny margin of one point.

In 1953, the matches were over two days. Day one was given over to four foursomes matches, followed by eight singles on day two. Each match was contested over thirty-six holes. Captain Henry Cotton decided on an all-Ireland pairing in the final match on day one. Fred Daly and Harry Bradshaw fought a tense and exciting battle against Walter Burkemo and 1949 US Open champion Cary Middlecoff, with the match going down to the wire. It was on the eighteenth green that Fred Daly complemented his playing colleague's high standard of play by holing a nerve-wracking four-foot putt under extreme pressure to win the match by one hole.

Fred Daly humiliated Ted Kroll in the second singles encounter on the second day by 9 and 7. The man from the South also came up trumps in his match when he disposed of Fred Haas by 3 and 2. Despite losing the overall team event by 5½ to 6½ points, both Fred and Harry were unbeaten.

1955 Thunderbird Golf and Country Club, Palm Springs, California, US
Fred Daly played his last Ryder Cup in 1953. However, another Irishman would join Harry Bradshaw when the event got underway in California – Christy O'Connor, Sr. Harry said at the time that this Irishman would become one of the greatest his country would ever produce. How prophetic Harry turned out to be. Christy O'Connor, Sr. became a legend in his own lifetime.

The Great Britain and Ireland team were beaten yet again. This time it was on American soil and by the very convincing margin of 8 points to 4. Both Harry and Christy might well like to forget the Thunderbird Golf and Country Club, because that was where they played the 1955 Ryder Cup matches. They didn't win a single point. Harry was now in a new foursomes pairing. He and Dai Rees were beaten by Sam Snead and Cary Middlecoff by 3 and 2. In the singles matches on the final day,

Harry lost out to Jack Burke by 3 and 2, who, it must be said, was absolutely brilliant. Bradshaw covered the first eighteen holes in 65 and he was only level with the American, who finally won out.

1957 Lindrick Golf Club, Sheffield, Yorkshire, England

'The Brad' played his last Ryder Cup in 1957 and finished on a high note. Oddly, he was left out of the captain's foursomes matches on day one. Welshman Dai Rees probably queried the wisdom of his own decision when Great Britain and Ireland trailed by 3 points to 1 after the first day's play. There would be better things to come on day two.

There were 8 points on offer from the man-to-man battles on the final day. The home side won 6½ of those to win the 1957 Ryder Cup at Lindrick. The half point was won by Harry Bradshaw in his match against the reigning US Open champion, Dick Mayer. Harry would finish his association with the Ryder Cup by bowing out on a winning high note.

Harry Junior, Breda and the entire Bradshaw family have donated all their photographic and allied golfing memorabilia to Portmarnock Golf Club, where their late father spent most of his professional career. There is a separate wing specially set aside where this entire collection is on permanent view. It is a fitting tribute.

NORMAN DREW

Norman Drew made one appearance in the Ryder Cup, in 1959

Norman Drew was born in 1932 in Northern Ireland. He won the Irish Amateur Championship in 1952 at the age of twenty and defended his title the following year. He played the Walker Cup in 1953, and when he made his one and only appearance in Ryder Cup matches at the Eldorado Country Club in Palm Springs, California, he became the first player in history to have represented Great Britain and Ireland in both Walker and Ryder Cup events. As a professional, Norman Drew won three tournaments in 1959: the Irish Championship, the Irish Dunlop Tournament and the *Yorkshire Evening News* Tournament and was runner-up in the prestigious Dunlop Masters.

It was as a result of his fine performances and consistency of play that he was selected to become a member of the 1959 Ryder Cup matches. On that occasion, matches were over two days. Welshman Dai Rees was the Great Britain and Ireland captain to lead his squad against Sam Snead's team at Eldorado Country Club. Christy O'Connor, Sr. was also a member of the team hoping to retain the cup they had won in 1957 at Lindrick.

There were just four foursomes matches on the first day, but Norman Drew didn't figure in any of them. After day one the US led by 2½ points to 1½. There were eight singles matches on the second and final day. Norman was put out first and immediately was in the firing line when he found himself up against a man ten years his senior. Doug Ford was playing his third Ryder Cup match. He would play his final Ryder Cup event in 1961 and finish with a very credible total of four wins and a half from his total of nine matches.

Matches in those days were thirty-six holes. Norman Drew was four down at an early stage during the opening eighteen holes, but managed to reduce the deficit to one hole by the end of the morning's eighteen holes. The Ulsterman was under enormous pressure on the eighteenth hole, the thirty-sixth in the match. He was one down with just the eighteenth to negotiate. He deliberated on what club to hit, but being anxious to make the green, finally decided on a three wood. He hit the 'spoon' and safely made the green and halved the game with Doug Ford. Unfortunately, the US team beat the Great Britain and Ireland squad by 8½ to 3½ points.

CHAPTER 9

The O'Connor Era

CHRISTY O'CONNOR, SR.

Christy played in the Ryder Cup on ten occasions: 1955, 1957, 1959, 1961, 1963, 1965, 1967, 1969, 1971 and 1973.

The year was 1960. Australian Kel Nagle won the centenary Open Championship and the Canada Cup (now the World Cup of Golf) was played in Portmarnock. Americans Arnold Palmer and Sam Snead were competitors at this world-renowned links, as were South Africans Gary Player and Harold Henning.

Spectators could wander in comfort around Portmarnock in 1960. Despite record spectator numbers of 60,000 throughout the week, there were no problems with crowd control. There were no barriers and no ropes to contend with. The marshals had little difficulty in controlling the enormous galleries, who respected the professionalism of the sport and enjoyed the open air and continuous sunshine that was theirs for the week.

When the official tournament got underway, my friends and I joined the gallery following the Irish players, Christy O'Connor and Norman Drew. I had never seen these golfers before and had heard little about them until Ireland hosted this event. However, when I saw the now-legendary Christy O'Connor, Sr. hit a tee shot to the par four fifth hole and finish with his characteristic low follow-through, it stopped me in my tracks.

My friends and I spent a fantastic week at the Canada Cup and were there to marvel at Gary Player's wonderful course record 65. For the record, Palmer and Snead won the event for the States, with Belgian's Flory van Donck winning the individual title.

Early years

Christy O'Connor, Sr. was born in Galway on 21 December 1924. He was one of eleven children and lived in Knocknacarra, a small village near the first green at Galway Golf Club. As a child, Christy made his pocket money from caddying. Interestingly enough, there was absolutely no association with golf in his family background. Pat Quinn was a local pro and he encouraged the young Christy's love for the game. After caddying for hours, Christy would spend much time hitting countless shots to improve his own game.

Another Galway pro, Bob Wallace, recognised the potential this young golfer showed and he took Christy on as his assistant in 1946, the year Sam Snead won the Open Championship. Working in the pro shop meant a lot of time would be taken up with menial tasks like making and repairing clubs. In whatever spare time there was, Bob helped develop Christy's very ordinary swing into something more traditionally acceptable.

In late 1948, Christy moved on to take up a position as resident pro cum green keeper at Tuam Golf Club. Three years later, he played in the 1951 British Open, which was played in Northern Ireland at Royal Portrush and won by the genial Max Faulkner. Christy finished in nineteenth position and earned £19. Not too long afterwards, he was approached by Bundoran Golf Club to become their resident professional, which he did.

Christy's preference seemed to focus on links courses. Bundoran offered him an excellent opportunity to develop his game on a links layout. Here he was exposed to the frequent whistling Atlantic winds with the accompanying threatening angry rains. He practised incessantly, hitting countless numbers of balls during any free time he had. There were occasions when the same winds and rains were so ferociously foreboding that he had to practise behind the clubhouse walls for protection. The Galway man would be the first to denounce those who say he is a 'natural' when it comes to swinging a club. His now grooved swing is the result of unimaginable long hours spent practising off the sandy beaches off our coastlines. Playing off sand requires a special kind of deftness and skill that O'Connor didn't develop overnight, but after years of disciplined devotion to practice. Years after he elevated this skill to a fine art, particularly with his iron play, people believed he was endowed with a natural ability, though nothing could be further from the truth.

At the top of Christy's swing, he still lets go very gently with the last two to three fingers of the left hand before he begins the downswing. This is unorthodox, but it works for Christy. In fact, this delicate movement arguably helped the great man develop a finely tuned whip-like wrist motion to initiate the downswing. Perhaps this explains why we refer to O'Connor as 'wristy Christy'.

Christy would find more time to practise in the winter season, when there weren't as many demands for lessons. Jimmy Kinsella, of the renowned golfing family, became O'Connor's assistant in Bundoran, leaving the maestro time to play the circuit. Playing the tour in those days was financially draining on a family. As was the situation earlier in Tuam, the Bundoran golf club members were very generous in supporting him financially so he could play the circuit. Christy entered and won the 1955 Swallow Penfold event, being the first player on tour to win a four-figure cheque of £1,000.

In 1956 Christy went on to win the Spalding and Dunlop Masters titles, followed by the *News of the World* Match Play Championship and the Irish Hennessy Tournament a year later. 1958 would see the talented player move yet again, when he was appointed resident pro at Killarney, one of the most picturesque locations in Ireland. Christy was thirty-three years old and at the peak of his career. His remuneration at Killarney would be a very acceptable retainer wage of £7 weekly.

The committee of this idyllic location also gave their new pro ample time off to play the circuit. He made use of that generous offer when he and his friend Harry Bradshaw from Portmarnock represented Ireland in the Canada Cup in Mexico in 1958 and won this prestigious world event. They beat the very best of competition, as the field included two of the world's greats, Hogan and Snead. It was significant that the Irish duo won, given the humidity on a course that lay 7,500 feet above sea level. Christy's 6,000-mile journey ended with a victory breakfast for himself and Harry Bradshaw at Shannon Airport, followed by a jubilant celebration from waiting crowds at the grotto on the Tralee road. It would culminate with a rapturous reception and torchlit welcome home procession in pony and trap to Killarney. Harry received an equally heart-warming reception in Dublin on his arrival home.

1958 Open at Royal Lytham and St Anne's, Lancashire, England

At thirty-three years old, Christy almost won the Claret Jug at Royal Lytham and St Anne's. Playing out of Killarney, Christy carded a first round 67 followed by a 68 to be on a very nice midway total of 135. A third-round 73 didn't have the magic of the earlier scores, but Christy carried on regardless. Going down the last hole of the final round, he needed a birdie three to win the coveted title. The crowds were there in large numbers, as were many from Killarney's committee and rank and file members. Everybody wanted the Galway man to win. O'Connor hit a very good drive only to take an unfortunate bounce left into a bunker. He had no option but to simply play out for safety. His third shot to the green ended some twelve feet beyond the cup. He rimmed the hole for a four and a tie, a huge disappointment after a final round of 71.

Christy O'Connor's career at this stage was on the rise and it demanded a great deal of travel, not only within Ireland itself, but also overseas. After one very happy year at Killarney, he felt the urge to move yet again. The preoccupying considerations were now to do with proximity to Dublin's main airport. So it was that Christy's very busy and successful playing schedule resulted in him moving to the renowned links at Royal Dublin on Dublin's north side. He has been there ever since.

It's hard to chronicle Christy O'Connor's winning career. Suffice it to say he won everything apart from a major. He was so close so many times to winning the British Open. He would have loved to have added this title to the others he won throughout his distinguished career. Among his worldwide wins are the 1961 Carling Tournament, the 1963 Martini International, the 1965

Senior Service Tournament (the same year Christy tied for second in the Open Championship) and the Dunlop Masters titles in 1956 and 1959. In the latter, which was staged at Portmarnock, the maestro, with a final round 66, came from behind as he so often did in his career to snatch victory from legendary amateur Joe Carr. Christy was also European and World Seniors Champion to boot.

On the home front, his victories included ten Irish PGA titles, two Irish Hospitals' Tournaments, four Carroll's International titles and three Gallagher Ulster Opens. One of his outstanding victories on home soil was the 1966 Carroll's International at Royal Dublin. The title was almost in the hands of Eric Brown. The Royal Dublin man stood on the sixteenth tee needing three birdies to force a play-off. He played virtuoso golf over the three holes. He hit a three-wood to the short par four sixteenth, holing a twenty-footer for an eagle. This was a sudden blow to the prospects of a Scottish victory.

Even more was to befall Eric Brown, who was sitting nervously in the clubhouse but still hopeful of a victory. Christy sank another monstrous birdie putt on the seventeenth. The two were now level. The pressure was huge, but the Irishman revelled in it and hit a courageous arrow-straight 'spoon' (a three wood, as we call it now) down the last hole, landing close to the ditch bordering the out-of-bounds garden to the right. His three iron second shot to the par five eighteenth hovered over the out of bounds for some time before unerringly finding its target a few feet from the pin. This was a fatal blow for Eric Brown, as O'Connor would hole out for an eagle and victory.

O'Connor was delighted with another fighting comeback that had been a feature of many of his final rounds in competitive events. He would later confess that the supportive crowds were worth shots to him. It was another big winning cheque. He was a master when it came to big-money events. In 1970 he won the-then largest first prize in golf – £25,000 in the John Player Classic in Hollinwell, Nottinghamshire, England.

1955 Thunderbird Ranch and Country Club, Palm Springs, California, US
The background to this event was the continuing dominance of the Americans, whose attitude to the biennial matches was luke-

warm. It was Christy O'Connor's debut, an occasion he might well want to forget. He was left out of the morning's foursomes series, after which the US led by 3 points to 1. The Royal Dublin man led the charge on the final day only to fall foul to tantrum-throwing Ryder Cup rookie, Tommy Bolt, who was 3 up on him after lunch, eventually beating the Irishman 4 and 2. The Americans won another Ryder Cup, yet again, by 8 points to 4. Despite the result, Christy O'Connor would begin a Ryder Cup journey of ten consecutive appearances.

1957 Lindrick, Yorkshire, England

Lindrick came in for much criticism as a venue, mainly because of its shortness of length at 6,541 yards. The same reservations about the feasibility of continuing the biennial event raised their ugly heads again. There was wholehearted support for the Ryder Cup matches on this side of the Atlantic, while in the US there was a total disinterest in them, as they were too one-sided.

The matches were played amidst this negative background. The Americans got a rude awakening when the final result went unexpectedly against the favourites. They were beaten by Great Britain and Ireland 7½ points to 4½. Harry Bradshaw halved his match with Dick Mayer. It was Christy's second appearance in a Ryder Cup match and it would prove to be a highly controversial one.

After partnering Eric Brown in a losing match against Dick Mayer and Tommy Bolt, Christy faced Dow Finsterwald in the singles clash on the final day. Many will remember how the American missed his first putt on the third green in the first eighteen holes and gave himself the short one back. The referee intervened and awarded the hole to O'Connor. From that moment on, there was a needle match between the two players. After eighteen holes, the two were level.

Later in the thirty-six-hole match, Finsterwald stormed off a green in anger when a losing putt was conceded to him. Christy assumed his own short winning putt had been given to him by the American. It wasn't, and Christy hadn't finished out. Dow Finsterwald claimed the hole on the next tee. The Irishman didn't relent until he pulverised his opponent by 7 and 6. It was no surprise that there were no handshakes after the match.

1959 Eldorado Country Club, Palm Springs, California, US

It was in California that the Peter Alliss/Christy O'Connor partnership saw the light of day. Their very first foursomes match was
against Art Wall and Doug Ford. Peter Alliss remembered apolo-
gising to Christy for hitting a bad shot early on in the match. The
Galway man's response was quick and effective: 'No apologies,
we're both doing our very best, let's go about it!' said Christy. They
did their best and defeated the opposition by 3 and 2.

The best, however, was not good enough for O'Connor in the
singles on the final day. Art Wall gave him a 7 and 6 humiliating
thrashing. Peter Alliss was more fortunate, for he managed a half
point in his singles against Jay Hebert.

The 1959 Ryder Cup will be remembered for another reason.
The Ryder Cup squad had travelled on the *Queen Elizabeth* to
America. The turbulent Atlantic Ocean waves caused much sea
sickness on board before finally docking at New York. Christy
O'Connor, Norman Drew and Peter Alliss, along with the rest of
the team, were later en route by plane from Los Angeles to Palm
Springs, where the thirteenth biennial matches would take place.
What they didn't reckon on was more turbulence, this time air
turbulence. As a result of a raging thunderstorm, their twin engine
propeller aircraft plummeted from 13,000 feet to 6,000 feet.

The pilot was left with no option but to return to base at Los
Angeles. Once their feet touched down on terra firma they vowed
to continue their journey by coach.

1961 Royal Lytham and St Anne's, Lancashire, England

Christy O'Connor loved playing in the Ryder Cup. He respected
the tradition and history associated with Sam Ryder's dream of
1927. Even though the American supremacy in the matches still
continued unabated, Christy felt it would level out over time and
become more popular.

From 1961 on, matches would be contested over eighteen
holes and not over thirty-six, as they had been previously.

On day one Peter and Christy were out first in their foursomes
match against Doug Ford and American rookie Gene Littler. Gene
would go on to play in a total of seven Ryder Cup events. The
Alliss/O'Connor partnership came up trumps again when they

defeated their American opposition by the convincing margin of 4 and 3.

In the afternoon foursomes, the Alliss/O'Connor 'invincibility' label suffered a mighty shock. On the very last hole, Art Wall and Jay Hebert won the point for the American squad. There were two sets of singles on the final day. In the morning session Christy's old adversary from 1957, Dow Finsterwald, would get a sweet revenge on him, beating him by 2 and 1. In the afternoon session of singles, Christy had a halved match with Gene Littler.

Unfortunately, the Americans triumphed again by 14½ points to 9½.

1963 East Lake Country Club, Atlanta, Georgia, US

The Ryder Cup would be officially played over three days, with fourball matches as part of the revised format. A surprise defeat of the Alliss/O'Connor combination in the morning foursomes on day one resulted in the partnership being dissolved for the remainder of the 1963 foursomes and fourball events. Billy Casper and Dave Ragan beat them by just one hole. On day two Bob Goalby and Dave Ragan beat the new morning fourball partnership of Neil Coles and Christy O'Connor by a mere one hole. The same Irish/English pairing suffered another defeat in the afternoon fourball match, when they were beaten 3 and 2 by Arnold Palmer and Dow Finsterwald.

Gene Littler got the better of Christy in the morning singles on the third day. Gene's one-hole victory ensured a point for his team. Christy O'Connor lost his second singles in the afternoon to Billy Maxwell, who played his one and only Ryder Cup event in 1963. The 1963 Ryder Cup was certainly one that the Royal Dublin man might well like to forget.

1965 Royal Birkdale, Southport, Lancashire, England

This was a special year for both O'Connor and Alliss. Their partnership status would be reinstated. O'Connor redeemed his Ryder Cup standing significantly at a venue where he had finished joint second to Peter Thomson in the Open Championship just a few months previously. Alliss failed to get a point in only one match out of six played. O'Connor had mixed fortunes. He and Peter defeated Ken Venturi and Don January by 5 and 4 on day one in the morning foursomes. The strong pairing continued their winning streak in the afternoon's foursomes, when they beat Billy Casper and Gene Littler. O'Connor and Alliss went out in 31, but were only one hole to the good. The American pair drew level four holes later, but the confident Alliss/O'Connor pairing closed the door on the seventeenth and won their match by 2 and 1.

Peter Alliss and Christy O'Connor were trounced 6 and 4 by Arnold Palmer and Dave Marr in the morning fourballs on day two. However, Peter and Christy got their revenge that afternoon in the fourballs, when they beat Palmer and Marr by two holes. The Irishman would be left out of the first series of singles on the final day, but played in the afternoon series, losing out to Tony Lema by 6 and 4.

The Americans won again, this time beating the Great Britain and Ireland team by 19½ points to 12½.

1967 Champions' Golf Club, Houston, Texas, US

Both Christy O'Connor and Peter Alliss might well regard the 1967 Ryder Cup as their *annus horibilis*. Christy played in four matches and lost each one. He lost the morning foursomes on day one with Alliss to Palmer and Dickenson by 2 and 1. Peter and Christy lost the afternoon foursomes to Bobby Nichols and Johnny Pott by 2 and 1. The second day's morning foursomes saw the same solid partnership go down, this time by 3 and 2 to the mighty Casper and Brewer. O'Connor would lose his one remaining match, a singles, to Bobby Nichols by 3 and 2. The match result was US 23½, Great Britain and Ireland 8½.

1969 Royal Birkdale, Southport, Lancashire, England

This links venue is one of Christy O'Connor's favourites. He had but one blemish on this otherwise envious performance. Christy played in four matches and earned points from three of them. The Alliss/O'Connor pairing was still a solid combination. They halved their opening foursomes encounter with Billy Casper and Frank Beard. Christy would go on to partner Peter Townsend in a successful fourball match on day two, when they defeated Dave Hill and rookie Dale Douglas by one hole. The Irish maestro would play both singles on the final day. In the morning session he accounted for Frank Beard's scalp by the very convincing margin of 5 and 4, but after lunch lost out to the classic swinger, Gene Littler, by 2 and 1. The Ryder Cup ended in a tie, with 16 points accumulated by both teams.

By 1969, Christy O'Connor, Sr. had played eight Ryder Cup matches. The 1969 Cup was Peter Alliss's last Ryder Cup appearance.

1971 Old Warson Country Club, St Louis, Missouri, US

Christy O'Connor's new partner would be Neil Coles from Coombe Hill. They were first out of the traps for the foursomes match on day one, beating Billy Casper and Miller Barber by 2 and 1. They created a positive momentum for others to emulate. In the first of the morning's fourballs on day two, Christy was partnered with former 'button boy' Brian Barnes. They lost 2 and 1 to Lee Trevino and Mason Rudolf.

Neil Coles and Christy O'Connor were back together as a partnership and earned a half point for their wounded team. The Irishman played in only one of the two series of singles on the final day. In this match he was well and truly beaten by Gardner Dickinson by 5 and 4.

It was a resounding victory for the Americans, who won 18½ points to 13½.

1973 Muirfield, Gullane, Scotland

This was the Royal Dublin man's final appearance in a Ryder Cup blazer. He would, however, go out on a relatively high note. Despite being on a losing side, Christy O'Connor, Sr. earned a half point in his halved match with the reigning British Open champion, Tom Weiskopf. Christy had mixed fortunes in his other matches.

He partnered Neil Coles yet again in the second foursomes match on day one. They beat the stiff opposition of Tom Weiskopf and Jesse Snead, nephew of the legendary Sam Snead, by 3 and 2. However, the same Great Britain and Ireland pairing would lose 2 and 1 in the afternoon fourball series to Lee Trevino and Homero Blancas, who incidentally played in this, his one and only Ryder Cup match. Christy and Neil would lose yet again on day two when Lee Trevino and Billy Casper would be responsible for their demise by 2 and 1 in the morning foursomes.

Christy took defeat on the chin but he was rightfully upbeat, having halved his singles match with the reigning Open champion.

Christy departed this historic scene with dignity and grace. He was proud of his Irish record in Ryder Cup matches. He has ten caps which, because of the biennial nature of the event, span twenty years. It's a wonderful Irish record that will prove difficult to emulate. Christy is a great golfing ambassador who has put Ireland on the map through his dedicated professionalism and his undoubted talents that have led to multiple wins throughout the golfing world. He is still the resident pro in Royal Dublin and lives in nearby Clontarf with his wife, Mary.

HUGH BOYLE

Hugh Boyle played in the Ryder Cup for Great Britain and Ireland only once, in 1967 in Houston, Texas. The year was a particularly good one for him, as he won a few tournaments on the circuit and played for Ireland in the World Cup of Golf. He was born in Omeath, County Louth, just a long par five away across the estuary from Warrenpoint where another great Ryder Cup player, Ronan Rafferty, comes from. Hugh spoke to me in January 2006 about his one and only experience in competition at this level.

It was his first visit to the States, although he had already been to Canada. Resurrecting memories going back some forty years wasn't easy, though he did recall facing the great Arnold Palmer on two occasions. 'The King' had flown into Houston in his own private jet – and that was in 1967! In Hugh's first match, he partnered Malcolm Gregson against Arnie and Gardner Dickinson in the afternoon foursome on the opening day's play. Dickinson modelled himself on his Ryder Cup captain, Ben Hogan.

Unfortunately, Boyle and Gregson suffered the humiliation of a 5 and 4 defeat. Day two sticks in Hugh's memory because victory was within reach. The occasion was the afternoon four-balls, when he and his partner, three-time Ryder Cup player George Will, fell foul of Arnold Palmer and his playing companion, Julios Boros, going down by just one hole. They enjoyed a commanding lead in the early part of the encounter against the Americans, who were the favourites. The highlight of this lead was George's eagle at the ninth, leaving the pair four up going into the home stretch.

They appeared invincible. 'But Arnie played like God, making four birdies in the second nine,' Hugh said. 'The sides were level going down the eighteenth. George made bunker off the tee shot while I made the fairway. Dusk had set in as the four of us prepared to hit our second shots. George was reluctant to finish out, as the light was fast fading. None of us could see the green. We had no say whether or not play would be suspended and had no option but to play on and plod our weary way to hole out for a bogey five while Palmer made a par four to close us out. And that was that. It was very sore and a very bitter pill to swallow.'

Hugh is convinced 'going European' in 1979 was the best thing to do. It was now a more level playing field. In addition, Hugh feels that players this side of the Atlantic are now far better players. In his day, the Americans excelled. They knew they were great, and much to their regret, the Great Britain and Ireland players were aware of this. Harsh reality had set in. They were at a huge disadvantage before they even hit a shot. This psychological warfare was to continue for decades, with the mighty Americans experiencing little difficulty in disposing of their weaker visitors. Of course, in more recent times the tables have been turned with fine, young, talented European players now competing on the world stage. This is a most welcome turn of events. Standards have risen and the home side's game has responded in splendid fashion. Despite this, Hugh sounded a note of caution about people thinking the Europeans would be favourites at the event when it would be hosted at the K Club in 2006. The odds will be even money.

Hugh Boyle spent over twenty years as a professional golfer at Royal Wimbledon before retiring in 2002. Hugh lives with his wife, Rosalind, in London. They have a family of two: a son, James, and a daughter, Cara.

Jimmy Martin

Jimmy made one Ryder Cup appearance, at Royal Birkdale in Southport, Lancashire in 1965, the same year his compatriot Christy O'Connor, Sr. finished joint runner-up to British Open champion, Peter Thomson.

Jimmy Martin, born in 1924 in Wicklow, was an assistant to his father in Greystones before doing likewise to Arthur Lees at Sunningdale. He returned to Ireland for a brief stint in

Edmonstwon as the resident pro at this club on Dublin's south side. He would later become full-time pro at Rush Golf Club, near Skerries, which is about twenty-five miles from the capital city. He was a second cousin of another Wicklow man, Eamonn Darcy, who himself honoured his country with Ryder Cup distinction. Jimmy had a small number of victories to his credit. He won the then Piccadilly Tournament in 1964, the Carroll's International in 1968 and the Madrid Open in 1972, and he represented Ireland in the Canada Cup (now the World Cup of Golf) on five occasions between 1962 and 1970.

1965 Royal Birkdale, Southport, Lancashire, England

Jimmy Martin would make only one brief match appearance in the 1965 Ryder Cup. He and fellow rookie player, Jimmy Hitchcock of Ashford Manor, were out in the afternoon foursomes on day one against the formidable partnership of Julios Boros and 'Champagne' Tony Lema. Nicky Lynch, who Jimmy played with in the Carroll's International in 1968, remembers the Rush man telling him about the pressure felt on that occasion. Jimmy tossed a coin on the first tee to see who would hit the opening tee shot. The Irishman won the toss, allowing him to decide whether he or Hitchcock would play first. Hitchcock was obliged to hit off. Hitchcock hit a very good opening drive and found the fairway.

Having avoided pressure on the first hole, it was now his turn. Jimmy chose a four wood for his long second shot to the green. Jimmy lined up the shot, took a few quick, wristy practice flicks and pulled the trigger. It was a fantastic second shot – his first – and it found its target with precision-like accuracy. If Jimmy did nothing else but this finely executed shot, he was a happy man, because he left his partner with a twelve-footer for an opening birdie. Not only did Hitchcock miss the birdie attempt, but he left the Irishman with a six-footer back for a par. The pressure was mounting by the second and they were only on the first hole.

The home pairing was eventually trounced by 5 and 4. Why the Great Britain and Ireland team captain, Harry Weetman, omitted the Irishman in the final day's singles is beyond compre-hension. The captain played his other team member, Jimmy Hitchcock, twice in the singles, morning and afternoon, and the Ashford Manor pro lost both games to Arnold Palmer and Julios Boros, respectively.

The US beat the Great Britain and Ireland squad by 19½ points to 12½.

EDDIE POLLAND

Eddie Polland was one of five Ryder Cup players from Northern Ireland. He made one Ryder Cup appearance, in 1973 at Muirfield, Gullane, Scotland.

Eddie Polland was born in 1947 in Northern Ireland, the same year his compatriot, Fred Daly, won the Open Championship at Hoylake. Eddie was a very accomplished professional golfer who won a number of tournaments in Ireland in the 1970s, with further wins in England and Spain. He represented Ireland in the World Cup of Golf on six occasions. He won the Swallow Penfold Tournament the same year he played in the Ryder Cup at Gullane, in 1973. Recognised as a very good match player, he won the 1975 PGA Match Play Championship and followed it up with an international win in the Spanish Open in 1976. His Ryder Cup pedigree was obvious.

However, the talented Ulsterman would receive a Ryder Cup baptism of fire on day one at Muirfield, the one and only time a Ryder Cup had been staged in Scotland. (Scotland has been selected to host the 2014 series of Ryder Cup matches.) In the opening foursomes on day one, Eddie Polland teamed up with Englishman Maurice Bembridge to face what was arguably the toughest opposition of the 1973 Ryder Cup matches. The Great Britain and Ireland partnership was 5 down at the turn to Jack Nicklaus and Arnold Palmer, who eventually devoured them by 6 and 5.

The baptism of fire was prolonged on day two for Polland, when he teamed up with fellow rookie Clive Clark to face Jack Nicklaus and the reigning British Open champion, Tom Weiskopf. The home side was beaten 3 and 2. Unfortunately, Bernard Hunt, who was the captain of the home team, decided to leave Eddie Polland out of the singles on the final day.

The dominance and supremacy of the Americans were confirmed again by the final result: America 19, Great Britain and Ireland 13.

Eddie Polland now plays on the British Seniors' Tour.

CHAPTER 10

The New Breed

DARREN CLARKE

Darren Clarke comes from Northern Ireland and has played in four Ryder Cups.

His debut was at Valderrama in Spain in 1997. He also played in 1999 at Brookline, the Belfry in 2002 and Oakland Hills in 2004.

Darren Clarke was born in Dugannon, County Tyrone, Northern Ireland in 1968, the same year Gary Player won another British Open Championship. He grew up in a golfing environment that would eventually bring the very best out of him. Royal Portrush was where he would play much of his golf as a youngster. This links course rates as one of the best in the world. Golf was a passion for Darren, as it was and is for the great players throughout history. He duly indulged in this passion, which would bring him to the top of his relatively short amateur career. In 1990, Darren won both the Irish Close Championship and the Spanish Amateur Open Championship.

In 1990 he gave serious thought to turning pro, but wondered if he should wait just a little longer in the hope of making the 1991 Walker Cup at Portmarnock. This would, in fact, be the zenith of an amateur career. He thought long and hard about his immediate future at that point in time, but made his decision rather swiftly. He would turn pro in 1990 with a handicap of plus four. A visit to the Qualifying School would follow. His first victory on the professional circuit was in the 1993 Alfred Dunhill Open, just three years after turning pro. This win confirmed Darren's earlier decision to have been the correct one. Within another three years he would add the 1996 Linde German Masters to his list of victories. He was also joint runner-up with Jesper Parnevik behind Justin Leonard at the 1997 British Open at Troon.

The future augured particularly well for the talented golfer from Northern Ireland. This would be copperfastened by additional wins for him in the 1998 Benson & Hedges International Open and the Volvo Masters at Andalucía in the same year. There was no stopping Darren, for he would continue to excel in the professional game, winning the 1999 English Open, the first of three English Opens. 1999 was another good year for Darren. I was at the European Open that summer and followed him around when he carded a record 60 at the K Club. He was the first player on the European Tour to score 60 on two occasions. The first time was also a record at the European Monte Carlo Open in 1992.

Harmony and balance

Darren Clarke's *annus mirabilis* came when he won the 2000 WGC-Accenture Match Play, beating Tiger Woods in the thirty-six-hole final. He won the 2001 Smurfit European Open, and two years later he notched up another world win, the WGC-NEC Invitational. On top of all these accolades, the Northern Ireland star was a member of the Alfred Dunhill Cup on nine occasions, a member of three World Cup teams and two Seve Trophy teams.

There was a time when Darren was easily annoyed with his bad play. In the past he was hot tempered and a little abrupt when things didn't go well on the golf course. These negative traits undermined his confidence and self-esteem.

But a new approach, outlined in his 2005 publication *Darren Clarke and Golf – The Mind Factor*, had positive implications for his attitude. Darren Clarke is now the consummate professional. He went from division three in the mental side of his game to the premiership. Fellow players and journalists acknowledged this. He was now giving his all to practice in the belief that it would pay handsome dividends. Although he tied thirteenth in the 2004 USPGA event at Whistling Straits, Darren led with an opening record round of 65.

Amongst the elite

The triumvirate of Clarke, Harrington and McGinley now all share the same frame of mind. All three are patient and unflappable in the fiercest of competition. They would fear nobody. This quality of mind would have its ultimate test in the thick of Ryder Cup battle. Clarke himself referred to the pressure in these biennial matches. No one knows what real pressure is unless they have played in Ryder Cup matches. Real pressure is not felt until you hit the very first shot in a Ryder Cup event. No wonder he was a member of three out of four winning Ryder Cup matches.

1997 Valderrama, Spain

Darren Clarke made his Ryder Cup debut at the 1997 event in Sotogrande. Seve's squad would take on Tom Kite's US team in the keenest of competition. The home side would score a very narrow winning victory over the visitors. Captain Seve Ballesteros would be a very proud captain indeed. It was a big disappointment for the Americans, who were obliged to return home without Sam Ryder's trophy. The European captain decided to leave Darren out on the first day. His very first game in his rookie year came in the Saturday morning fourballs, when he was paired with the rock-solid Colin Montgomerie, who has an enviable track record in Ryder Cup matches. The two proved to be a sound partnership when they beat the strong American pairing of Fred Couples and Davis Love III by one hole.

After the end of play on day two, the European team led by 10½ points to 5½. The Spanish captain needed only 3½ points to retain the trophy and 4 to win.

Meanwhile, the American captain, Tom Kite, was in a quandry. He couldn't believe the unenviable predicament he and his team found themselves in. He had done all his homework and preparations well in advance. He had even researched the weather patterns that were peculiar to Valderrama over the previous thirty years.

The feedback was that there was little or no rain expected at that time of the year. Yet there were heavy downpours in Ryder Cup week and matches on day one were delayed because of the heavy rains. Thankfully, the green keeping and ground staff put in a mammoth effort to ensure that play would in fact take place on day one. In addition, Valderrama as a course came out on top, as their drainage system responded magnificently to the heavy rains.

Tom Kite, on the other hand, saw his team 'drained' of much mental energy, self-esteem and confidence as they faced the final day's twelve singles matches. America needed 9 points from these encounters to win the Ryder Cup. This was a stern test. Team member Tom Lehman felt America could turn the tables. In desperation, Kite had a chat with former US president, George Bush, Sr., who was at the event, asking him to give his team a pep talk in the hope of instilling an element of pride into a team that had suffered a serious setback over the opening few days of competition. It had the intended result, for the underdogs came out with guns blazing in the singles. They all but managed it, scoring 8 points from the singles. Had they got another half point they would have tied the event. The European team got their 4 points and won the Ryder Cup.

Darren Clarke played his heart out in his match against favourite Phil Mickelson, but lost out to the world's best left-hander by 2 and 1. The overall result was a salutary reminder to the home team that they should never sit on their laurels, no matter how commanding a lead they might have going into the final day's singles of a Ryder Cup. Darren learned a great deal from his first experience in a Ryder Cup match, which would stand him in good stead.

1999 Brookline, US

Darren would have had mixed fortunes during the three days of Ryder Cup competition at Brookline. Darren teamed up with Englishman and best friend Lee Westwood to take on the mighty partnership of America's Tiger Woods and David Duval in the four-ball matches on day one. The European partnership proved to be a solid one. They beat the opposition by one hole. However, Westwood and Clarke lost the afternoon foursomes, succumbing to the supremacy of their opponents, Jeff Maggert and Hal Sutton, by

3 and 2. Mark James, the European captain, kept the same pairing for the Saturday morning fourballs against Phil Mickelson and Tom Lehman. Unfortunately, it would be a second loss in a row for the visitors, who were beaten 2 and 1. However, the same pairing was put out into battle once more, and this time they regained much pride by disposing of Jim Furyk and Mark O'Meara by 3 and 2.

At the end of play on the second day, the Europeans led the Americans by 10 points to 6. Day three got off to a very good start for the Americans, who won the first six of the singles matches to lead by 12 points to 10. The Europeans experienced an almost fatal blow at an early stage. Clarke was one of the casualties. He lost out to Hal Sutton by the convincing margin of 4 and 2. In fact, the only European wins came from Irishman Padraig Harrington, Colin Montgomerie and reigning British Open champion Paul Lawrie. There was one halved match, an infamous one at that. Olazábal and Leonard got a half point each. The US won the 1999 Ryder Cup by one point. Ireland's Darren Clarke had gained much experience, which would be put to use the time the next Ryder Cup matches took place at the Belfry in 2002.

2002 The Belfry, Sutton Coldfield, West Midlands, England

The thirty-fourth Ryder Cup got underway a year after being postponed due to 9/11 at the Belfry. Darren Clark would be on the team, along with fellow Irishmen Padraig Harrington and Paul McGinley. Sam Torrance was the captain, and he and his team were acutely aware how victory had been dramatically snatched from their grasp last time out. The Scotsman had fire in his belly and he studied his players well.

First out of the trap in the Friday fourballs on the opening day would be Darren Clarke, paired with the reliable Thomas Björn. Clarke was a superb ball striker and was, according to Sam Torrance, a very impressive and intimidating player when on form. Sam had been a little concerned about another Westwood/Clarke partnership, which was his reason for putting Clarke with 'the Great Dane'. Björn had a great track record and pedigree. He won the 2002 Dubai Desert Classic, playing with the world's number one in all four rounds. That was pressure at its best. Darren Clarke had also beaten Tiger Woods to take top spot in the thirty-six-hole final of the 2002 Accenture Match Play Championship in America. Clarke and Björn beat Tiger Woods and Paul Azinger. The Europeans won the first point. The important momentum had been set in motion, for the Europeans won the first three matches out.

There would be a disappointment for the up-to-now solid partnership of Clarke and Björn when they lost out in afternoon foursomes to Hal Sutton and Scott Verplank by 2 and 1. In the Saturday morning foursomes they would suffer another setback, this time going down to Tiger Woods and Davis Love III by 4 and 3. Darren would be in an all-Irish pairing in the afternoon four-balls. He and Paul McGinley would earn a half point in their match with Scott Hoch and Jim Furyk.

The Americans and Europeans were tied at 8 points apiece going into the singles on Sunday. Americans were always favourites when going into the final day. However, the tables would be turned when Sam's squad won 7½ points out of 12 to snatch the Ryder Cup back from the Americans' jaws. Clarke contributed significantly to the result when he halved with the great David Duval. He certainly had shed the nasty shackles of being an underachiever and lacking in goal commitment in his earlier career. Clarke would play his fourth Ryder Cup in a row when next staged at Oakland Hills in 2004.

2004 Oakland Hills, Michigan, US

Darren Clarke played in five matches at Oakland Hills, winning points in four. He had another partner in this outing. Bernhard Langer felt Darren was the kind of player who could team up with virtually anyone and still come out on top, which is what happened when he and Miguel Angel Jiménez beat Davis Love III and Chad Campbell in the second fourball match out on day one by 5 and 4. In the afternoon foursomes clash against Tiger Woods and Phil Mickelson, Darren had his old friend Lee Westwood on board. This was a clever move on the part of captain Bernhard Langer. He knew of their friendship and was also aware of how well they had played together in the past. Bernhard also made another shrewd observation – he knew that there was no love lost friendship-wise between Woods and Mickelson, who would play against Darren and Lee. Sure enough, the Europeans came out on top.

Darren lost his only point when he once again got a new partner in Ian Poulter. The Europeans were beaten 4 and 3 by

Tiger Woods and Chris Riley. Darren Clarke was back yet again with Lee Westwood when they inflicted a 5 and 4 thrashing on Jay Haas and Chris DiMarco on Saturday afternoon.

After day two, the Europeans led by 11 points to 5. This was a huge lead going into the final day on American soil. The visitors weren't complacent, however. They went on to win 7½ points out of 12. Darren Clarke won his half point against Davis Love III. The result was Europe 18½, US 9½. The Europeans were a golfing force to be reckoned with. They no longer played second fiddle on the world stage. Northern Ireland's Darren Clarke was now an established player in this modern crusade.

EAMONN DARCY

Eamonn Darcy played in the Ryder Cup on four occasions, twice with the Great Britain and Ireland team in 1975 and 1977, and twice as a member of the European team in 1981 and 1987.

I met with Eamonn in January 2005 at Druids Glen in County Wicklow. Eamonn comes from Harry Bradshaw country, where the Wicklow air is commensurate with the playing of this great game. He knew and had a great respect for 'The Brad', as he was affectionately known. Eamonn is a native of Delgany and as a youngster considered becoming a jockey, but as time marched on he grew rather tall and later decided on golf as a career. He joined the professional ranks in 1969. Critics would describe his swing as being anything but graceful. However, as the Wicklow man made steady progress throughout his professional career, he got significant praise from a number of his golfing colleagues.

Christy O'Connor, Sr. said Eamonn's left-hand grip on the shaft was something special. Others regarded his short game as being world class. John O'Leary said he was one of the greatest wedge players the world had ever witnessed. Even Severiano Ballesteros and Bernhard Langer are reputed to have spent some considerable time observing him on the practice ground hitting wedge shots. There was a gentle, delicate full swing of the club, followed by an authoritative, confident hit resulting in a very high trajectory, with the ball falling softly onto the green. Darcy could practically stop a ball on a concrete green.

In the 1970s, Eamonn managed to get himself into the top ten of the Order of Merit, certainly no mean feat. He would later win the Dubai Desert Classic and the New Zealand, Spanish and Kenyan Opens. Eamonn was the leading European player in the 1991 Open Championship, when he tied for fifth place. That was the same year he finished eighteenth in the Order of Merit and agonisingly missed out on automatic selection for the Ryder Cup. He decided not to compete in the final qualifying tournament, the German Open, perhaps thinking he had done enough to gain an automatic place. Eamonn missed competing at Kiawah Island by the narrowest of margins: IR£58, or 58 points (every pound was equal to a point). Had he only played in that last official event and, of course, qualified for the final thirty-six holes, he would have played in five Ryder Cups instead of four.

The 1975 Ryder Cup was an inauspicious inaugural occasion for Eamonn Darcy. It was in America, where the home side always won. This time would be no different, as captain Arnold Palmer led the US to a resounding victory over the visitors by 21 points to 11. Laurel Valley, Pennsylvania was the venue, a place that holds anything but happy Ryder Cup memories for Eamonn. He was paired on the opening day in the afternoon fourballs with his good friend Christy O'Connor, Jr. They proved no match for the American partnership of Tom Weiskopf and Lou Graham, who beat the two Irishmen by the convincing margin of 3 and 2.

The result of the morning fourballs on day two was somewhat more acceptable, as Eamonn partnered Englishman Guy Hunt to a halved match against Al Geiberger and Ray Floyd. Darcy and Hunt teamed up again for the afternoon foursomes, this time against the formidable opposition of Al Geiberger and Lou Graham. Unfortunately, the Americans beat them with cruise-like control by 3 and 2. To add insult to injury, in-form Billy Casper disposed of Eamonn by a similar 3 and 2 margin in the singles on the final day. The 1975 Ryder Cup, albeit his debut, was to prove to be the Irishman's *annus horibilis*.

By 1977, American interest in the continuance of the Ryder Cup was once again on a significant downward curve. It was now regarded by them to be a damp squib. A new format had already been put in place in advance of the matches at Royal Lytham and St Anne's. The fiery little Welshman, Brian Huggett, would lead his team with five foursomes on the first day and five fourballs on the second day. Day three, as before, would be devoted to the singles matches. Eamonn Darcy partnered Tony Jacklin to a halved match against Ed Sneed and Don January on the opening day's play, and the same Great Britain and Ireland partnership suffered a crushing blow from Dave Stockton and Dave Hill in the fourballs on the second day.

Another singles defeat beckoned on the final day for Darcy. This time Hubert Green, a winner of the 1977 Irish Open at Portmarnock, beat him on the final green for the narrow one-hole victory. The final result was 12½ points to 7½, recording yet another win for the Americans.

1981 Walton Health, England

Although Eamonn didn't feature in the 1979 matches at Greenbrier, West Virginia, his appearance in the 1981 Ryder Cup at Walton Heath was an affair to remember. It was no longer the Great Britain and Ireland side, but rather Europe that would play against the US.

Darcy would feature on the 1981 European team. Once again the Americans were to notch up another home victory, with 18½ points to 9½, and Eamonn was to be a casualty, along with Scotland's Bernard Gallacher, in the afternoon foursomes on the first day against Hale Irwin and Ray Floyd, going down 2 and 1. Tragically, in his only other match, this time the singles, he would succumb to one of the finest exponents the game has ever seen, Jack Nicklaus. Eamonn suffered a humiliating 5 and 3 defeat at the hands of the 'Golden Bear'.

1987 Muirfield Village, Ohio, US

Eamonn would balance the record books in 1987, when he was to emerge a hero of the event in Jack Nicklaus's own backyard at Muirfield Village. The Americans had never been beaten on home soil. Eamonn relived the experience for me. European captain Tony Jacklin left him out of the entire first day's play, much to Eamonn's disappointment. To compound the agony, Jacklin left the Irishman out of the morning foursomes on day two. Experts regard this to be psychologically detrimental, starving Darcy of vital playing experience leading up to the final day's one-to-one singles.

Eamonn did get to play in the fourball series in the afternoon of day two. Playing alongside Gordon Brand, Jr., he suffered defeat at the hands of the late Payne Stewart and his partner, Andy Bean, by the convincing margin of 3 and 2. Going into the final day's man-to-man singles matches, the home side led by a slender margin of 4½ to 3½. As always, the US team was confident of victory.

Eamonn Darcy was drawn against Ben Crenshaw on the Sunday. 'Gentleman Ben' was the favourite. Former Masters champion Ben was third in the US money list in 1987. In his head-to-head clash with Ireland's Eamonn Darcy, he found the going very rough. After six holes, the US Masters champion found himself two down. Much has been spoken in golfing circles about this sixth hole featuring the Crenshaw/Darcy match. It's true Crenshaw went two down to Darcy. Some say Ben broke his putter in total disgust and extreme anger at three-putting to lose the hole. What really happened was completely different, according to Eamonn Darcy.

Eamonn actually didn't notice anything untoward on the sixth green. It was only after the singles match that he realised that Ben had actually broken his putter on the sixth and had had to improvise for the rest of the match with his one iron, and to good effect, on the greens. Occasionally, he successfully used the leading edge of his sand wedge to good effect also. The truth is that Ben Crenshaw had a very old, reliable, intimate putter whose shaft had rusted away from the inside over time and had finally broken. When he missed the short putt on the sixth, he did what most golfers do – he took a gentle swipe at the ground in dismay. There was no aggression, no unbridled anger and no uncontrolled outburst.

In fact, despite being two behind after six, Ben actually managed to square the match with his improvised putting, eventually to go one up at the difficult sixteenth. Eamonn remembers the occasion vividly. The sixteenth was a difficult par three with the pin placement hovering over a yawning bunker. Eamonn was awestruck at the tee shot executed by Ben. It was a four iron which seemed to soar 200 feet into the air with a gentle cut and fell 'like a wet blanket a few feet from the hole. It was one of the greatest shots I've ever seen,' he said. It was that finely executed shot that put Crenshaw into a one-hole lead.

Eamonn played a career-best second shot to the seventeenth in reply, leaving him with a three-footer, which he duly holed to square the match with just one to play. The tension was electrifying. 'It knocked Ben off his perch,' said the Irishman. Darcy had the honour. The news spread like wildfire around Muirfield Village: 'The Irishman has squared the match with our Ben on the seventeenth.'

The best was yet to come. Darcy hit a three wood down the difficult eighteenth hole, making the fairway. Ben Crenshaw hooked his tee shot, his second into a stream and coaxed his third into a greenside bunker. Darcy's second ended up in the same trap but for two. The galleries were huge at this stage. The word about the closeness of the contest had spread round the course. Ben's rescue attempt from sand left him with a longer putt than he wished for. Eamonn, with his 'agricultural swing' incorporating a flying right elbow, exploded from the bunker, leaving him with a tricky but manageable four- to five-footer. Crenshaw holed his difficult, testing putt for a bogey 5. The pressure was now on Darcy.

Irish golf journalist Colm Smith was around the eighteenth green and overheard a comment from a small gallery of Americans, which included some of the players from the American team, who were with captain Jack Nicklaus eagerly awaiting the outcome of the Darcy/Crenshaw duel. One of the American supporters is reputed to have said 'Darcy will hole out', but someone replied, 'I wouldn't be too sure about that.' The American asked, 'How do you know?' 'I designed the course,' was the response – it was the great Jack Nicklaus himself. However, Eamonn was confident he could give Tony Jacklin a point, such was his buoyant mood on the final green. The Delgany man carefully studied his tricky, slippery five-foot downhill putt and then calmly holed out for a fantastic one-hole victory.

Darcy was ecstatic. He was somewhat distracted on the eighteenth green, but distinctly recalls Jack Nicklaus throwing his arms around him and guiding him off, saying, 'Eamonn, you will remember that putt for the rest of your life.' Eamonn still cherishes that comment, coming as it did from one of the greatest exponents the game has ever seen. For the very first time in the history of the Ryder Cup, the Americans were beaten by 7½ to 4½ points on home soil.

DAVID FEHERTY

David Feherty played in one Ryder Cup, and that was in 1991 at Kiawah Island, in South Carolina.

In the golfing world of 2006, the name David Feherty is synonymous with golf reporting and commentating on American television sports channels. He has that Irish appeal and charm that goes down well with the American golfing public. It's not what he says during his commentaries, but rather the way he says it, using a hilarious amalgam of comic metaphors and anecdotes to illustrate a golfing point. Behind this veneer, though, is a serious golfer who joined the professional ranks in 1979. David needed three attempts at the Qualifying School before making the grade, however.

David Feherty was born in Northern Ireland in 1958. He was the last player from that part of the country to play in a Ryder Cup up to and including the event to be played at the K Club in September 2006. David followed in the illustrious footsteps of fellow Northerners Fred Daly, Norman Drew, Eddie Polland and Ronan Rafferty in making it into the Ryder Cup in 1991, when Europe played at Kiawah Island in South Carolina, which incidentally was the venue where Padraig Harrington and Paul McGinley would triumph in the World Cup of Golf six years later.

Playing on the European Tour earlier in his career, David Feherty would finish in the top fifty in the Order of Merit in 1982. After an initial tournament win in South Africa, he continued to work hard at his game, which propelled him to two victories on the circuit in 1986, the Italian and Scottish Opens. He finished the 1986 season in the top twenty of the money list. In 1989, two years before his Ryder Cup debut, he felt the compunction to seek out a sports psychologist to help him focus better and get back on track with his game. It paid handsome dividends, for soon after David won the BMW International Open and the Cannes Open, and he was one of the team members that led Ireland to win the Dunhill Cup in the same year. Shortly before embarking on a Ryder Cup venture, David Feherty finished a credible joint seventh in the USPGA Championship of the same year.

1991 Kiawah Island, South Carolina, US

Captain Bernard Gallacher came to South Carolina in the hopes of beating the Americans on their own ground. In the opening fourballs on day one, David Feherty partnered his best friend, Sam Torrance, in a tense and exciting match against their American opponents, Lanny Wadkins and Mark O'Meara. The match went down to the wire and resulted in a very acceptable draw with a half point earned for the two sides. Feherty's Ryder Cup debut opened in reasonable fashion.

However, David and Sam would succumb to the supremacy of Hale Irwin and Lanny Wadkins in the first foursomes match out on day two, being convincingly beaten by 4 and 2. Both Feherty and Torrance were rested from afternoon play. At the end of play on day two, Bernard Gallacher's hopes of a win were still alive. The two teams were tied on 8 points; 6½ points were required from the singles on the final day for the Europeans to capture the Ryder Cup.

The inimitable Nick Faldo led the charge on day three with a solid win over former US Masters champion Ray Floyd. The momentum was there for Feherty to build on. He was playing in match number two directly behind his playing colleague, Faldo. The Ulsterman's self-esteem and confidence soared and he continued to play mercurial golf against the reigning US Open champion, the late Payne Stewart, whom he comfortably beat by 2 and 1. The only other European to win a match on the final day was Severiano Ballesteros. The US side, captained by Dave Stockton, won the Ryder Cup by a slender margin of 14½ points to 13½.

PADRAIG HARRINGTON

Padraig Harrington has played in three Ryder Cup matches, in 1999, 2002 and 2004.

Padraig Harrington is a Dubliner and learned a lot of his golf at Stackstown Golf Club, situated on the slopes of the Dublin Mountains. His late father, Paddy, was a garda (policeman) and founder member of Stackstown, often referred to as the 'garda club'. Padraig is the youngest of five brothers.

In 2004, Padraig was sixth in the world golf rankings. This was a marvellous achievement by any standards. Climbing to the top rung of the golfing ladder didn't happen overnight, though. Padraig worked very hard over a long period of time to become the great golfer he undoubtedly is today. His 'Ben Hogan' work ethic is second to none today. Harrington loves to practise. Three, four or even five hours spent on the practice range is not unusual for Bob Torrance's player. The Dubliner thrives on the discipline he has learned over the years.

Padraig Harrington entered the professional ranks in 1995 after a magnificent amateur career which included three Walker Cup caps. One of these was a winning occasion at Royal Porthcawl in 1995. In 1996 he made every cut in each one of his first ten outings and won the Spanish Open in his eleventh event. Nine runner-up finishes in the early part of his professional career seemed to confine Padraig Harrington to the back benches, but this didn't deter him. He almost made it to the play-off stage in the 2002 Open Championship. A bogey on the seventy-second hole prevented him from joining four others in a play-off. He finished a credible fifth. He was on eight Irish World Cup teams and with his friend, Paul McGinley, followed in the illustrious footsteps of Christy O'Connor, Sr. and the late Harry Bradshaw by winning the World Cup of Golf at Kiawah Island in 1997.

Other fine performances and victories came Padraig's way at home in Ireland and on the European Tour. He won the Irish PGA Championship in 1998 and 2004. He tied for second place in the 2004 Nissan Irish Open. He played in five Alfred Dunhill Cup events from 1996 to 2000. Other victories included the Brazil, Asian, Deutsche Bank and Hong Kong Opens as well as the Volvo Masters and Linde German Masters. In 2002 he tied fifth with South Africa's Ernie Els in the US Masters, with rounds of 69, 70, 72 and 71 and tied eighth in the US Open with rounds of 70, 68, 73 and 75.

His record in recent years on the American circuit has been phenomenal. He missed out in winning the 2004 Buick Open when Sergio Garcia beat him in a play-off. In 2002 he won the Target World Challenge in America. On this side of the Atlantic, Padraig was on three Seve Trophy team events played against Europe in 2000, 2002 and 2003.

There were more exceptional performances in 2005, when he won two tournaments on the demanding US circuit. After a three-way play-off with Joe Olgivie and world number-two player, Vijay Singh, the Stackstown player won the number one spot in the

Honda Classic. He became the first player from the Republic of Ireland to win on the regular American tour since 1922, when Pat O'Hara from Greenore, County Louth won the North and South Championship at Pinehurst. Another title came Harrington's way in June 2005 when he beat former US Open champion Jim Furyk by sinking a sixty-five-foot eagle putt on the last hole to win the Barclays Classic.

1999 Brookline, US

The 1999 Ryder Cup was Padraig's first. Although he lost his morning foursomes match on day two in partnership with Miguel Angel Jiménez against Steve Pate and Tiger Woods by the very slender margin of one hole, his overall Ryder Cup initiation was significant. In his other two encounters he accumulated 1½ points. A half point came from the morning foursomes on day one playing alongside Jiménez and defeating Davis Love III and the late Payne Stewart. The feather in his cap came when he beat former British Open and Masters champion, Mark O'Meara, and chalked up a point for his captain, Mark James. The Americans won the 1999 Ryder Cup in dramatic fashion by 14½ points to 13½.

Those who followed Padraig over the three days couldn't help being impressed by his determination and discipline in the fiercest of competition. He relished the entire occasion, especially the cut and thrust of Ryder Cup encounters. He would prove to be a force to be reckoned with on the world stage.

2002 The Belfry, Sutton Coldfield, West Midlands, England

Over 35,000 spectators turned up for this fantastic occasion at the Belfry in 2002. The Irishman wasn't up to his usual game and was on the losing side in the fourballs and foursomes on the first day. His form was so out of sync that he asked his captain, Sam Torrance, to omit him from the morning foursomes on day two to allow him time to sort out his bad form. Torrance, whose father is Harrington's coach, was reluctant at first to leave the Irishman out, but finally agreed to rest him.

Under the guidance and direction of Bob Torrance, much practice took place into the evening's darkness and Padraig got to the root of his problem. He came out firing on all cylinders for the fourball matches on the second day and for the man-to-man duel on the final day. He teamed up with Scotland's Colin Montgomerie on the Saturday and was responsible for disposing of the strong pairing of Phil Mickelson and David Toms. He was in devastating form in the singles when he crushed America's Mark Calcavecchia by 5 and 4. In the meantime, Paul McGinley had holed that nerve-wracking 'Benson & Hedges' putt on the last hole to win the all-important half point to ensure a European victory: Europe 15½, US 12½. The Cup was back.

The mention of Benson & Hedges doesn't resonate too well with Padraig. Every golf enthusiast will recall the 2000 Benson & Hedges International Open, when the man from Stackstown failed to sign a score card. After consolidating his lead by five shots on moving day (the third round), he was informed before teeing off on the final that he had failed to sign his card after his opening first round of 71. A five-shot lead certainly made him a firm favourite to scoop the £166,000 first prize. But he was in breach of Rule 6.6b and was disqualified from the tournament.

2004 Oakland Hills, Michigan

The 2004 Ryder Cup at Oakland Hills would be Padraig Harrington's *annus mirabilis*. In the Friday morning foursomes he partnered the rock-solid Colin Montgomerie to a convincing 5 and 4 thrashing of Tiger Woods and Phil Mickelson. Padraig and Montgomerie sidelined Davis Love III and Fred Funk by a cruise-control margin of 4 and 2. The only 2004 blemish for the same partnership happened on the Saturday morning in the fourballs, when they lost out to Stewart Cink and Davis Love III by 3 and 2.

The Irishman recharged his batteries for the singles battle against Jay Haas, beating the American by one hole after sinking a thirty-footer on the final green. Padraig's compatriot and great friend, Paul McGinley, played in the final match and delivered another point for Bernhard Langer, beating Stewart Cink by 3 and 2. The Americans were beaten yet again on home soil.

PAUL MCGINLEY

Paul McGinley has played two Ryder Cup matches to date: the 2002 matches in the Belfry at Sutton Coldfield, West Midlands and in 2004 at Oakland Hills, Michigan.

Paul McGinley was born in Dublin in 1966. Golf wasn't his first sporting love – it was Gaelic football. He played hurling and football at his school, Coláiste Eanna, in Rathfarnham. He also played the two sports at senior level at St Enda's football club in Ballyboden. Padraig Harrington also attended Coláiste Eanna, but there was a five-year age gap between the two. Little did they know they would be playing in the same 1991 Walker Cup at Portmarnock.

Paul's one ambition was to play for The Dubs in a Croke Park final. The transformation of taking on a new dream of wanting to become a Ryder Cup player happened literally by accident. He broke his patella (kneecap) during football training. It was his left knee that posed the problem. That sounded the death knell for his future ambitions as far as football was concerned. At the time he was studying marketing, and upon completing his studies he decided to pursue an interest in that area by spending a short time in Brussels with the then European Economic Community.

As a young man he would have played golf, but it was very much a secondary sport given his passion at the time for Gaelic football. He used to caddy for his father, who was a key influence in his upbringing as a golfer. Paul was attracted to the etiquette and spirit associated with the game. He joined the Grange at nineteen, where the former Walker Cup player, David Sheehan, was a member.

Wattie Sullivan was the resident pro at the Grange at the time and he turned out to be a great help to Paul McGinley. David Kinsella was one of a family of golfing brothers and it was he who taught the young Paul McGinley much about the rudiments and techniques of the game. The more he played, the better he got and it wasn't very long before he turned his attention to the States, thinking he might get a sports scholarship there. This didn't materialise. Paul later enrolled as a student at San Diego International University. During his few years there, Paul travelled all over California and played very successfully as an amateur in many of the professional tournaments going on at the time.

Paul McGinley's pedigree gradually improved. He went from a single handicap golfer to scratch over a few years. In 1988 he won the Irish Youths' Championship and the Scottish Youths' Amateur Open Stroke Play Championship. The following year he won the Irish Amateur Close Championship. In 1991 Paul also won a much-coveted Irish title: the Mullingar Scratch Cup. He also won the South of Ireland Championship the same year and, of course, he was a Walker Cup player alongside his compatriot, Padraig Harrington, when the matches were played in Portmarnock. With a handicap of plus four, Paul McGinley turned pro in 1991.

Paul McGinley secured his European Tour Playing Card on his first attempt in the Qualifying School. His first win was in the 1996 Hohe Bruecke Open, followed by a win in the Oki Pro-Am the following year. The same year, 1997, he won the World Cup of Golf along with Padraig Harrington for Ireland at Kiawah Island. He has played on ten World Cups. He has also played on seven Alfred Dunhill Cups. In 2001, after surviving a five-hole sudden death play-off, he won the Welsh Open, when the event was curtailed to thirty-six holes after torrential rains made it impossible to play the final two days. Paul was also on the 2002 Seve Trophy team that beat Europe.

He posted eight top-ten finishes in 2004. This included two second place finishes, one behind Mark O'Meara in the Dubai Desert Classic and one second to David Lynn in the KLM Open. He clinched his Ryder Cup place by finishing in a tie for sixth place in the final qualifying event, the BMW International. Later, Paul missed out on golf's richest first prize, £1 million (€1.479 million), when he was beaten by the reigning US Open champion, Michael Campbell, in the final of the 2005 HSBC World Match Play Championship at Wentworth. He was devastated at the loss. He blamed it at having played the man rather than the course. However, he bounced back and won one of the most sought-after titles on the European Tour, the Volvo Masters at Valderrama in November 2005. This was the final event in the 2005 European Tour Order of Merit. McGinley finished in third position with official earnings of €2,296,422.77.

Paul McGinley's rich pedigree has been really and truly recognised.

2002 The Belfry, Sutton Coldfield, West Midlands, England

The 2002 Ryder Cup was strongly identified with Ireland's Paul McGinley. It was he who holed 'the Benson & Hedges' putt that ensured victory for Europe, who beat the US by 15½ to 12½ points.

This was Paul McGinley's Ryder Cup debut. He would partner Padraig Harrington in the afternoon foursomes on day one against Phil Mickelson and David Toms. Captain Sam Torrance felt this would be a very strong Irish partnership capable of doing the required task. After all, they had done it in the Seve Trophy. However, they were convincingly beaten by 3 and 2. At the end of play on day one, the Europeans had a comfortable one point lead over the visiting team.

Paul was left out of the morning play for a second day running but would partner another Irishman, Darren Clarke, in the afternoon fourballs against the firm opposition of Scott Hoch and Jim Furyk. Paul and Darren were two down with four holes remaining, but rallied to halve the match on the eighteenth to earn a well-deserved half point for Europe.

The two teams were level going into the twelve singles on Sunday. The last time this had happened was at Kiawah Island in 1991. Sam Torrance and his crew would not be complacent, for he was well aware of the dominance of the Americans going into the final day's battle. The balance was strongly in the Americans' favour. Since 1981 they had come out on top in the singles six times out of eight.

Sam had decided on his team to engage in man-to-man matches, but he kept on revisiting his list. Was it the correct one? McGinley couldn't be considered the favourite against Furyk. He made his list, he made his mind up and put his singles plan into action. The focus would soon be on Ireland's Paul McGinley. There were six holes to go and he was two down to the tenacious Jim Furyk. The Irishman clawed back the deficit, leaving him going down the eighteenth all square. Could he salvage a half point for his team? Sam Torrance had just made his way across the bridge at the eighteenth a few minutes earlier, sensing the unfolding drama. He was there to observe the finish of the match ahead of McGinley's. Niclas Fasth was one up on Paul Azinger, who found greenside sand off his second shot. A huge American roar went up as Azinger holed out from sand for a birdie and a half point. Fasth was shattered and Sam Torrance was in bits.

Everything was now moving at speed. McGinley must have been thunderstruck when he heard the roar ahead. Enormous pressure was now on the rookie's shoulders. Furyk found the greenside bunker in two. Paul pulled his shot way left of the green and bunker and played a deft pitch almost to perfection, but leaving him a putt of some eight to ten feet from the cup. Furyk almost replicated Azinger's bunker shot of a few minutes earlier. After a little discussion with his caddie as to the exact line of the putt, Paul McGinley holed that tricky 'Benson & Hedges' pressure putt to halve his match with Furyk and win the Ryder Cup for Europe.

The home team had accumulated 14½ points following McGinley's win, the minimum necessary points to win the cup.

Torrance's strategy for the Sunday singles worked wonders. The Europeans won 7½ out of a possible 12 points. The Americans' proud singles results in recent times had been reversed. They only managed 4½ points.

2004 Oakland Hills, Michigan, US

Bernhard Langer led the Europeans at the 2004 Ryder Cup. This time, however, the Americans were on their own turf and would be favourites to bring the Ryder Cup trophy back to the States. On the other hand, the Europeans were on a winning streak and were reluctant to let Sam's trophy be snatched from their firm grasp.

Paul McGinley was no longer a rookie. He was a firmly established and respected Ryder Cup player. He emerged from this Cup with an almost 100 per cent record. His worst performance was in gaining a half point in his fourball match along with Luke Donald against Chris Riley and Stewart Cink. The rest were all wins.

The European team was in a buoyant mood when the 2004 Ryder Cup matches got underway. Colin Montgomerie and Ireland's Padraig Harrington played in the opening match against Tiger Woods and Phil Mickelson and confidently disposed of the Americans by 5 and 4. Paul played with Luke Donald and delivered an important half point to their captain, Bernhard Langer.

The afternoon matches kicked off for Harrington and Montgomerie much as it had in the morning session. They annihilated Davis Love III and Fred Funk by 4 and 2. American skipper Hal Sutton was in anything but a good mood when his pre-match strategy was torn into shreds. His side trailed by 1½ points to 6½ at the end of play on day one.

After a rest from the afternoon matches on the opening day, Paul McGinley teamed up with compatriot Padraig Harrington on day two to face one of the strongest American partnerships of Davis Love III and Tiger Woods. The Irish pair delivered a 4 and 3 defeat to the Americans. Day two drew to a close, with the visitors leading by 11 points to 5.

Matters were to worsen for Hal Sutton's side on the final day. All they could come up with were 4½ points out of 12 in the singles. Paul McGinley's match was the final one of the 2004 event. He duly obliged his captain with another win and a point, beating Stewart Cink by 3 and 2. Bernhard Langer's squad won 7½ points from the singles encounter. The 2004 Ryder Cup was won by Europe beating the Americans by the huge margin of 18½ points to 9½.

CHRISTY O'CONNOR, JR.

Christy Junior played in the Ryder Cup on two occasions, in 1975 and 1989.

The name Christy O'Connor has a special resonance in Ireland. There are two O'Connors. Christy O'Connor, Sr. is synonymous with golf in Ireland and indeed throughout the globe. His nephew is Christy O'Connor, Jr. and he is held in equally high regard at home and abroad. Like his famous uncle, Junior hails from the same family homestead in a small village in Galway called Knocknacarra.

After watching his uncle play in the Carroll's Sweet Afton Tournament in Dublin in 1964, Junior returned to Galway and sought out Bob Wallace, the pro who had taught Senior the techniques and rudiments of the game in his early years and who would surely do the same for his nephew. Christy Junior wasn't happy with the off-putting response that awaited him: 'Forget it. You won't make the grade.' Junior was stunned at Bob's reaction. He decided to go it alone, and after some time made his way to South Shields in England, where he became assistant pro to Bob's son, Kevin. He came home after a brief spell and was fortunate to be taken on as an assistant to his Uncle Christy at Royal Dublin. It just so happened that there was a vacancy at the club. Fortune would continue to favour Junior, as Christy Senior invited him to stay with him in the family home in Clontarf, just a stone's throw from Royal Dublin.

Young Christy had a 7.00 a.m. daily rise followed by a strict working routine that incorporated a thorough cleaning of clubs and grips together with all the other menial tasks that are part and parcel of a resident professional golfer's working day. Uncle Christy was a hard task master, but very fair.

Whenever there was a rare respite from daily chores, Christy Senior would help Junior with his game. They spent considerable time with the grip. Young Christy asked his uncle how he'd developed his own grip. The answer was abrupt: simply through trial and error.

Uncle Christy dissected Junior's swing and drew attention to his overpowering right hand. His uncle repeated time and time again that no one hand should dominate in the swing. The hands should work in unison. Junior would achieve this expertise over time.

Christy O'Connor, Jr. would spend a short time in Holland before returning to take up appointments in Carlow and eventually in Shannon. He joined the European Tour in 1970 and actually played in the John Player Classic when his uncle won the then biggest first prize in the world of £25,000.

Christy Junior would go on to raise his own level of golf and was rewarded with a win in the 1973 Carroll's Match Play event in Kilkenny. He was subsequently a proud winner of the 1975 revived Irish Open at Woodbrook. In the same event, his uncle holed out in one on the par three seventeenth and shared his prize of a bottle of champagne with Junior to celebrate his own big win. Young Christy went on to win the Martini event in England. Through a twist of fate, the two O'Connors would represent Ireland in the World Cup of Golf that same year. Eamonn Darcy was due to play with O'Connor Senior, but unfortunately had to withdraw from the event. Junior would play in five World Cups in all.

At twenty-eight years old, Christy Junior finished sixth in the 1976 British Open Championship behind winner Johnny Miller at Royal Birkdale. He would go on to win the 1978 Sumrie Better Ball Tournament with fellow Irishman Eamonn Darcy at Queen's Park. He finished third in the 1985 Open Championship at Royal St George's course in Kent. After being the in-form player of the time, however, he was overlooked by Tony Jacklin as a captain's pick for the 1985 Ryder Cup, which was a huge disappointment for him. Christy went on to win the Jersey Open at La Moye and the Kenya Open in 1989 and 1990, respectively. A great feather in his cap was capturing one of the most prestigious titles on the European circuit, the British Masters at Woburn, in 1992. Christy Junior had well and truly arrived on the world scene.

As a result of his greatly improved performances in the 1980s, he was a captain's pick for the 1989 Ryder Cup team to face the Americans at the Belfry.

1975 Laurel Valley, Pennsylvania, US

Christy O'Connor, Jr. played in two matches and lost both of them. Bernard Hunt was the captain and didn't include the Irishman in the final day's singles.

Junior's first loss came in the afternoon fourball match with Eamonn Darcy on day one. They were beaten 3 and 2 by Tom Weiskopf and Lou Graham. Another Irishman, John O'Leary, would partner Christy on day two in their match against Tom Weiskopf and Johnny Miller in the afternoon fourball series. The Irish pair was beaten 5 and 3. There was little they could do against the scintillating performance of the opposition. Weiskopf in particular could do nothing wrong. He went to the turn in an unbelievable 30.

Captain Arnold Palmer's US team beat the Great Britain and Ireland squad by 21 points to 11.

1989 The Belfry, Sutton Coldfield, West Midlands, England

Christy O'Connor, Jr. would justify being his captain's pick at this event. Uncle Christy would be there to support his golfing nephew.

Christy didn't play any match on the opening day, but he played the morning foursomes on day two with Ronan Rafferty. Unfortunately, it was to be another loss for Christy, for they were defeated by Mark Calcavecchia and Ken Green by 3 and 2. After day two, the home side led by 9 points to 7. The captain, Tony Jacklin, was in a buoyant mood. Ballesteros and Langer were first out in the final day's singles, but lost their matches. Jacklin had placed great importance on these two players coming up trumps and inspiring the rest of the team. It was Ireland's Christy O'Connor, Jr. who would rise to the pressure of the occasion.

Christy was out in match seven against big-hitting Fred Couples, who had a great pedigree behind him. There was huge shoulder pressure on the Galway man going down the eighteenth. The two were all square after seventeen holes. Both made the fairway with their tee shots. O'Connor faced a 200-yards plus shot over troubled waters, while Couples had a relatively easy nine iron in. Lining up his two iron second Christy recalled the praise his uncle had given him on the practice ground at the Belfry. He took careful aim and rifled the shot unerringly towards its target, finishing only a few feet away. The shock waves unnerved Couples, who was further up the fairway by some fifty yards, and he missed his relatively easy approach to the final hole. Still not on the green, he pitched, leaving him an awkward putt which he eventually missed, and he ended up with a bogey five. Christy's birdie putt was conceded. It was a proud moment for Tony Jacklin and his European team and for their devout followers. It was an especially proud moment for Christy Senior, who knows exactly what an occasion like this does to you.

The Europeans tied the 1989 series of Ryder Cup matches and because of their 1987 win at Muirfield Village in Columbus, Ohio, they would remain the proud custodians of Sam Ryder's trophy.

JOHN O'LEARY

John O'Leary played his one and only Ryder Cup at Laurel Valley, Pennsylvania in 1975. The author interviewed him early in 2006.

John was born in 1949, the year Harry Bradshaw was beaten in a play-off by South African Bobby Locke in the Open Championship. He comes from Dublin's south side and in his amateur days was a member of Foxrock Golf Club, a few miles from Dublin. He took up golf by accident while he was on holiday at Butlin's Holiday Camp in Skerries in north County Dublin. He made use of his holidays by hitting a few shots every day and when he returned home he paid the odd visit to John Jacobs's driving range at Leopardstown. John Jacobs himself was a well-respected professional golfer at the time and it was he who recognised John O'Leary's talent. He became John's coach, the only coaching commitment Jacobs undertook at the time. John Jacobs himself made a Ryder Cup appearance in 1995 and later went on to captain a Ryder Cup squad on two occasions, in 1979 and 1981. The 1979 captaincy coincided with the inaugural European team to play against the Americans.

O'Leary's game progressed by leaps and bounds, so much so that he hoped he would make the 1971 Walker Cup side to meet his amateur counterparts at St Andrew's, but was regrettably over-looked by the British and Irish Walker Cup selectors. John O'Leary turned pro almost immediately and began his profes-sional career from his base in Richmond, Surrey. He would have loved to have done this from Ireland, but the prohibitive air travel costs at the time left him with little option but to reside within close range of where the circuit was.

He was a great friend of Australian Jack Newton, who tied with Tom Watson for the 1975 British Open at Carnoustie. Jack lost out by one shot in the eighteen-hole play-off. Both John O'Leary and Jack Newton teamed up to win the Sumrie Fourball Tournament in 1975, the same year as John's appearance in the Ryder Cup.

The following year John O'Leary won the Greater Manchester Open and finished the season in sixteenth place in the Order of Merit. His best performance came in 1982, when he came out tops by winning the 1982 Irish Open at the world-famous links in Portmarnock. In March 2006 I had a brief conversation with John after he returned from Cape Town, and he recalled that great Irish Open win. It was something very special to him. In fact, no Irishman has won that coveted title since John's 1982 victory.

He remembers the very strong field breathing down his neck at the time. Players like Faldo, Ballesteros and Langer were some of the serious challengers. However, the threat he felt most came not from this group, but rather from a seasoned campaigner called Christy O'Connor, Sr. 'Himself', as the elder statesman was affec-tionately known, suddenly emerged from the chasing pack to threaten the Foxrock man. He was acutely aware of the renowned legacy and capabilities of the Royal Dublin maestro, especially when he would mount a last-day final charge and snatch victory from your grasp. 'I was fortunate to hold my nerve and come through the ordeal,' said John.

What was it about Christy that caused this type of reaction? John was very definite in his response. 'He was one of the best players in the world. His iron play was superb. I have travelled the golfing world ten times over and everyone I meet on my travels knows the name of O'Connor. They too recognise him as one of the finest strikers of a golf ball in the world. He was a quality player,' said John.

John was carried shoulder high after his winning 287 aggregate score.

1975 Laurel Valley, Pennsylvania, US

The US beat the visiting Great Britain and Ireland Ryder squad at Laurel Valley by 21 points to 11. There were three Irish players on the team: Eamonn Darcy, Christy O'Connor, Jr. and John O'Leary. The outing wasn't a particularly happy one for O'Leary. He played in four matches. In the opening foursomes on day one he partnered Tommy Horton against the formidable pairing of Lee Trevino and Jesse Snead (nephew of the legendary Sam Snead). Unfortunately, the Irishman was on the receiving end when he and Horton went down by 2 and 1.

In the afternoon fourballs, the same Great Britain and Ireland pairing lost out again to Lee Trevino and his new partner, Hale Irwin, by a similar margin. John's woe was prolonged when the all-Irish partnership of O'Connor and O'Leary was trounced 5 and 3 by Tom Weiskopf and Johnny Miller. The final nail in the coffin came when John's earlier adversary, Hale Irwin, disposed of him by 2 and 1 in the singles.

John O'Leary withdrew from the tournament scene in the late 1980s as a result of a car crash. He was only thirty-eight at the time. His insatiable passion for golf was still burning, though. He came back to the professional scene a number of times afterwards, but lower back problems hampered his progress. He had several operations to try and rectify the situation, but after a while things worsened significantly. He recalled one day he was hitting a bunker shot when his legs gave way. He decided there and then that was enough. His professional golfing days were at an end. He was then chairman of the Tournament Players' Committee for a number of years, directing his administrative talents towards serving the interests of the European Tour. He was a member of the past five prestigious Ryder Cup Committees. John is very proud to see this historic event coming to the K Club in September 2006.

RONAN RAFFERTY

Ronan Rafferty played in the Ryder Cup on one occasion, in 1989 at the Belfry in England.

Ronan Rafferty was born in 1964 just across the border from County Louth. It was the same year that Ken Venturi won the US Open and fellow American 'Champagne' Tony Lema won the British Open. Ronan played most of his golf at Warrenpoint, County Down, which is situated across the estuary from Greenore. He began golf at the age of nine and by the time he was fifteen he was down to scratch when he took the British Boys' title.

At the age of seventeen, this talented player from Warrenpoint would become the youngest golfer ever to play in the Walker Cup. It was inevitable that he would soon join the professional ranks and become a serious contender on the circuit. However, Ronan was more than upset when he failed to get his playing card at Qualifying School. Undaunted by this unexpected turn of events, he played with distinction on the Safari circuit and qualified by the circuitous route to compete on the European Tour. He continued to play exceptionally well in overseas events and won the Venezuelan, South Australian and New Zealand Opens. In 1989, the same year he made his Ryder Cup debut, he won the Australian Match Play Championship. They were all prestigious titles. It wasn't long afterwards before he would lay a certain ghost aside and win his first European event, the Italian Open. Ronan topped the Order of Merit in 1989.

The year 1990 would see Ronan still in contention on the circuit, when he and David Feherty represented Ireland in the World Cup of Golf and finished second. Ronan ended the season with a fifth place in the Order of Merit. Then Rafferty went off form. Some suggested he had wrist problems which prevented him playing at his best. He later suffered shoulder injuries and was generally out of sync with his game for the whole of the season, finishing thirty-fifth in the Order of Merit. Ronan Rafferty would reverse this unacceptable downward trend the following year by winning the lucrative Daiyko Cup in Australia. What seemed to be a feature of his early days, he would win overseas and then come back rejuvenated and win at home, which he did after his Daiyko Cup success when he captured the Portuguese title a few weeks later.

However, as the years progressed, Ronan's game suffered a setback. He would play the occasional event without really distinguishing himself. He seems to have gone into semi-retirement, devoting much of his talents and energies into golf commentating on Sky Sports. Perhaps he will recharge his batteries, rediscover what has eluded him in recent years and come back and successfully play the circuit once more before turning his undoubted talents to the seniors circuit six years from now. After all, he was a quality player.

1989 The Belfry, Sutton Coldfield, West Midlands, England

The 'Jacklin years' would come to an end after the 1989 series of Ryder Cup matches. This was Tony Jacklin's fourth captaincy in a row. During his reign, the Europeans were narrowly beaten in the first series in 1983 and were victorious in 1985 and 1987. It was now 1989 and Ronan Rafferty would be on the team.

The home side would start out as favourites. Ronan was paired with German Bernhard Langer in the fourth morning foursomes on the opening day. Unfortunately, they found themselves three down after nine holes, going out in a dismal 41. Their opponents, the reigning British Open champion, Mark Calcavecchia, and his compatriot, Ken Green, had little difficulty in beating them by 2 and 1.

In the morning foursomes on the second day, Ronan got a new partner in Christy O'Connor, Jr. to face the same opposition of Calcavecchia and Green. Once again, Ronan found himself on the losing side, succumbing to the Americans by 3 and 2. Ronan got sweet revenge in the singles when he beat the Open champ by one hole, earning a precious point from this tense battle. It was very precious indeed, for Tony Jacklin's side tied the 1989 event, going out on an extremely high note, as the Europeans would be the custodians of 'Sam's chalice' for three series in a row. Ronan Rafferty played a significant role in that feat.

DES SMYTH

Des Smyth played in two Ryder Cups, in 1979 and 1981.

Des himself became one of Ireland's great players over a long period of time. At the age of forty-eight, approaching the autumn of a very successful career, he won the Madeira Island Open. He was only two years away from earning the right to compete on the Seniors Tour on this side of the Atlantic and the Champions Tour in America, where he won two events.

He made two Ryder Cup appearances, one in 1979 and the other in 1981. I met with Des early in 2006 and summoned up many memories.

The Drogheda man lived less than a mile from the Laytown and Bettystown links. As a child he and his friends would creep unnoticed underneath the course boundary fence and chip to and putt on the first green. He had an early attraction to the game, and before too long he became a junior member, got a handicap and improved his game before entering the upper echelons of senior golf. His handicap continued to tumble and he would play many of the boys' championships around the country, winning some of them. At the age of seventeen he became a scratch player and a year later he was a +1 golfer. The professional life beckoned and he was keen to embark on a career that would span more than thirty years. He turned pro at age twenty in 1974.

By his own admission, Des struggled badly in the early stages. He began to question the wisdom of his undertaking. However, he persisted in his aspiration to play professional golf and after a few years began to establish himself. In 1979 he won his first tournament, the Sun Alliance European Match Play Championship. Throughout his successful European Tour, which embraced twenty seasons, he had eight victories, culminating in that magnificent 2001 Madeira Island Open at the age of forty-eight, becoming the oldest winner on the regular tour. In addition, Des won six Irish National Championships, the 1995 Glen Dimplex Irish Match Play event and was a member of the Irish trio that won the coveted 1998 Alfred Dunhill Cup at St Andrew's. Des's official career earnings on the European Tour were €2,539,101.

A rich pedigree

After reaching fifty, Des, the natural optimist, turned his thoughts to the 2003 Champions Tour in the States. He was in no way underestimating the difficulties that faced him in this venture. Against the fiercest of competition, Des won top spot in the 2002 Qualifying School to allow him entry to the 2003 season. It was one of his toughest challenges, as there were some 600 challengers for eight places. That's real pressure. He rose to the occasion by winning twice in 2005 on the American circuit: the SBC Classic and the Liberty Mutual Legends of Golf. On the European Seniors Tour he had his first win in the 2005 Arcapita Tour Championship in Bahrain. He also narrowly missed out on winning the Claret Jug at the Senior British Open when he was beaten by Tom Watson at the third play-off hole.

1979 Greenbrier, West Virginia, US

As a boy Des nourished one dream: he wanted to play in the Ryder Cup. He played in two: 1979 and 1981.

I asked Des what Ryder Cup pressure is like. He has strong feelings on this point. 'The pressure is enormous. It's a far different pressure than the "normal" pressure. When you're forging your own career as an individual professional golfer, you just have yourself very much in mind. When you're thrown into a team situation, it's profoundly different. You spend a year trying to qualify. That's pressure! Then when you're on the team you don't want to let the side down. It's the same in other sports. Team pressure on individuals contributing to the overall result is hugely demanding,' Des admitted.

I recall comments attributed to Scotland's Colin Montgomerie about Ryder Cup pressure, who feels the pressure is unique and unbearable. He remembers playing in the 1993 matches with Nick Faldo. Their opponents were former US Open champion Corey Pavin and Lanny Wadkins. Hitting the opening tee shot, Pavin's hand was shaking so much his ball fell off the tee.

Des's Ryder Cup debut was in 1979 at the Greenbrier, West Virginia. Unfortunately, Europe, under captain John Jacobs, could do little against the might of Billy Casper's American side. It was the European team's first outing as a unit. They were just beginning their honeymoon period, so it was a little premature to judge the performance after only one series.

Des was paired on day one with Ken Brown in the foursomes match against Hale Irwin and Tom Kite, losing by the humiliating margin of 7 and 6. It was an unpleasant initiation for Des, as his partner had been targeted earlier in the week for conduct unbecoming of a member of the European team. It arguably militated against their performance in the match.

Des Smyth was left out of play on day two but was called to do battle with Hale Irwin in the singles on the final day. Hale Irwin got the better of the Irishman yet again, this time by the very convincing margin of 5 and 3. It was a Ryder Cup baptism of fire for the gentle giant from Drogheda. Better times lay ahead, however.

1981 Walton Heath, Surrey, England

The 1981 matches were played on home soil at Walton Heath in Surrey. John Jacobs captained the side yet again. There was another controversial climate which had a negative effect on the home side. Tony Jacklin and Severiano Ballesteros were regarded by many as two 'wild card' certainties. Appearance money willing to be paid to Seve by various tournament sponsors throughout the golfing year was vehemently opposed by British officialdom. Jacklin, one of the home side's stronger players, supported the Spaniard. The wild cards went to Peter Oosterhuis and Mark James. The American team could have fielded a second or third division and still have been favourites for the 1981 matches.

Against that unpleasant background, Des Smyth played his second and final Ryder Cup. In partnership with Scotsman Bernard Gallacher in the morning foursomes, Des avenged the humiliation of 1979 when the strong American partnership of Hale Irwin and Raymond Floyd were beaten 3 and 2. In the afternoon fourballs with Spain's José Maria Canizares, Des played a significant part in crushing their opponents Bill Rogers and Bruce Lietzke by 6 and 5. Des and José Maria were on a roll.

However, facing the formidable opposition of Tom Watson and Jack Nicklaus, they were beaten 3 and 2 in the morning fourballs on the second day. Des and Bernard Gallacher also lost their afternoon foursomes battle against Tom Kite and Larry Nelson 3 and 2. The same fate awaited Des in his singles clash with America's Ben Crenshaw. This time it was by the more convincing margin of 6 and 4.

Modern-day Ryder Cup

What does Des Smyth think of the modern-day Ryder Cup – is it too commercially oriented? 'No, on the contrary,' he said. 'Everything is commercial nowadays. Nothing comes cheap. It's a huge television success and because of this it must generate enough finance to cover an event like this which brings on board the corporate business sector. The Ryder Cup is the better for it.'

What does Des think of the choice of the K Club over Portmarnock as a venue for Ireland's hosting of the 2006 Ryder Cup? 'Portmarnock is a great course. There is absolutely no doubt whatever but that it would be a success there as well. Politics, business and investment all play a part in the modern game. Considering the event from a transportation point of view, the K Club comes out on top. The hotels on site at the K Club can house the two teams and officials. That's a huge problem taken out of the equation to begin with. The Smurfit organisation has been working extremely hard over the years and has invested a lot of finance in promoting European golf tournaments. The European Open has been staged there since 1995, it has already staged two PGA Cups and the Junior Ryder Cup. The Smurfit group played their cards perfectly. They deserve it. It's a wonderful course.'

Des Smyth will be one of the two vice-captains destined for the K Club in September 2006. Woosie and Des are good friends. 'Of course we are. But I'm friendly with nearly all the players. I'm that type of person. I'm fortunate having gone through life without making real enemies. I do have opinions, you know! I convey these in a way I believe will not offend. Yes, Woosie and I go back a long way. I'm absolutely thrilled to be asked to become a vice-captain. I look forward to the involvement. He could have asked others. I'm delighted to be one of the chosen two. I have always been a fan of the Ryder Cup for years, even before my dream was realised. I remember as a young man I would have cordoned off the Ryder Cup event in my diary. If for some reason or another I couldn't be at the event itself, I would follow every shot that was on television,' Des enthused.

How does he see his role at the K Club? 'I attended one or two functions with Peter Baker, who's the other vice-captain. In fairness to Woosie, he and the Ryder Cup Committee would have been working two or three years in advance of the event. The hard work is all but done. A vice-captain's role is to support the captain. This comes very much into play when the series gets underway in Ryder Cup week. Along with Peter Baker I would keep a watchful eye on the players during the week – at practice and also during the event proper. We would keep in touch with team players who are very much in form or as the case might be on those who are not in form. Part of the role is listening to players themselves. They have requests too. They may have certain preferences about a choice of partner in foursomes and fourballs. The point is to have a team that's in good shape.'

As a result of Des's successful performance on the Champions Tour in 2005, he was back there again in 2006, starting with event number one in Hawaii. He is a professional golfer to his core.

PHILIP WALTON

Philip Walton turned professional in 1983, the same year Europe lost their Ryder Cup battle by a single point at Palm Beach Gardens in Florida. He had a great amateur career. He was a member of the 1982 Eisenhower Trophy team and a member of two Walker Cup teams in 1981 and 1983. As a tournament professional he distinguished himself by being part of the Dunhill Cup squad in 1989, 1990, 1992, 1994 and 1995. He also played in Ireland's World Cup the same year. He reached his zenith when making the 1995 Ryder Cup and being the man responsible for holing the winning putt that brought Sam Ryder's trophy back to Europe.

Unfortunately, in more recent times his game has taken somewhat of a tumble. Things got so bad that he was obliged to visit the Tour School on a number of occasions only to miss out on obtaining his playing card. The few events he played in were as a result of sponsors' invitations. The thought of him quitting the professional tournament scene was uppermost in his mind. Although the immediate future looked bleak, fortune shone on him in 2005. After he contested the Tour School for a sixth successive time, he retrieved his playing card after finishing in the top fifteen places.

I interviewed former Ryder Cup player Philip Walton at the European Open at the K Club in 2005. The season hadn't been too kind to Philip. Out of twelve starts he managed to qualify for the final thirty-six holes only once, and that was in the Indonesian Open at the beginning of the year, where he played in the extreme heat.

1995 Oak Hill Country Club, Rochester, New York, US

Philip Walton made one Ryder Cup appearance and that was in 1995 at the Oak Hill Country Club in Rochester, New York. His contribution to this one and only clash with the Americans was enormous. Some experts say it was Faldo who won the event for Europe when he closed out Curtis Strange on the final hole. While acknowledging Faldo's great triumph over Strange, and indeed the entire team's contribution to a European victory, it must be stated for the record that Irishman Philip Walton was the player who officially got the winning point for Europe.

Philip vividly recalls the two matches he played in. He was left out of both foursomes and fourball matches on the opening day. On day two he partnered Ian Woosnam in the foursomes against the American opposition of Loren Roberts and Peter Jacobsen, losing out to them on the final hole. Philip said, 'Woosie played absolute rubbish, and to think that the European team captain, Bernard Gallacher, walked off the eighteenth green with his arms around the Welshman, telling him he would be playing in the afternoon matches with Rocca! This did not impress me at all.' Philip was left with no option but to sit it out until his call for the singles matches.

Was he anxious about the impending challenge? 'When I met Jay Haas on the first tee he was actually snow white with fear. He cheered me up because I was really nervous. I started off bogey, par and he started double bogey! This settled me down and we both began to play well after that.' Things progressed very much in Philip's favour as this penultimate match went down the final stretch. Philip continues, 'I was three up with three to play and I remember a guy from Malahide Golf Club always telling me to expect the worst to happen in match play. Haas was in a greenside bunker, quite close to the green, about twenty-five feet from the flag. I actually said to myself that this guy might hole it. He played a terrible shot out, a low, thin one that hit the pin head on and dropped. I smiled at him.' The Malahide man's words rang true and Philip Walton missed his putt for a half.

Haas was dormie two down and anxious to win a half point for his team. The par four seventeenth demanded a well-hit tee shot. Walton went too far right, played a four iron short, leaving him with a very awkward chip. He played a very good shot to within four feet of the cup only to pull his putt. Another hole lost, two in a row. The Malahide man's voice echoed yet again. Imagine the thoughts of both players going down the last hole. Haas was buoyant, having pulled two holes back. The galleries were increasing by the minute, as the buzz that went round the course was infectious.

Bernard Gallacher and Lanny Wadkins were on tenterhooks. Wadkins was banking on America winning three Ryder Cups in a row. Bernard Gallacher didn't relish the thought, as he had captained the last two losses for Europe. Philip was dead on line with his second shot but was surprisingly short and in heavy rough. Haas, having played four, was past the hole. The hole was halved, giving the Irishman a one-hole victory. Europe won on American soil by 14½ to 13½.

Philip confessed the winning feeling to be great, not just in beating Jay Haas, but in his team winning the Ryder Cup. The enormity of the occasion took some time to sink in for the player from north County Dublin. The pressures as well as the occasion were huge, he acknowledged.

Philip also had strong feelings about Europe being a strong force in recent times. He felt European players were getting the edge on the old enemy, who was no longer working together as a team.

I asked Philip what the future held for him. He was very direct in admitting things hadn't being going well in recent years. He was in the doldrums. He confessed to being regarded as too old for the tour by some of his playing colleagues, which greatly upset him.

He also admitted to having met the Belgian golf psychologist Jos Vanstiphout in the hope he might trigger something to put Philip back on track. After a couple of weeks with Vanstiphout, he was told he had too much negativity within him. He had to download this negativity before he could begin to focus on a comeback.

Philip was a world-class player. Apart from his stint as a successful Ryder Cup player, his pedigree includes beating two of the world's best exponents of the game. He beat Bernhard Langer into second place in the 1990 French Open and Colin Montgomerie into the same spot in the 1995 English Open at the Forest of Arden.

Everyone knows Philip can regain his former glory. Everyone *wants* him to regain it. Philip is the only person who can bring this about. At forty-three, he can successfully challenge on the European Tour for another seven years. Des Smyth did it at the age of forty-eight, when he won the Madeira Island Open.

SECTION 4

Statistics

THE RYDER CUP MATCHES

1927 WORCESTER COUNTRY CLUB, WORCESTER, MASSACHUSETTS, JUNE 3–4

Captains: E. Ray (GB), W. Hagen (USA)

Great Britain		USA	
Foursomes		**Foursomes**	
E. Ray and F. Robson	0	W. Hagen and J. Golden (2 and 1)	1
G. Duncan and A. Compston	0	J. Farrell and J. Turnesa (8 and 6)	1
A.G. Havers and H.C. Jolly	0	G. Sarazen and A. Watrous (3 and 2)	1
A. Boomer and C.A. Whitcombe (7 and 5)	1	L. Diegel and W. Melhorn	0
Singles		**Singles**	
A. Compston	0	W. Mehlhorn (1 hole)	1
A. Boomer	0	J. Farrell (5 and 4)	1
H.C. Jolly	0	J. Golden (8 and 7)	1
E. Ray	0	L. Diegel (7 and 5)	1
C.A. Whitcombe (halved)	½	G. Sarazen (halved)	½
A.G. Havers	0	W. Hagen (2 and 1)	1
F. Robson	0	A. Watrous (3 and 2)	1
G. Duncan (1 hole)	1	J. Turnesa	0

Great Britain 2 ½   USA 9 ½

1929 MOORTOWN, LEEDS, MAY 26–27

Captains: G. Duncan (GB), W. Hagen (USA)

Great Britain		USA	
Foursomes		**Foursomes**	
C.A. Whitecomb and A. Compston (halved)	½	J. Farrell and Turnesa (halved)	½
A. Boomer and G. Duncan	0	L. Diegel and A. Espinosa (7 and 5)	1
A. Mitchell and F. Robson (2 and1)	1	G. Sarazen and E. Dudley	0
E.R. Whitcombe and T.H. Cotton	0	G. Holden and W. Hagen (2 holes)	1

Singles			Singles	
C.A.Whitcombe (8 and 6)	1		J. Farrell	0
G. Duncan (10 and 8)	1		W. Hagen	0
A. Mitchell	0		L. Diegel (9 and 8)	1
A. Compston (6 and 4)	1		G. Sarazan	0
A. Boomer (4 and 3)	1		J.Turnesa	0
F. Robson	0		H. Smith (4 and 2)	1
T.H. Cotton (4 and 3)	1		A.Watrous	0
E.R.Whitcombe (halved)	½		A. Espinosa (halved)	½

Great Britain 7   USA 5

1931 SCIOTO COUNTRY CLUB, COLUMBUS, OHIO, JUNE 26-27

Captains: C. A. Whitcombe (GB), W. Hagen (USA)

Great Britain   **USA**

Foursomes			Foursomes	
A. Compston and W. H. Davies	0		G. Sarazen and J. Farrell (8 and 7)	1
G. Duncan and A. G. Havers	0		W. Hagen and D. Shute (10 and 9)	1
A. Mitchell and F. Robson (3 and 1)	1		L. Diegel and A. Espinosa	0
S. Easterbrook and E.R.Whitcombe	0		W. Burke and W. Cox (3 and 2)	1
Singles			Singles	
A. Compston	0		W. Burke (7 and 6)	1
F. Robson	0		G. Sarazen (7 and 6)	1
W.H. Davies (4 and 3)	1		J. Farrell	0
A. Mitchell	0		W. Cox (3 and 1)	1
C.A.Whitcombe	0		W. Hagen (4 and 3)	1
B. Hodson	0		D. Shute (8 and 6)	1
E.R.Whitcombe	0		A. Espinosa (2 and 1)	1
A.G. Havers (4 and 3)	1		C. Wood	0

Great Britain 3   USA 9

1933 SOUTHPORT AND AINSDALE, SOUTHPORT, JUNE 26-27

Captains: J. H. Taylor (GB), W. Hagen (USA)

Great Britain   **USA**

Foursomes			Foursomes	
P.Alliss and C.A.Whitcombe (halved)	½		G. Sarazen and W. Hagen (halved)	½
A. Mitchell and A. G. Havers (3 and 2)	1		O. Dutra and D. Shute	0
W. H. Davies and S. Easterbrook (1 hole)	1		C.Wood and P. Runyan	0
A. H. Padgham and A. Perry	0		E. Dudley and W. Burke (1 hole)	1

Singles		Singles	
A.H. Padgham	0	G. Sarazen (6 and 4)	1
A. Mitchell (9 and 8)	1	O. Dutra	0
A. J. Lacey	0	W. Hagen (2 and 1)	1
W. H. Davies	0	C. Wood (4 and 3)	1
P. Alliss (2 and 1)	1	P. Runyan	0
A.G. Havers (4 and 3)	1	L. Diegel	0
S. Easterbrook (1 hole)	1	D. Shute	0
C.A. Whitcombe	0	H. Smith (2 and 1)	1

Great Britain 6 ½   USA 5 ½

1935 Ridgewood Country Club, Ridgewood, New Jersey, September 28-29

Captains: C. A. Whitcombe (GB), W. Hagen (USA)

Great Britain   **USA**

Foursomes		Foursomes	
A. Perry and J.J. Busson	0	G. Sarazen and W. Hagen (7 and 6)	1
A. H. Padgham and P. Alliss	0	H. Picard and J. Revolta (6 and 5)	1
W. J. Cox and E. W. Jarman	0	P. Runyaan and H. Smith (9 and 8)	1
C.A. Whitcombe and E. R. Whitcombe (1 hole)	1	O. Dutra and K. Laffoon (1 hole)	0

Singles		Singles	
J.J. Busson	0	G. Sarazen (3 and 2)	1
R. Burton	0	P. Runyan (5 and 3)	1
R.A. Whitcombe	0	J. Revolta (2 and 1)	1
A.H. Padgham	0	O. Dutra (4 and 2)	1
P. Alliss (1 hole)	1	C. Wood	0
W. J. Cox (halved)	½	H. Smith (halved)	½
E. R. Whitcombe	0	H. Picard (3 and 2)	1
A. Perry (halved)	½	S. Parks (halved)	½

Great Britain 3   USA 9

1937 Southport and Ainsdale, Southport, June 29-30

Captains: C. A. Whitcombe (GB), W. Hagen (USA)

Great Britain   **USA**

Foursomes		Foursomes	
A. H. Padgham and T. H. Cotton	0	E. Dudley and B. Nelson (4 and 2)	1
A. J. Lacey and W. J. Cox	0	R. Guldahl and T. Manero (2 and 1)	1
C. A. Whitcombe and D. J. Rees (halved)	½	G. Sarazen and D. Shute (halved)	½
P. Alliss and R. Burton (2 and 1)	1	H. Picard and J. Revolta	0

191

Singles			Singles	
A. H. Padgham	0		R. Guldahl (8 and 7)	1
S. L. King (halved)	½		D. Shute (halved)	½
D. J. Rees (3 and 1)	1		B. Nelson	0
T. H. Cotton (5 and 3)	1		T. Manero	0
P. Alliss	0		G. Sarazen (1 hole)	1
R. Burton	0		S. Snead (5 and 4)	1
A. Perry	0		E. Dudley (2 and 1)	1
A. J. Lacey	0		H. Picard (2 and 1)	1

Great Britain 4   USA 8

1947 PORTLAND GOLF CLUB, PORTLAND, OREGON, NOVEMBER 1-2
Captains: T. H. Cotton (GB), B. Hogan (USA)

Great Britain   **USA**

Foursomes			Foursomes	
T. H. Cotton and A. Lees	0		E. Oliver and L. Worsham (10 and 9)	1
F. Daly and C. H. Ward	0		S. Snead and L. Mangrum (6 and 5)	1
J. Adams and M. Faulkner	0		B. Hogan and J. Demaret (2 holes)	1
D. J. Rees and S. L. King	0		B. Nelson and H. Barron (2 and 1)	1

Singles			Singles	
F. Daly	0		E. J. Harrison (5 and 4)	1
J. Adams	0		L. Worsham (3 and 2)	1
M. Faulkner	0		L. Mangrum (6 and 5)	1
C. H. Ward	0		E. Oliver (4 and 3)	1
A. Lees	0		B. Nelson (2 and 1)	1
T. H. Cotton	0		S. Snead (5 and 4)	1
D. J. Rees	0		J. Demaret (3 and 2)	1
S. L. King (4 and 3)	1		H. Keiser	0

Great Britain 1   USA 11

1949 GANTON, SCARBOROUGH, SEPTEMBER 16-17
Captains: C. A. Whitcombe (GB), B. Hogan (USA)

Great Britain   **USA**

Foursomes			Foursomes	
M. Faulkner and J. Adams (2 and 1)	1		E. J. Harrison and J. Palmer	0
F. Daly and K. Bousfield (4 and 2)	1		R. Hamilton and S. Alexander	0
C. H. Ward and S. L. King	0		J. Demaret and C. Heafner (4 and 3)	1
R. Burton and A. Lees (1 hole)	1		S. Snead and L. Mangrum	0

Singles			Singles	
M. Faulkner	0		E. J. Harrison (8 and 7)	1
J. Adams (2 and 1)	1		J. Palmer	0
C. H. Ward	0		S. Snead (6 and 5)	1
D. J. Rees (6 and 4)	1		R. Hamilton	0
R. Burton	0		C. Heafner (3 and 2)	1
S. L. King	0		C. Harbert (4 and 3)	1
A. Lees	0		J. Demaret (7 and 6)	1
F. Daly	0		L. Mangrum (4 and 3)	1

Great Britain 5   USA 7

1951 PINEHURST COUNTRY CLUB, PINEHURST NORTH CAROLINA, NOVEMBER 2 AND 4

Captains: A. J. Lacey (GB), S. Snead (USA)

Great Britain			**USA**	
Foursomes			Foursomes	
M. Faulkner and D. J. Rees	0		C. Heafner and J. Burke (5 and 3)	1
C. H. Ward and A. Lees (2 and 1)	1		E. Oliver and H. Ransom	0
J. Adams and J. Panton	0		S. Snead and L. Mangrum (5 and 4)	1
F. Daly and K. Bousfield	0		B. Hogan and J. Demaret (5 and 4)	1
Singles			Singles	
J. Adams	0		J. Burke (4 and 3)	1
D. J. Rees	0		J. Demaret (2 holes)	1
F. Daly (halved)	½		C. Heafner (halved)	½
H. Weetman	0		L. Mangrum (6 and 5)	1
A. Lees (2 and 1)	1		E. Oliver	0
C. H. Ward	0		B. Hogan (3 and 2)	1
J. Panton	0		S. Alexander (8 and 7)	1
M. Faulkner	0		S. Snead (4 and 3)	1

Great Britain 2 ½   USA   9 ½

1953 WENTWORTH CLUB, VIRGINIA WATER, OCTOBER 2-3

Captains: T. H. Cotton (GB and Ireland), L. Mangrum (USA)

Great Britain, Ireland			**USA**	
Foursomes			Foursomes	
H. Weetman and P. Alliss	0		D. Douglas and E. Oliver (2 and 1)	1
E. C. Brown and J. Panton	0		L. Mangrum and S. Snead (8 and 7)	1
J. Adams and B. J. Hunt	0		T. Kroll and J. Burke (7 and 5)	1
F. Daly and H. Bradshaw (1 hole)	1		W. Burkemo and C. Middlecoff	0

Singles		Singles	
D. J. Rees	0	J. Burke (2 and 1)	1
F. Daly (9 and 7)	1	T. Kroll	0
E. C. Brown (2 holes)	1	L. Mangrum	0
H. Weetman (1 hole)	1	S. Snead	0
M. Faulkner	0	C. Middlecoff (3 and 1)	1
P. Alliss	0	J. Turnesa (1 hole)	1
B. J. Hunt (halved)	½	D. Douglas (halved)	½
H. Bradshaw (3 and 2)	1	F. Haas	0

Great Britain and Ireland 5 ½   USA 6 ½

1955 THUNDERBIRD GOLF AND COUNTRY CLUB, CALIFORNIA, NOVEMBER 5-6

Captains: D. J. Rees (GB and Ireland), C. Harbert (USA)

Great Britain, Ireland   **USA**

Foursomes		Foursomes	
J. Fallon and J. R. M. Jacobs (1 hole)	1	C. Harper and J. Barber	0
E. C. Brown and S. S. Scott	0	D. Ford and T. Kroll (5 and 4)	1
A. Lees and H. Weetman	0	J. Burke and T. Bolt (1 hole)	1
H. Bradshaw and D. J. Rees	0	S. Snead and C. Middlecoff (3 and 2)	1
Singles		Singles	
C. O'Connor	0	T. Bolt (4 and 2)	1
S. S. Scott	0	C. Harbert (3 and 2)	1
J. R. M. Jacobs (1 hole)	1	C. Middelcoff	0
D. J. Rees	0	S. Snead (3 and 1)	1
A. Lees (3 and 2)	1	M. Furgol	0
E. C. Brown (3 and 2)	1	J. Barber	0
H. Bradshaw	0	J. Burke (3 and 2)	1
H. Weetman	0	D. Ford (3 and 2)	1

Great Britain and Ireland 4   USA 8

1957 LINDRICK GOLF CLUB, SHEFFIELD, OCTOBER 4-5

Captains: D. J. Rees (GB and Ireland), J. Burke (USA)

Great Britain, Ireland   **USA**

Foursomes		Foursomes	
P. Alliss and B. J. Hunt	0	D. Ford and D. Finsterwald (2 and 1)	1
K. Bousfield and D. J. Rees (3 and 2)	1	A. Wall and F. Hawkins	0
M. Faulkner and H. Weetman	0	T. Kroll and J. Burke (4 and 3)	1
C. O'Connor and E. C. Brown	0	R. Mayer and T. Bolt (7 and 5)	1

Singles		Singles	
E. C. Brown (4 and 3)	1	T. Bolt	0
R. P. Mills (5 and 3)	1	J. Burke	0
P. Alliss	0	F. Hawkins (2 and 1)	1
K. Bousfield (4 and 3)	1	L. Hebert	0
D. J. Rees (7 and 6)	1	E. Furgol	0
B. J. Hunt (6 and 5)	1	D. Ford	0
C. O'Connor (7 and 6)	1	D. Finsterwald	0
H. Bradshaw (halved)	½	R. Mayer (halved)	½

Great Britain and Ireland 7 ½   USA 4 ½

1959 ELDORADO COUNTRY CLUB, CALIFORNIA, NOVEMBER 6-7
Captains: D. J. Rees (GB and Ireland), S. Snead (USA)

Great Britain, Ireland **USA**

Foursomes		Foursomes	
B. J. Hunt and E. C. Brown	0	R. Rosburg and M. Souchak (5 and 4)	1
D. J. Rees and K. Bousfield	0	J. Boros and D. Finsterwald (2 holes)	1
C. O'Connor and P. Alliss (3 and 2)	1	A. Wall and D. Ford	0
H. Weetman and D. C. Thomas (halved)	½	S. Snead and C. Middlecoff (halved)	½

Singles		Singles	
N. V. Drew (halved)	½	D. Ford (halved)	½
K. Bousfield	0	M. Souchak (3 and 2)	1
H. Weetman	0	R. Rosburg (6 and 5)	1
D. C. Thomas	0	S. Snead (6 and 5)	1
C. O'Connor	0	A. Wall (7 and 6)	1
D. J. Rees	0	D. Finderwald (1 hole)	1
P. Alliss (halved)	½	J. Hebert (halved)	½
E. C. Brown (4 and 3)	1	C. Middlecoff	0

Great Britain and Ireland 3 ½   USA 8 ½

1961 ROYAL LYTHAM AND ST. ANNES, ST. ANNES, OCTOBER 13-14
Captains: D. J. Rees (GB and Ireland), J. Barber (USA)

Great Britain, Ireland **USA**

Foursomes		Foursomes	
Morning		*Morning*	
C. O'Connor and P. Alliss (4 and 3)	1	D. Ford and G. Littler	0
J. Panton and B. J. Hunt	0	A. Wall and J. Hebert (4 and 3)	1
D. J. Rees and K. Bousfield	0	W. Casper and A. Palmer (2 and 1)	1
T. B. Haliburton and N. C. Coles	0	W. Collins and M. Souchak (1 hole)	1

Afternoon		*Afternoon*	
C. O'Connor and P. Alliss	0	A. Wall and J. Herbert (1 hole)	1
J. Panton and B. J. Hunt	0	W. Casper and A. Palmer (5 and 4)	1
D. J. Rees and K. Bousfield (4 and 2)	1	W. Collins and M. Souchak	0
T. B. Haliburton and N. C. Coles	0	J. Barber and D. Finsterwald (1 hole)	1

Singles		Singles	
Morning		*Morning*	
H. Weetman	0	D. Ford (1 hole)	1
R. L. Moffitt	0	M. Souchak (5 and 4)	1
P. Alliss (halved)	½	A. Palmer (halved)	½
K. Bousfield	0	W. Casper (5 and 3)	1
D. J. Rees (2 and 1)	1	J. Hebert	0
N. C. Coles (halved)	½	G. Littler (halved)	½
B. J. Hunt (5 and 4)	1	J. Barber	0
C. O'Connor	0	D. Finsterwald (2 and 1)	1

Afternoon		*Afternoon*	
H. Weetman	0	A. Wall (1 hole)	1
P. Alliss (3 and 2)	1	W. Collins	0
B. J. Hunt	0	M. Souchak (2 and 1)	1
T. B. Haliburton	0	A. Palmer (2 and 1)	1
D. J. Rees (4 and 3)	1	D. Ford	0
K. Bousfield (1 hole)	1	J. Barber	0
N. C. Coles (1 hole)	1	D. Finsterwald	0
C. O'Connor (halved)	½	G. Littler (halved)	½

Great Britain and Ireland 9 ½   USA 14 ½

1963 EAST LAKE COUNTRY CLUB, ATLANTA, GEORGIA, OCTOBER 11–13

Captains: J. Fallon (GB and Ireland), A. Palmer (USA)

Great Britain, Ireland		**USA**	
Foursomes		Foursomes	
Morning		*Morning*	
B. Huggett and G. Will (3 and 2)	1	A. Palmer and J. Pott	0
P. Alliss and C. O'Connor	0	W. Casper and D. Ragan (1 hole)	1
D. Thomas and H. Weetman (halved)	½	G. Littler and D. Finsterwald (halved)	½
N. C. Coles and B. J. Hunt (halved)	½	J. Boros and A. Lema (halved)	½

Afternoon		*Afternoon*	
D. Thomas and H. Weetman	0	W. Maxwell and R. Goalby (4 and 3)	1
B. Huggett and G. Will	0	A. Palmer and W. Casper (5 and 4)	1
N. C. Coles and G. M. Hunt	0	G. Littler and D. Finsterwald (2 and1)	1
T. B. Haliburton and B. J. Hunt	0	J. Boros and A. Lema (1 hole)	1

Fourballs		Fourballs	
Morning		*Morning*	
B. Huggett and D. Thomas	0	A. Palmer and D. Finsterwald (5 and 4)	1
P. Alliss and J. Hunt (halved)	½	G. Littler and J. Borros (halved)	½
H. Weetman and G. Will	0	W. Casper and W. Maxwell (3 and 2)	1
N. C. Coles and C. O'Connor (1 hole)	1	R. Goalby and D. Ragan	0
Afternoon		*Afternoon*	
N. C. Coles and C. O'Connor	0	A. Palmer and D. Finsterwald (3 and 2)	1
P. Alliss and B. J. Hunt	0	A. Lema and J. Pott (1 hole)	1
T. B. Haliburton and G. M. Hunt	0	W. Casper and W. Maxwell (2 and 1)	1
B. Huggett and D. Thomas (halved)	½	R. Goalby and D. Ragan (halved)	½

Singles		Singles	
Morning		*Morning*	
G. M. Hunt	0	A. Lema (5 and 3)	1
B. Huggett (3 and 1)	1	J. Pott	0
P. Alliss (1 hole)	1	A. Palmer	0
N. C. Coles (halved)	½	W. Casper (halved)	½
D. Thomas	0	R. Goalby (3 and 2)	1
C. O'Connor	0	G. Littler (1 hole)	1
H. Weetman (1 hole)	1	J. Boros	0
B. J. Hunt (2 holes)	1	D. Finsterwald	0
Afternoon		*Afternoon*	
G. Will	0	A. Palmer (3 and 2)	1
N.C. Coles	0	D. Ragan (2 and 1)	1
P. Alliss (halved)	½	A. Lema (halved)	½
T. B. Haliburton	0	G. Littler (6 and 5)	1
H. Weetman	0	J. Boros (2 and 1)	1
C. O'Connor	0	W. Maxwell (2 and 1)	1
D. Thomas	0	D. Finsterwald (4 and 3)	1
B. J. Hunt	0	R. Goalby (2 and 1)	1

Great Britain and Ireland 9   USA 23

1965 ROYAL BIRKDALE, SOUTHPORT, OCTOBER 7-9

Captains: H. Weetman (GB and Ireland), B. Nelson (USA)

Great Britain, Ireland		USA	
Foursomes		Foursomes	
Morning		*Morning*	
L. Platts and P. J. Butler	0	J. Boros and A. Lema (1 hole)	1
D. C. Thomas and G. Will (6 and 5)	1	A. Palmer and D. Marr	0
B. J. Hunt and N. C. Coles	0	W. Casper and G. Littler (2 and 1)	1
P. Alliss and C. O'Connor (5 and 4)	1	K. Venturi and D. January	0

Afternoon			*Afternoon*	
D. C. Thomas and G. Will	0		A. Palmer and D. Marr (6 and 5)	1
P. Alliss and C. O'Connor (2 and 1)	1		W. Casper and G. Littler	0
J. Martin and J. Hitchcock	0		J. Boros and A. Lema (5 and 4)	1
B. J. Hunt and N. C. Coles (3 and 2)	1		K. Venturi and D. January	0

Fourballs
Morning

D. C. Thomas and G. Will	0		D. January and T. Jacobs (1 hole)	1
L. Platts and P. J. Butler (halved)	½		W. Casper and G. Littler (halved)	½
P. Alliss and C. O'Connor	0		A. Palmer and D. Marr (6 and 4)	1
B. J. Hunt and N. C. Coles (1 hole)	1		J. Boros and A. Lema	0

Afternoon			*Afternoon*	
P. Alliss and C. O'Connor (1 hole)	1		A. Palmer and D. Marr	0
D. C. Thomas and G. Will	0		D. January and T. Jacobs (1 hole)	1
L. Platts and P. J. Butler (halved)	½		W. Casper and G. Littler (halved)	½
B. J. Hunt and N. C. Coles	0		K. Venturi and A. Lema (1 hole)	1

Singles
Morning

J. Hitchcock	0		A. Palmer (3 and 2)	1
L. Platts	0		J. Boros (4 and 2)	1
P. J. Butler	0		A. Lema (1 hole)	1
N. C. Coles	0		D. Marr (2 holes)	1
B. J. Hunt (2 holes)	1		G. Littler	0
D. C. Thomas	0		T. Jacobs (2 and 1)	1
P. Alliss (1 hole)	1		W. Casper	0
G. Will (halved)	½		D. January (halved)	½

Afternoon			*Afternoon*	
C. O'Connor	0		A. Lema (6 and 4)	1
J. Hitchcock	0		J. Boros (2 and 1)	1
P. J. Butler	0		A. Palmer (2 holes)	1
P. Alliss (3 and 1)	1		K. Venturi	0
N. C. Coles (3 and 2)	1		W. Casper	0
G. Will	0		G. Littler (2 and 1)	1
B. J. Hunt	0		D. Marr (1 hole)	1
L. Platts (1 hole)	1		T. Jacobs	0

Great Britain and Ireland 12 ½   USA 19 ½

1967 CHAMPION GOLF CLUB, HOUSTON, TEXAS, OCTOBER 20-22
Captains: D. J. Rees (GB and Ireland), B. Hogan (USA)

Great Britain, Ireland		**USA**	
Foursomes		Foursomes	
Morning		*Morning*	
B. G. C. Huggett and G. Will (halved)	½	W. Casper and J. Boros (halved)	½
P. Alliss and C. O'Connor	0	A. Palmer and G. Dickinson (2 and 1)	1
A. Jacklin and D.C. Thomas (4 and 3)	1	D. Sanders and G. Brewer	0
B. J. Hunt and N.C. Coles	0	R. Nicholas and J. Pott (6 and 5)	1
Afternoon		*Afternoon*	
B.G.C. Huggett and G. Will	0	W. Casper and J. Boros (1 hole)	1
M. Gregson and H. Boyle	0	G. Dickinson and A. Palmer (5 and 4)	1
A. Jacklin and D.C. Thomas (3 and 2)	1	G. Litter and A. Geiberger	0
P. Alliss and C. O'Connor	0	R. Nichols and J. Pott (2 and 1)	1
Fourballs		Fourballs	
Morning		*Morning*	
P. Alliss and C. O'Connor	0	W. Casper and G. Brewer (3 and 2)	1
B.J. Hunt and N.C. Coles	0	R. Nichols and J. Pott (1 hole)	1
A. Jacklin and D. C. Thomas	0	G. Littler and A. Geiberger (1 hole)	1
B.G.C. Huggett and G. Will	0	G. Dickinson and D. Sanders (3 and 2)	1
Afternoon		*Afternoon*	
B. J. Hunt and N.C. Coles	0	W. Casper and G. Brewer (5 and 3)	1
P. Alliss and M. Gregson	0	G. Dickinson and D. Sanders (3 and 2)	1
G. Will and H. Boyle	0	A. Palmer and J. Boros (1 hole)	1
A. Jacklin and D. C. Thomas (halved)	½	G. Littler and A. Geilberger (halved)	½
Singles		*Singles*	
Morning		Morning	
H. Boyle	0	G. Brewer (4 and 3)	1
P. Alliss	0	W. Casper (2 and 1)	1
A. Jacklin	0	A. Palmer (3 and 2)	1
B.G.C. Huggett (1 hole)	1	J. Boros	0
N.C. Coles (2 and 1)	1	D. Sanders	0
M. Gregson	0	A. Geiberger (4 and 2)	1
D.C. Thomas (halved)	½	G. Littler (halved)	½
B.J. Hunt (halved)	½	R. Nichols (halved)	½
Afternoon		*Afternoon*	
B.G.C. Huggett	0	A. Palmer (5 and 3)	1
P. Alliss (2 and 1)	1	G. Brewer	0
A. Jacklin	0	G. Dickinson (3 and 2)	1
C. O'Connor	0	R. Nichols (3 and 2)	1
G. Will	0	J. Pott (3 and 1)	1
M. Gregson	0	A. Geiberger (2 and 1)	1
B.J. Hunt (halved)	½	J. Boros (halved)	½
N.C. Coles (2 and 1)	1	D. Sanders	0

Great Britain and Ireland 8 ½   USA 23 ½

1969 ROYAL BIRKDALE, SOUTHPORT, SEPTEMBER 18-20

Captains: E. C. Brown (GB and Ireland), S. Snead (USA)

Great Britain, Ireland   **USA**

Foursomes   Foursomes
Morning   *Morning*
N. C. Coles and B. G. C.Huggett (3 and 2)	1	M. Barber and R. Floyd	0
B. Gallacher and M. Bernbridge (2 and 1)	1	L. Trevino and K. Still	0
A. Jacklin and P. Townsend (3 and 1)	1	D. Hill and T. Aaron	0
C. O'Connor and P. Alliss (halved)	½	W. Casper and F. Beard (halved)	½

Afternoon   *Afternoon*
N. C. Coles and B. G. C. Huggett	0	D. Hill and T. Aaron (1 hole)	1
B. Gallacher and M. Bernbridge	0	L. Trevino and G. Littler (2 holes)	1
A. Jacklin and P. Townsend (1 hole)	1	W. Casper and F. Beard	0
P. J. Butler and B. J. Hunt	0	J. Nicklaus and D. Sikes (1 hole)	1

Fourballs   Fourballs
Morning   *Morning*
C. O'Connor and P. Townsend (1 hole)	1	D. Hill and D. Douglass	0
B. G. C. Huggett and G. A. Caygill (halved)	½	R. Floyd and M. Barber (halved)	½
B. Barnes and P. Alliss	0	L. Trevino and G. Littler (1hole)	1
A. Jacklin and N. C. Coles (1 hole)	1	J. Nicklaus and D. Sikes	0

Afternoon   *Afternoon*
P. J. Butler and P. Townsend	0	W. Casper and F. Beard (2 holes)	1
B. G. C. Huggett and B. Gallacher	0	D. Hill and K. Still (2 and 1)	1
M. Bernbridge and B. J. Hunt (halved)	½	T. Aaron and R. Floyd (halved)	½
A. Jacklin and N. C. Coles (halved)	½	L. Trevino and M. Barber (halved)	½

Singles   *Singles*
Morning   Morning
P. Alliss	0	L. Trevino (2 and 1)	1
P. Townsend	0	D. Hill (5 and 4)	1
N. C. Coles (1 hole)	1	T. Aaron	0
B. Barnes	0	W. Casper (1 hole)	1
C. O'Connor (5 and 4)	1	F. Beard	0
M. Bernbridge (1 hole)	1	K. Still	0
P. J. Butler (1 hole)	1	R. Floyd	0
A. Jacklin (4 and 3)	1	J. Nicklaus	0

Afternoon   *Afternoon*
B. Barnes	0	D. Hill (4 and 2)	1
B. Gallacher (4 and 3)	1	L. Trevino	0
M. Bernbridge	0	M. Barber (7 and 6)	1
P. J. Butler (3 and 2)	1	D. Douglass	0
N.C. Coles	0	D. Sikes (4 and 3)	1
C.O'Connor	0	G. Littler (2 and 1)	1
B.G.C. Huggett (halved)	½	W. Casper (halved)	½
A. Jacklin (halved)	½	J. Nicklaus (halved)	½

Great Britain and Ireland 16   USA 16

1971 Old Warson Country Club, St. Louis, Missouri, September 16–18

Captains: E. C. Brown (GB and Ireland), J. Hebert (USA)

Great Britain, Ireland		USA	
Foursomes		**Foursomes**	
Morning		*Morning*	
N.C. Coles and C. O'Connor (2 and 1)	1	W. Casper and M. Barber	0
P. Townsend and P. Oosterhuis	0	A. Palmer and G. Dickinson (2 holes)	1
B.G.C. Huggett and A. Jacklin (3 and 2)	1	J. Nicklaus and D. Stockton	0
M. Membridge and P. J. Butler (1 hole)	1	C. Coody and F. Beard	0
Afternoon		*Afternoon*	
H. Bannerman and B. Gallacher (2 and 1)	1	W. Casper and M. Barber	0
P. Townsend and P. Oosterhuis	0	A. Palmer and G. Dickinson (1 hole)	1
B.G.C. Huggett and A. Jacklin (halved)	½	L. Trevino and M. Rudolph (halved)	½
M. Bembridge and P. J. Butler	0	J. Nicklaus and J. C. Snead (5 and 3)	1
Fourballs		**Fourballs**	
Morning		*Morning*	
C. O'Connor and B. Barnes	0	L. Trevino and M. Rudolph (2 and 1)	1
N.C. Coles and J. Garner	0	F. Beard and J. C. Snead (2 and 1)	1
P. Oosterhuis and P. Gallacher	0	A. Palmer and G. Dickinson (5 and 4)	1
P. Townsend and H. Bannerman	0	J. Nicklaus and G. Littler (2 and 1)	1
Afternoon		*Afternoon*	
B. Gallacher and P. Oosterhuis (1 hole)	1	L. Trevino and W. Casper	0
A. Jacklin and B. G. C. Huggett	0	G. Littler and J. C. Snead (2 and 1)	1
P. Townsend and H. Bannerman	0	A. Palmer and J. Nicklaus (1 hole)	1
N.C. Coles and C. O'Connor (halved)	½	C. Coody and F. Beard (halved)	½
Singles		**Singles**	
Morning		*Morning*	
A. Jacklin	0	L. Trevino (1 hole)	1
B. Gallacher (halved)	½	D. Stockton (halved)	½
B. Barnes (1 hole)	1	M. Rudolph	0
P. Oosterhuis (4 and 3)	1	G. Littler	0
P. Townsend	0	J. Nicklaus (3 and 2)	1
C. O'Connor	0	G. Dickinson (5 and 4)	1
H. Bannerman (halved)	½	A. Palmer (halved)	½
N.C. Coles (halved)	½	F. Beard (halved)	½
Afternoon		*Afternoon*	
B. G. C. Huggett	0	L. Trevino (7 and 6)	1
A. Jacklin	0	J.C. Snead (1 hole)	1
B. Barnes (2 and 1)	1	M. Barber	0
P. Townsend	0	D. Stockton (1 hole)	1
B. Gallacher (2 and 1)	1	C. Coody	0
N.C. Coles	0	J. Nicklaus (5 and 3)	1
P. Oosterhuis (3 and 2)	1	A. Palmer	0
H. Bannerman (2 and 1)	1	G. Dickinson	0

Great Britain and Ireland 13 ½   USA   18 ½

1973 MUIRFIELD, SCOTLAND, SEPTEMBER 20-22

Captains: B. J. Hunt (GB and Ireland), J. Burke (USA)

Great Britain and Ireland		USA	
Foursomes		**Foursomes**	
Morning		*Morning*	
B. W. Barnes and B. J. Gallacher (1 hole)	1	L. Trevino and W. J. Casper	0
C. O'Connor and N. C. Coles (3 and 2)	1	T. Weiskopf and J. C. Snead	0
A. Jacklin and P. A. Oosterhuis (halved)	½	J. Rodriguez and L. Graham (halved)	½
M. E. Bembridge and E. Polland	0	J. W. Nicklaus and A. Palmer (6 and 5)	1
Fourballs		**Fourballs**	
Afternoon		*Afternoon*	
B. W. Barnes and B. J. Gallacher (5 and 4)	1	T. Aaron and G. Brewer	0
M. E. Bembridge and B. G. C. Huggett (3 and 1)	1	A. Palmer and J. W. Nicklaus	0
A. Jacklin and P. A. Oosterhuis (3 and 1)	1	T. Weiskopf and W. J. Casper	0
C. O'Connor and N. C. Coles	0	L. Trevino and H. Blancas (2 and 1)	1
Foursomes		**Foursomes**	
Morning		*Morning*	
B. W. Barnes and P. J. Butler	0	J. W. Nicklaus and T. Weiskopf (1 hole)	1
P. A. Oosterhuis and A. Jacklin (2 holes)	1	A. Palmer and D. Hill	0
M. E. Bembridge and B. G. C. Huggett (5 and 4)	1	J. Rodriguez and L. Graham	0
N. C. Coles and C. O'Connor	0	L. Trevino and W. Casper (2 and 1)	1
Fourballs		**Fourballs**	
Afternoon		*Afternoon*	
B. W. Barnes and P. J. Butler	0	J. C. Snead and A. Palmer (2 holes)	1
A. Jacklin and P. A. Oosterrhuis	0	G. Brewer and W. J. Casper (3 and 2)	1
C. Clark and E. Polland	0	J. W. Nicklaus and T. Weiskopf (3 and 2)	1
M. E. Bembridge and B. G. C. Huggett (halved)	½	L. Trevino and H. Blancas (halved)	½
Singles		**Singles**	
Morning		*Morning*	
B. W. Barnes	0	W. J. Casper (2 and 1)	1
B. J. Gallacher	0	T. Weiskopf (3 and 1)	1
P. J. Butler	0	H. Blancas (5 and 4)	1
A. Jacklin (2 and 1)	1	T. Aaron	0
N. C. Coles (halved)	½	G. Brewer (halved)	½
C. O'Connor	0	J. C. Snead (1 hole)	1
M. E. Bembridge (halved)	½	J. W. Nicklaus (halved)	½
P. A. Oosterhuis (halved)	½	L. Trevino (halved)	½
Afternoon		*Afternoon*	
B. G. C. Huggett (4 and 2)	1	H. Blancas	0
B. W. Barnes	0	J. C. Snead (3 and 1)	1
B. J. Gallacher	0	G. Brewer (6 and 5)	1
A. Jacklin	0	W. J. Casper (2 and 1)	1

N. C. Coles	0	L. Trevino (6 and 5)	1
C. O'Connor (halved)	½	T. Weiskopf (halved)	½
M. E. Bembridge	0	J. W. Nicklaus (2 holes)	1
P. A. Oosterhuis (4 and 2)	1	A. Palmer	0

Great Britain and Ireland 13   USA 19

1975 Laurel Valley Golf Club, Liognier, Pennsylvania, September 19-21

Captains: B. J. Hunt (GB and Ireland), A. Palmer (USA)

Great Britain and Ireland		USA	
Foursomes		Foursomes	
Morning		*Morning*	
B. W. Barnes and B. J. Gallacher	0	J. W. Nicklaus and T. Weiskopf (5 and 4)	1
N. Wood and M. Bembridge	0	G. Littler and H. Irwin (4 and 3)	1
A. Jacklin and P. Oosterhuis	0	A. Geiberger and J. Miller (3 and 2)	1
T. Horton and J. O'Leary	0	L. Trevino and J. C. Snead (2 and 1)	1
Fourballs		Fourballs	
Afternoon		*Afternoon*	
P. Oosterhuis and A. Jacklin (2 and 1)	1	W. J. Casper and R. Floyd	0
E. Darcy and C. O'Connor, Jnr	0	T. Weiskopf and L. Graham (3 and 2)	1
B. W. Barnes and B. J. Gallacher (halved)	½	J. W. Nicklaus and R. Murphy (halved)	½
T. Horton and J. O'Leary	0	L. Trevino and H. Irwin (2 and 1)	1
Fourballs		Fourballs	
Morning		*Morning*	
P. Oosterrhuis and A. Jacklin (halved)	½	W. J. Casper and J. Miller (halved)	½
T. Horton and N. Wood	0	J. W. Nicklaus and J. C. Snead (4 and 2)	1
B. W. Barnes and B. J. Gallacher	0	G. Littler and L. Graham (5 and 3)	1
E. Darcy and G. L. Hunt (halved)	½	A. Geiberger and R. Floyd (halved)	½
Foursomes		Foursomes	
Afternoon		*Afternoon*	
A. Jacklin and B. G. C. Huggett (3 and 2)	1	L. Trevino and R. Murphy	0
C. O'Connor, Jnr and J. O'Leary	0	T. Weiskopf and J. Miller (5 and 3)	1
P. Oosterhuis and M. Bembridge	0	H. Irwin and W. J. Casper (3 and 2)	1
E. Darcy and G. L. Hunt	0	A. Geiberger and L. Graham (3 and 2)	1
Singles		Singles	
Morning		*Morning*	
A. Jacklin	0	R. Murphy (2 and 1)	1
P. Oosterhuis (2 holes)	1	J. Miller	0
B. J. Gallacher (halved)	½	L. Trevino (halved)	½
T. Horton (halved)	½	H. Irwin (halved)	½
B. G. C. Huggett	0	G. Littler (4 and 2)	1
E. Darcy	0	W. J. Casper (3 and 2)	1
G. L. Hunt	0	T. Weiskopf (5 and 3)	1
B. W. Barnes (4 and 2)	1	J. W. Nicklaus	0

Afternoon			Afternoon	
A. Jacklin	0		R. Floyd (1 hole)	1
P. Oosterhuis (3 and 2)	1		J. C. Snead	0
B. J. Gallacher (halved)	½		A. Geiberger (halved)	½
T. Horton (2 and 1)	1		L. Graham	0
J. O'Leary	0		H. Irwin (2 and 1)	1
M. Bembridge	0		R. Murphy (2 and 1)	1
N. Wood (2 and 1)	1		L. Trevino	0
B. W. Barnes (2 and 1)	1		J. W. Nicklaus	0

Great Britain and Ireland 11   USA 21

1977 ROYAL LYTHM AND ST ANNES, ST ANNES, SEPTEMBER 15–17

Captains: B. Huggett (GB and Ireland), D. Finsterwald (USA)

Great Britain and Ireland		**USA**	
Foursomes		Foursomes	
B. J. Gallacher and B. W. Barnes	0	L. Wadkins and H. Irwin (3 and 1)	1
N. C. Coles and P. Dawson	0	D. Stockton and J. McGee (1 hole)	1
N. Faldo and P. Oosterrhuis (2 and 1)	1	R. Floyd and L. Graham	0
E. Darcy and A. Jacklin (halved)	½	E. Sneed and D. January (halved)	½
T. Horton and M. James	0	J. W. Nicklaus and T. Watson (5 and 4)	1
Fourballs		Fourballs	
B. W. Barnes and T. Horton	0	T. Watson and H. Green (5 and 4)	1
N. C. Coles and P. Dawson	0	E. Sneed and L. Wadkins (5 and 3)	1
N. Faldo and P. Oosterhuis (3 and 1)	1	J. W. Nicklaus and R. Floyd	0
A. Jacklin and E. Darcy	0	D. Hill and D. Stockton (5 and 3)	1
M. James and K. Brown	0	H. Irwin and L. Graham (1 hole)	1
Singles		Singles	
H. Clark	0	L. Wadkins (4 and 3)	1
N. C. Coles	0	L. Graham (5 and 3)	1
P. Dawson (5 and 4)	1	D. January	0
B. W. Barnes (1 hole)	1	H. Irwin	0
T. Horton	0	D. Hill (5 and 4)	1
B. J. Gallacher (1 hole)	1	J. W. Nicklaus	0
E. Darcy	0	H. Green (1 hole)	1
M. James	0	R. Floyd (2 and 1)	1
N. Faldo (1 hole)	1	T. Watson	0
P. Oosterhuis (2 holes)	1	J. McGee	0

Great Britain and Ireland 7 ½   USA 12 ½

1979 THE GREENBRIER, WHITE SULPHUR SPRINGS, WEST VIRGINIA, SEPTEMBER 14-16

Captains: J. Jacobs (Europe), W. Casper (USA)

Europe		USA	
Fourballs		**Fourballs**	
Morning		*Morning*	
A. Garrido and S. Ballesteros	0	L. Wadkins and L. Nelson (2 and 1)	1
K. Brown and M. James	0	L. Trevino and F. Zoeller (3 and 2)	1
P. Oosterhuis and N. Faldo	0	A. Bean and L. Elder (2 and 1)	1
B. Gallacher and B. Barnes (2 and 1)	1	H. Irwin and J. Mahaffey	0
Foursomes		Foursomes	
Afterrnoon		*Afternoon*	
K. Brown and D. Smyth	0	H. Irwin and T. Kite (7 and 6)	1
S. Ballesteros and A. Garrido (3 and 2)	1	F. Zoeller and H. Green	0
A. Lyle and A. Jacklin (halved)	½	L. Trevino and G. Morgan (halved)	½
B. Gallacher and B. Barnes	0	L. Wadkins and L. Nelson (4 and 3)	1
Foursomes		Foursomes	
Morning		*Morning*	
A. Jacklin and A. Lyle (5 and 4)	1	L. Elder and J. Mahaffey	0
N. Faldo and P. Oosterrhuis (6 and 5)	1	A. Bean and T. Kite	0
B. Gallacher and B. Barnes (2 and 1)	1	F. Zoeller and M. Hayes	0
S. Ballesterones and A. Garrido	0	L. Wadkins and L. Nelson (3 and 2)	1
Fourballs		Fourballs	
Afternoon		*Afternoon*	
S. Ballesteros and A. Garrido	0	L. Wadkins and L. Nelson (5 and 4)	1
A. Jacklin and A. Lyle	0	H. Irwin and T. Kite (1 hole)	1
B. Gallacher and B. Barnes (3 and 2)	1	L. Trevino and F. Zoeller	0
N. Faldo and P. Oosterhuis (1 hole)	1	L. Elder and M. Hayes	0
Singles		Singles	
Morning		*Morning*	
B. Gallacher (3 and 2)	1	L. Wadkins	0
S. Ballesteros	0	L. Nelson (3 and 2)	1
A. Jacklin	0	T. Kite (1hole)	1
A. Garrido	0	M. Hayes (1 hole)	1
M. King	0	A. Bean (4 and 3)	1
B. Barnes	0	J. Manhaffey (1 hole)	1
Afternoon		*Afternoon*	
N. Faldo (3 and 2)	1	L. Elder	0
D. Smyth	0	H. Irwin (5 and 3)	1
P. Oosterhuis	0	H. Green (2 holes)	1
K. Brown (1 hole)	1	F. Zoeller	0
A. Lyle	0	L. Trevino (2 and 1)	1
M. James, injured (halved, match not played)	½	G. Morgan (halved, match not played)	½

Europe 11   USA 17

205

1981 WALTON HEATH, SURREY, SEPTEMBER 18-20

Captains: J. Jacobs (Europe), D. Marr (USA)

Europe		**USA**	
Foursomes		**Foursomes**	
Morning		*Morning*	
B. Langer and M. Piñero	0	L. Trevino and L. Nelson (1 hole)	1
A. Lyle and M. James (2 and 1)	1	B. Rodgers and B. Lietzke	0
B. Gallacher and D. Smyth (3 and 2)	1	H. Irwin and R. Floyd	0
P. Oosterhuis and N. Faldo	0	T. Watson and J. Nicklaus (4 and 3)	1
Fourballs		**Fourballs**	
Afternoon		*Afternoon*	
S. Torrance and H. Clark (halved)	½	T. Kite and J. Miller (halved)	½
A. Lyle and M. James (3 and 2)	1	B. Crenshaw and J. Pate	0
D. Smyth and J. M. Cañizares (6 and 5)	1	B. Rodgers and B. Lietzke	0
D. Gallacher and E. Darcy	0	H. Irwin and R. Floyd (2 and 1)	1
Fourballs		**Fourballs**	
Morning		*Morning*	
N. Faldo and S. Torrance	0	L. Trevino and J. Pate (7 and 5)	1
A. Lyle and M. James	0	L. Nelson and T. Kite (1 hole)	1
B. Langer and M. Piñero (2 and 1)	1	R. Floyd and H. Irwin	0
J. M. Cañizares and D. Smyth	0	J. Nicklaus and T. Watson (3 and 2)	1
Foursomes		**Foursomes**	
Afternoon		*Afternoon*	
P. Oosterrhuis and S. Torrance	0	L. Trevino and J. Pate (2 and 1)	1
B. Langer and M. Piñero	0	J. Nicklaus and T. Watson (3 and 2)	1
A. Lyle and M. James	0	B. Rogers and R. Floyd (3 and 2)	1
D. Smyth and B. Gallacher	0	T. Kite and L. Nelson (3 and 2)	1
Singles		**Singles**	
S. Torrance	0	L. Trevino (5 and 3)	1
A. Lyle	0	T. Kite (3 and 2)	1
B. Gallacher (halved)	½	B. Rogers (halved)	½
M. James	0	L. Nelson (2 holes)	1
S. Smyth	0	B. Crenshaw (6 and 4)	1
B. Langer (halved)	½	B. Lietzke (halved)	½
M. Piñero (4 and 2)	1	J. Pate	0
J. M. Cañizares	0	H. Irwin (1 hole)	1
N. Faldo (2 and 1)	1	J. Miller	0
H. Clark (4 and 3)	1	T. Watson	0
P. Oosterhuis	0	R. Floyd (1 hole)	1
E. Darcy	0	J. Nicklaus (5 and 3)	1

Europe 9 ½   USA 18 ½

1983 PGA NATIONAL GOLF CLUB, PALM BEACH GARDENS, FLORIDA, OCTOBER 14-16

Captains: A. Jacklin (Europe), J. Nicklaus (USA)

Europe		USA	
Foursomes		**Foursomes**	
Morning		*Morning*	
B. Gallacher and A. Lyle	0	T. Watson and B. Crenshaw (5 and 4)	1
N. Faldo and B. Langer (4 and 2)	1	L. Wadkins and C. Stadler	0
J. M. Cañizares and S. Torrance (4 and 3)	1	R. Floyd and B. Gilder	0
S. Ballesteros and P. Way	0	T. Kite and C. Peete (2 and 1)	1
Fourballs		**Fourballs**	
Afterrnoon		*Afternoon*	
B. Waites and K. Brown (2 and 1)	1	G. Morgan and F. Zoeller	0
N. Faldo and B. Langer	0	T. Watson and J. Haas (2 and 1)	1
S. Ballesteros and P. Way (1 hole)	1	R. Floyd and C. Strange	0
S. Torrance and I. Woosnam (halved)	½	B. Crenshaw and C. Peete (halved)	½
Fourballs		**Fourballs**	
Morning		*Morning*	
B. Waites and K. Brown	0	L. Wadkins and C. Stadler (1 hole)	1
N. Faldo and B. Langer (4 and 2)	1	B. Crenshaw and C. Peete	0
S. Ballesteros and P. Way (halved)	½	G. Morgan and J. Haas (halved)	½
S. Torrence and I. Woosnam	0	T. Watson and B. Gilder (5 and 4)	1
Foursomes		**Fourballs**	
Afternoon		*Afternoon*	
N. Faldo and B. Langer (3 and 2)	1	T. Kite and R. Floyd	0
S. Torrance and J. M. Cañizares	0	G. Morgan and L. Wadkins (7 and 5)	1
S. Ballesteros and P. Way (2 and 1)	1	T. Watson and B. Gilder	0
B. Waites and K. Brown	0	J. Haas and C. Strange (3 and 2)	1
Singles		**Singles**	
S. Ballesteros (halved)	½	F. Zoeller (halved)	½
N. Faldo (2 and 1)	1	J. Haas	0
B. Langer (2 holes)	1	G. Morgan	0
G. J. Brand	0	B. Gilder (2 holes)	1
A. Lyle	0	B. Crenshaw (3 and 1)	1
B. Waites	0	C. Peete (1 hole)	1
P. Way (2 and 1)	1	C. Strange	0
S. Torrance (halved)	½	T. Kite (halved)	½
I. Woosnam	0	C. Stadler (3 and 2)	1
J. M. Cañizares (halved)	½	L. Wadkins (halved)	½
K. Brown (4 and 3)	1	R. Floyd	0
B. Gallacher	0	T. Watson (2 and 1)	1

Europe 13 ½   USA 14 ½

1985 The De Vere Belfry, Sutton Coldfield, W. Midlands, September 13-15

Captains: A. Jacklin (Europe), L. Trevino (USA)

Europe		USA	
Foursomes		**Foursome**	
Morning		*Morning*	
S. Ballesteros and M. Piñero (2 and 1)	1	C. Strange and M. O'Meara	0
B. Langer and N. Faldo	0	C. Peete and T. Kite (3 and 2)	1
A. Lyle and K. Brown	0	L. Wadkins and R. Floyd (4 and 3)	1
H. Clark and S. Torrance	0	C. Stadler and H. Sutton (3 and 2)	1
Fourballs		**Fourballs**	
Afternoon		*Afternoon*	
P. Way and I. Woosnam (1 hole)	1	F. Zoeller and H. Green	0
S. Ballesteros and M. Piñero (2 and 1)	1	A. North and P. Jacobsen	0
B. Langer and J. M. Cañizares (halved)	½	C. Stadler 7 H. Sutton (halved)	½
S. Torrance and H. Clark	0	R. Floyd and L. Wadkins (1 hole)	1
Fourballs		**Fourballs**	
Morning		*Morning*	
S. Torrance and H. Clark (2 and 1)	1	T. Kite and A. North	0
P. Way and I. Woosnam (4 and 3)	1	H. Green and F. Zoeller	0
S. Ballesteros and M. Piñero	0	M. O'Meara and L. Wadkins (3 and 2)	1
B. Langerr and A. Lyle (halved)	½	C. Stadler and C. Strange (halved)	½
Foursomes		**Fourballs**	
Afternoon		*Afternoon*	
J. M. Cañizares and J. Rivero (7 and 5)	1	T. Kite and C. Peete	0
S. Ballesteros and M. Piñero (5 and 4)	1	C. Stadler and H. Sutton	0
P. Way and I. Woosnam	0	C. Strange and P. Jacobsen (4 and 2)	1
B. Langer and K. Brown (3 and 2)	1	R. Floyd and L. Wadkins	0
Singles		**Singles**	
M. Piñero (3 and 1)	1	L. Wadkins	0
I. Woosnam	0	C. Stadler (2 and 1)	1
P. Way (2 holes)	1	R. Floyd	0
S. Ballesteros (halved)	½	T. Kite (halved)	½
A. Lyle (3 and 2)	1	P. Jacobsen	0
B. Langer (5 and 4)	1	H. Sutton	0
S. Torrance (1 hole)	1	A. North	0
H. Clark (1 hole)	1	M. O'Meara	0
N. Faldo	0	H. Green (3 and 1)	1
J. Rivero	0	C. Peete (1 hole)	1
J. M. Cañizares (2 holes)	1	F. Zoeller	0
K. Brown	0	C. Strange (4 and 2)	1

Europe 16 ½   USA 11 ½

1987 MUIRFIELD VILLAGE, COLUMBUS, OHIO, SEPTEMBER 25-27
Captains: A. Jacklin (Europe), J. W. Nicklaus (USA)

Europe		USA	
Foursomes		**Foursomes**	
Morning		*Morning*	
S. Torrance and H. Clark	0	C. Strange and T. Kite (4 and 2)	1
K. Brown and B. Langer	0	H. Sutton and D. Pohl (2 and 1)	1
N. Faldo and I. Woosnam (2 holes)	1	L. Wadkins and L. Mize	0
S. Ballesteros and J. M. Olazábal (1 hole)	1	L. Nelson and P. Stewart	0
Fourballs		**Fourballs**	
Afternoon		*Afternoon*	
G. Brand Jnr. and J. Rivero (3 and 2)	1	B. Crenshaw and S. Simpson	0
A. Lyle and B. Langer (1 hole)	1	A. Bean and M. Calcavecchia	0
N. Faldo and I. Woosnam (2 and 1)	1	H. Sutton and D. Pohl	0
S. Ballesteros and J. M. Olazábal (2 and 1)	1	C. Strange and T. Kite	0
Foursomes		**Foursomes**	
Morning		*Morning*	
J. Rivero and G. Brand Jnr	0	C. Strange and T. Kite (3 and 1)	1
N. Faldo and I. Woosnam (halved)	½	H. Sutton and L. Mize (halved)	½
A. Lyle and B. Langer (2 and 1)	1	L. Wadkins and L. Nelson	0
S. Ballesteros and J. M. Olazábal (1 hole)	1	B. Crenshaw and P. Stewart	0
Fourballs		**Fourballs**	
Afternoon		*Afternoon*	
N. Faldo and I. Woosnam (5 and 4)	1	C. Strange and T. Kite	0
E. Darcy and G. Brand Jnr.	0	A. Bean and P. Stewart (3 and 2)	1
S. Ballesteros and J. M. Olazábal	0	H. Sutton and L. Mize (2 and 1)	1
A. Lyle and B. Langer (1 hole)	1	L. Wadkins and L. Nelson	0
Singles		**Singles**	
I. Woosnam	0	A. Bean (1 hole)	1
H. Clark (1 hole)	1	D. Pohl	0
S. Torrance (halved)	½	L. Mize (halved)	½
N. Faldo	0	M. Calcavecchia (1 hole)	1
J. M. Olazábal	0	P. Stewart (2 holes)	1
E. Darcy (1 hole)	1	B. Crenshaw	0
J. Rivero	0	S. Simpson (2 and 1)	1
B. Langer (halved)	½	L. Nelson (halved)	½
A. Lyle	0	T. Kite (3 and 2)	1
S. Ballesteros (2 and 1)	1	C. Strange	0
G. Brand Jnr. (halved)	½	H. Sutton (halved)	½
K. Brown	0	L. Wadkins (3 and 2)	1

Europe 15 USA 13

1989 The De Vere Belfry, Sutton Coldfield, W. Midlands, September 22–24

Captains: A. Jacklin (Europe), R. Floyd (USA)

Europe		USA	
Foursomes		**Foursomes**	
Morning		*Morning*	
N. Faldo and I. Woosnam (halved)	½	T. Kite and C. Strange (halved)	½
H. Clark and M. James	0	L. Wadkins and P. Stewart (1 hole)	1
S. Ballesteros and J. M. Olazábal (halved)	½	T. Watson and C. Beck (halved)	½
B. Langer and R. Rafferty	0	M. Calcavecchia and K. Green (2 and 1)	1
Fourballs		**Fourballs**	
Afternoon		*Afternoon*	
S. Torrance and G. Brand Jnr (1 hole)	1	C. Strange and P. Azinger	0
H. Clark and M. James (3 and 2)	1	F. Couples and L. Wadkins	0
N. Faldo and I. Woosnam (2 holes)	1	M. Calcavecchia and M. McCumber	0
S. Ballesteros and J. M. Olazábal (6 and 5)	1	T. Watson and M. O'Meara	0
Foursomes		**Foursomes**	
Morning		*Morning*	
I. Woosnam and N. Faldo (3 and 2)	1	L. Wadkins and P. Stewart	0
G. Brand Jnr. and S. Torrance	0	C. Beck and P. Azinger (4 and 3)	1
C. O'Connor Jnr. and R. Rafferty	0	M. Calcavecchia and K. Green (3 and 2)	1
S. Ballesteros and J. M. Olazábal (1 hole)	1	T. Kite and C. Strange	0
Fourballs		**Fourballs**	
Afternoon		*Afternoon*	
N. Faldo and I. Woosnam	0	C. Beck and P. Azinger (2 and 1)	1
B. Langer and J. M. Cañizares	0	T. Kite and M. Mc Cumber (2 and 1)	1
H. Clark and M. James (1 hole)	1	P. Stewart and C. Strange	0
S. Ballesteros and J. M. Olazábal (4 and 2)	1	M. Calcavecchia and K. Green	0
Singles		**Singles**	
S. Ballesteros	0	P. Azinger (1 hole)	1
B. Langer	0	C. Beck (3 and 1)	1
J. M. Olazábal (1 hole)	1	P. Stewart	0
R. Rafferty (1 hole)	1	M. Calcavecchia	0
H. Clark	0	T. Kite (8 and 7)	1
M. James (3 and 2)	1	M. O'Meara	0
C. O'Connor Jnr. (1 hole)	1	F. Couples	0
J. M. Cañizares (1 hole)	1	K. Green	0
G. Brand Jnr.	0	M. McCumber (1 hole)	1
S. Torrance	0	T. Watson (3 and 1)	1
N. Faldo	0	L. Wadkins (1 hole)	1
I. Woosnam	0	C. Strange (2 holes)	1

Europe 14   USA 14

1991 OCEAN COURSE, KIAWAH ISLAND, SOUTH CAROLINA, SEPTEMBER 27-29

Captains: B. Gallacher (Europe), D. Stockton (USA)

Europe		USA	
Foursomes		**Foursomes**	
Morning		*Morning*	
S. Ballesteros and J. M. Olazábal (2 and 1)	1	P. Azinger and C. Beck	0
B. Langer and M. James	0	R. Floyd and F. Couples (2 and 1)	1
D. Gilford and C. Montgomerie	0	L. Wadkins and H. Irwin (4 and 2)	1
N. Faldo and I. Woosnam	0	P. Stewart and M. Calcavecchia (1 hole)	1
Fourballs		**Fourballs**	
Afternoon		*Afternoon*	
S. Torrance and D. Feherty (halved)	½	L. Wadkins and M. O'Meara (halved)	½
S. Ballesteros and J. M. Olazábal (2 and 1)	1	P. Azinger and C. Beck	0
S. Richardson and M. James (5 and 4)	1	C. Pavin and M. Calcavecchia	0
N. Faldo and I. Woosnam	0	R. Floyd and F. Couples (5 and 3)	1
Foursomes		**Foursomes**	
Morning		*Morning*	
S. Torrance and D. Feherty	0	H. Irwin and L. Wadkins (4 and 2)	1
M. James and S. Richardson	0	M. Calcavecchia and P. Stewart (1 hole)	1
N. Faldo and D. Gilford	0	P. Azinger and M. O'Meara (7 and 6)	1
S. Ballesteros and J. M. Olazábal (3 and 2)	1	F. Couples and R. Floyd	0
Fourballs		**Fourballs**	
Afternoon		*Afternoon*	
I. Woosnam and P. Broadhurst (2 and 1)	1	P. Azinger and H. Irwin	0
B. Langer and C. Montgomerie (2 and 1)	1	S. Pate and C. Pavin	0
M. James and S. Richardson (3 and 1)	1	L. Wadkins and W. Levi	0
S. Ballesteros and J. M. Olazábal (halved)	½	F. Couples and P. Stewart (halved)	½
Singles		**Singles**	
N. Faldo (2 holes)	1	R. Floyd	0
D. Feherty (2 and 1)	1	P. Stewart	0
C. Montgomerie (halved)	½	M. Calcavecchia (halved)	½
J. M. Olazábal	0	P. Azinger (2 holes)	1
S. Richardson	0	C. Pavin (2 and 1)	1
S. Ballesteros (3 and 2)	1	W. Levi	0
I. Woosnam	0	C. Beck (3 and 1)	1
P. Broadhurst (3 and 1)	1	M. O'Meara	0
S. Torrance	0	F. Couples (3 and 2)	1
M. James	0	L. Wadkins (3 and 2)	1
B. Langer (halved)	½	H. Irwin (halved)	½
D. Gilford (halved)★	½	S. Pate (halved)	½

Europe 13 ½   USA 14 ½

★Pate withdrawn at start of day

1993 THE DE VERE BELFRY, SUTTON COLDFIELD, W. MIDLANDS, SEPTEMBER 24–26

Captains: B. Gallacher (Europe), T. Watson (USA)

Europe		USA	
Foursomes		**Foursomes**	
Morning		*Morning*	
S. Torrance and M. James	0	L. Wadkins and C. Pavin (4 and 3)	1
I. Woosnam and B. Langer (7 and 5)	1	P. Azinger and P. Stewart	0
S. Ballesteros and J. M. Olazábal	0	T. Kite and D. Love III (2 and 1)	1
N. Faldo and C. Montgomerie (4 and 3)	1	R. Floyd and F. Couples	0
Fourballs		**Fourballs**	
Afternoon		*Afternoon*	
I. Woosnam and P. Baker (1 hole)	1	J. Gallagher Jnr. and L. Janzen	0
B. Langer and B. Lane	0	L. Wadkins and C. Pavin (4 and 2)	1
N. Faldo and C. Montgomerie (halved)	½	P. Azinger and F. Couples (halved)	½
S. Ballesteros and J. M. Olazábal (4 and 3)	1	D. Love III and T. Kite	0
Foursomes		**Foursomes**	
Morning		*Morning*	
N. Faldo and C. Montgomerie (3 and 2)	1	L. Wadkins and C. Pavin	0
B. Langer and I. Woosnam (2 and 1)	1	F. Couples and P. Azinger	0
P. Baker and B. Lane	0	R. Floyd and P. Stewart (3 and 2)	1
S. Ballesterros and J. M. Olazábal (2 and 1)	1	D. Love III and T. Kite	0
Fourballs		**Fourballs**	
Afternoon		*Afternoon*	
N. Faldo and C. Montgomerie	0	J. Cook and C. Beck (2 holes)	1
M. James and C. Rocca	0	C. Pavin and J. Gallagher Jnr. (5 and 4)	1
I. Woosnam and P. Baker (6 and 5)	1	F. Couples and P. Azinger	0
J. M. Olazábal and J. Haeggman	0	R. Floyd and P. Stewart (2 and 1)	1
Singles		**Singles**	
I. Woosnam (halved)	½	F. Couples (halved)	½
B. Lane	0	C. Beck (1 hole)	1
C. Montgomerie (1 hole)	1	L. Janzen	0
P. Baker (2 holes)	1	C. Pavin	0
J. Haeggman (1 hole)	1	J. Cook	0
M. James	0	P. Stewart (3 and 2)	1
C. Rocca	0	D. Love III (1 hole)	1
S. Ballesteros	0	J. Gallagher Jnr. (3 and 2)	1
J. M. Olazábal	0	R. Floyd (2 holes)	1
B. Langer	0	T. Kite (5 and 3)	1
N. Faldo (halved)	½	P. Azinger (halved)	½
S. Torrance (halved)★	½	L. Wadkins (halved)	½

Europe 13 USA 15

★ Torrance withdrawn at start of day

1995 OAK HILL COUNTRY CLUB, ROCHESTER, NEW YORK, SEPTEMBER 22-24

Captains: B. Gallacher (Europe), L. Wadkins (USA)

Europe		USA	
Foursomes		**Foursomes**	
Morning		*Morning*	
N. Faldo and C. Montgomerie	0	C. Pavin and T. Lehman (1 hole)	1
S. Torrance and C. Rocca (3 and 2)	1	J. Haas and F. Couples	0
H. Clark and M. James	0	D. Love III and J. Maggert (4 and 3)	1
B. Langer and P. -U. Johansson (1 hole)	1	B. Crenshaw and C. Strange	0
Fourballs		**Fourballs**	
Afternoon		*Afternoon*	
D. Gilford and S. Ballesteros (4 and 3)	1	B. Faxon and P. Jacobsen	0
S. Torrance and C. Rocca	0	J. Maggert and L. Roberts (6 and 5)	1
N. Faldo and C. Montgomerie	0	F. Couples and D. Love III (3 and 2)	1
B. Langer and P. -U. Johansson	0	C. Pavin and P. Mickelson (6 and 4)	1
Foursomes		**Foursomes**	
Morning		*Morning*	
N. Faldo and C. Montgomerie (4 and 2)	1	C. Strange and J. Haas	0
S. Torrance and C. Rocca (6 and 5)	1	D. Love III and J. Maggert	0
I. Woosnam and P. Walton	0	L. Roberts and P. Jacobsen (1 hole)	1
B. Langer and D. Gilford (4 and 3)	1	C. Pavin and T. Lehman	0
Fourballs		**Fourballs**	
Afternoon		*Afternoon*	
S. Torrance and C. Montgomerie	0	B. Faxon and F. Couples (4 and 2)	1
I. Woosnam and C. Rocca (3 and 2)	1	D. Love III and B. Crenshaw	0
S. Ballesteros and D. Gilford	0	J. Haas and P. Mickelson (3 and 2)	1
N. Faldo and B. Langer	0	C. Pavin and L. Roberts (1 hole)	1
Singles		**Singles**	
S. Ballesteros	0	T. Lehman (4 and 3)	1
H. Clark (1 hole)	1	P. Jacobsen	0
M. James (4 and 3)	1	J. Maggert	0
I. Woosnam (halved)	½	F. Couples (halved)	½
C. Rocca	0	D. Love III (3 and 2)	1
D. Gilford (1 hole)	1	B. Faxon	0
C. Montgomerie (3 and 1)	1	B. Crenshaw	0
N. Faldo (1 hole)	1	C. Strange	0
S. Torrance (2 and 1)	1	L. Roberts	0
B. Langer	0	C. Pavin (3 and 2)	1
P. Walton (1 hole)	1	J. Haas	0
P. -U. Johansson	0	P. Mickelson (2 and 1)	1

Europe 14 ½   USA 13 ½

1997 Club de Golf Valderrama, Sotogrande, Spain, September 26-28

Captains: S. Ballesteros (Europe), T. Kite (USA)

Europe		USA	
Fourballs		**Fourballs**	
Morning		*Morning*	
J. M. Olazábal and C. Rocca (1 hole)	1	D. Love III and P. Mickelson	0
N. Faldo and L. Westwood	0	F. Couples and B. Faxon (1 hole)	1
J. Parnevik and P.-U. Johansson (1 hole)	1	T. Lehman and J. Furyk	0
B. Langer and C. Montgomerie	0	T. Woods and M. O'Meara (3 and 2)	1
Foursomes		**Foursomes**	
Afternoon		*Afternoon*	
J. M. Olazábal and C. Rocca	0	S. Hoch and L. Janzen (1 hole)	1
B. Langer and C. Montgomerie (5 and 3)	1	T. Woods and M. O'Meara	0
N. Faldo and L. Westwood (3 and 2)	1	J. Leonard and J. Maggert	0
I. Garrido and J. Parnevik (halved)	½	P. Mickelson and T. Lehman (halved)	½
Fourballs		**Fourballs**	
Morning		*Morning*	
C. Montgomerie and D. Clarke (1 hole)	1	F. Couples and D. Love III	0
I. Woosnam and T. Björn (2 and 1)	1	J. Leonard and B. Faxon	0
N. Faldo and L. Westwood (2 and 1)	1	T. Woods and M. O'Meara	0
J. M. Olazábal and I. Garrido (halved)	½	P. Mickleson and T. Lehman (halved)	½
Foursomes		**Foursomes**	
Afternoon		*Afternoon*	
C. Montgomerie and B. Langer (1 hole)	1	L. Janzen and J. Furyk	0
N. Faldo and L. Westwood	0	S. Hoch and J. Maggert (2 and 1)	1
J. Parnevik and I. Garrido (halved)	½	T. Woods and J. Leonard (halved)	½
J. M. Olazábal and C. Rocca (5 and 4)	1	F. Couples and D. Love III	0
Singles		**Singles**	
I. Woosnam	0	F. Couples (8 and 7)	1
P. -U. Johansson (3 and 2)	1	D. Love III	0
C. Rocca (4 and 2)	1	T. Woods	0
T. Björn (halved)	½	J. Leonard (halved)	½
D. Clarke	0	P. Mickelson (2 and 1)	1
J. Parnevik	0	M. O'Meara (5 and 4)	1
J. M. Olazábal	0	J. Lanzen (1 hole)	1
B. Langer (2 and 1)	1	B. Faxon	0
L. Westwood	0	J. Maggert (3 and 2)	1
C. Montgomerie (halved)	½	S. Hoch (halved)	½
N. Faldo	0	J. Furyk (3 and 2)	1
I. Garrido	0	T. Lehman (7 and 6)	1

Europe 14 ½   USA 13 ½

1999 THE COUNTRY CLUB, BROOKLINE, MASSACHUSETTS, SEPTEMBER 24-26

Captains: M. James (Europe), B. Crenshaw (USA)

Europe		USA	
Foursomes		**Foursomes**	
Morning		*Morning*	
C. Montgomerie and P. Lawrie (3 and 2)	1	D. Duval and P. Mickelson	0
J. Parnevik and S. Garcia (2 and 1)	1	T. Lehman and T. Woods	0
M. A. Jiménez and P. Harrington (halved)	½	D. Love III and P. Stewart (halved)	½
D. Clarke and L. Westwood	0	H. Sutton and J. Maggert (3 and 2)	1
Fourballs		**Fourballs**	
Afternoon		*Afternoon*	
C. Montgomerie and P. Lawrie (halved)	½	D. Love III and J. Leonard (halved)	½
J. Parnevik and S. Garcia (1 hole)	1	P. Mickelson and J. Furyk	0
M. A. Jiménez and J. M. Olazábal (2 and 1)	1	H. Sutton and J. Maggert	0
D. Clarke and L. Westwood (1 hole)	1	D. Duval and T. Woods	0
Foursomes		**Foursomes**	
Morning		*Morning*	
C. Montgomerie and P. Lawrie	0	H. Sutton and J. Maggert (1 hole)	1
D. Clarke and L. Westwood (3 and 2)	1	J. Furyk and M. O'Meara	0
M. A. Jiménez and P. Harrington	0	S. Pate and T. Woods (1 hole)	1
J. Parnevik and S. Garcia (3 and 2)	1	P. Stewart and J. Leonard	0
Fourballs		**Fourballs**	
Afterrnoon		*Afternoon*	
D. Clarke and L. Westwood	0	P. Mickelson and T. Lehman (2 and 1)	1
J. Parnevik and S. Garcia (halved)	½	D. Love III and D. Duval (halved)	½
M. A. Jiménez and J. M. Olazábal (halved)	½	J. Leonard and H. Sutton (halved)	½
C. Montgomerie and P. Lawrie (2 and 1)	1	S. Pate and T. Woods	0
Singles		**Singles**	
L. Westwood	0	T. Lehman (3 and 2)	1
D. Clarke	0	H. Sutton (4 and 2)	1
J. Sandelin	0	P. Mickelson (4 and 3)	1
J. Van de Velde	0	D. Love III (6 and 5)	1
A. Coltart	0	T. Woods (3 and 2)	1
J. Parnevik	0	D. Duval (5 and 4)	1
P. Harrington (1 hole)	1	M. O'Meara	0
M. A. Jiménez	0	S. Pate (2 and 1)	1
J. M. Olazábal (halved)	½	J. Leonard (halved)	½
C. Montgomerie (1 hole)	1	P. Stewart	0
S. Garcia	0	J. Furyk (4 and 3)	1
P. Lawrie (4 and 3)	1	J. Maggert	0

Europe 13 ½   USA 14 ½

2002 THE DE VERE BELFRY, SUTTON COLDFIELD, W. MIDLANDS, SEPTEMBER 27-29

MATCHES POSTPONED FROM 2001

Captains: S. Torrance (Europe), C. Strange (USA)

Europe		USA	
Fourballs		**Fourballs**	
Morning		*Morning*	
D. Clarke and T. Björn (1 hole)	1	T. Woods and P. Azinger	0
S. Garcia and L. Westwood (4 and 3)	1	D. Duval and D. Love III	0
C. Montgomerie and B. Langer (4 and 3)	1	S. Hoch and J. Furyk	0
P. Harrington and N. Fasth	0	P. Mickelson and D. Toms (1 hole)	1
Foursomes		**Foursomes**	
Afternoon		*Afternoon*	
D. Clarke and T. Björn	0	H. Sutton and S. Verplank (2 and 1)	1
S. Garcia and L. Westwood (2 and 1)	1	T. Woods and M. Calcavecchia	0
C. Montgomerie and B. Langer (halved)	½	P. Mickelson and D. Toms (halved)	½
P. Harrington and P. McGinley	0	S. Cink 7 J. Furyk (3 and 2)	1
Foursomes		**Foursomes**	
Morning		*Morning*	
P. Fulke and P. Price	0	P. Mickelson and D. Toms (2 and 1)	1
L. Westwood and S. Garcia (2 and 1)	1	S. Cink and Furyk	0
C. Montgomerie and B. Langer (1 hole)	1	S. Verplank and S. Hoch	0
D. Clarke and T. Björn	0	T. Woods and D. Love III (4 and 3)	1
Fourballs		**Fourballs**	
Afternoon		*Afternoon*	
N. Fasth and J. Parnevik	0	M. Calcavecchia and D. Duval (1 hole)	1
C. Montgomerie and P. Harrington (2 and 1)	1	P. Mickelson and D. Toms	0
S. Garcia and L. Westwood	0	T. Woods and D. Love III (1 hole)	1
D. Clarke and P. McGinley (halved)	½	S. Hoch and J. Furyk (halved)	½
Singles		**Singles**	
C. Montgomerie (5 and 4)	1	S. Hoch	0
S. Garcia	0	D. Toms (1 hole)	1
D. Clarke (halved)	½	D. Duval (halved)	½
B. Langer (4 and 3)	1	H. Sutton	0
P. Harrington (5 and 4)	1	M. Calcavecchia	0
T. Björn (2 and 1)	1	S. Cink	0
L. Westwood	0	S. Verplank (2 and 1)	1
N. Fasth (halved)	½	P. Azinger (halved)	½
P. McGinely (halved)	½	J. Furyk (halved)	½
P. Fulke (halved)	½	D. Love III (halved)	½
P. Price (3 and 2)	1	P. Mickelson	0
J. Parnevik (halved)	½	T. Woods (halved)	½

Europe 15 ½   USA 12 ½

2004 OAKLAND HILLS CC, BLOOMFIELD TOWNSHIP, MICHIGAN, SEPTEMBER 17–19

Captains: B. Langer (Europe), H. Sutton (USA)

Europe		USA	
Fourballs		**Fourballs**	
Morning		*Morning*	
C. Montgomerie and P. Harrington (2 and 1)	1	P. Mickelson and T. Woods	0
D. Clarke and M. A. Jiménez (5 and 4)	1	D. Love III and C. Campbell	0
P. McGinley and L. Donald (halved)	½	C. Riley and S. Cink (halved)	½
S. Garcia and L. Westwood (5 and 3)	1	D. Toms and J. Furyk	0
Foursomes		**Foursomes**	
Afternoon		*Afternoon*	
M. A. Jiménez and T. Levet	0	C. DiMarco and J. Haas (3 and 2)	1
C. Montgomerie and P. Harrington (4 and 2)	1	D. Love III and F. Funk	0
D. Clarke and L. Westwood (1 hole)	1	P. Mickelson and T. Woods	0
S. Garcia and L. Donald (2 and 1)	1	K. Perry and S. Cink	0
Fourballs		**Fourballs**	
Morning		*Morning*	
S. Garcia and L. Westwood (halved)	½	J. Haas and C. DiMarco (halved)	½
D. Clarke and I. Poulter	0	T. Woods and C. Riley (4 and 3)	1
P. Casey and D. Howell (1 hole)	1	J. Furyk and C. Campbell	0
C. Montgomerie and P. Harrington	0	S. Cink and D. Love III (3 and 2)	1
Foursomes		**Foursomes**	
Afternoon		*Afternoon*	
D. Clarke and L. Westwood (5 and 4)	1	J. Haas and C. DiMarco	0
M. A. Jiménez and T. Levet	0	P. Mickelson and D. Toms (4 and 3)	1
S. Garcia and L. Donald (1 hole)	1	J. Furyk and F. Funk	0
P. Harrington and P. McGinley (4 and 3)	1	D. Love III and T. Woods	0
Singles		**Singles**	
P. Casey	0	T. Woods (3 and 2)	1
S. Garcia (3 and 2)	1	P. Mickelson	0
D. Clarke (halved)	½	D. Love III (halved)	½
D. Howell	0	J. Furyk (6 and 4)	1
L. Westwood (1 hole)	1	K. Perry	0
C. Montgomerie (1 hole)	1	D. Toms	0
L. Donald	0	C. Campbell (5 and 3)	1
M. A. Jiménez	0	C. DiMarco (1 hole)	1
T. Levet (1 hole)	1	F. Funk	0
I. Poulter (3 and 2)	1	C. Riley	0
P. Harrington (1 hole)	1	J. Haas	0
P. McGinley (3 and 2)	1	S. Cink	0

Europe 18 ½   USA 9 ½

217

SECTION 5

Appendices

APPENDIX 1

THE SEVENTEEN IRISH RYDER CUP PLAYERS

Records
1. Hugh Boyle
2. Harry Bradshaw
3. Darren Clarke
4. Fred Daly
5. Eamonn Darcy
6. Norman Drew
7 David Feherty
8. Padraig Harrington
9. Jimmy Martin
10. Paul McGinley
11. Christy O'Connor, Jr.
12. Christy O'Connor, Sr.
13. John O'Leary
14. Eddie Polland
15. Ronan Rafferty
16. Des Smyth
17. Philip Walton

HUGH BOYLE PLAYED IN ONE RYDER CUP MATCH: 1967.

1967 Houston, Texas, US

Captain: Great Britain and Ireland: D.J. Rees; US: B. Hogan

Day 1 Foursomes (p.m.)
H. Boyle and M. Gregson lost to G. Dickinson and A. Palmer 5 and 4   0

Day 2 Fourballs (p.m.)
H. Boyle and G. Will lost to A. Palmer and J. Boros 1 up   0

Day 3 Singles
H. Boyle lost to G. Brewer 4 and 3   0
Total 0

HARRY BRADSHAW PLAYED IN THREE RYDER CUP MATCHES: 1953, 1955, 1957.

1953 Wentworth, Surrey, England

Captain: Great Britain and Ireland: T.H. Cotton; US: L. Mangrum

Day 1 Foursomes
H. Bradshaw and F. Daly beat W. Burkemo and C. Middlecoff 1 up   1

Day 2 Singles
H. Bradshaw beat F. Haas 3 and 2   1
Total 2

1955 California, US

Captain: Great Britain and Ireland: D.J. Rees; US: C. Harbert

Day 1 Foursomes
H. Bradshaw and D.J. Rees lost to S. Snead and C. Middlecoff 3 and 2   0

Day 2 Singles
H. Bradshaw lost to J. Burke 3 and 2   0
Total 0

1957 Yorkshire, England

Captain: Great Britain and Ireland: D.J Rees; US: J. Burke

Day 2 Singles
H. Bradshaw halved with R. Mayer ½

Total ½

DARREN CLARKE PLAYED IN FOUR RYDER CUP MATCHES: 1997, 1999, 2002 AND 2004.

1997 Valderrama, Andalucía, Spain

Captain: Europe: S. Ballesteros; US: T. Kite

Saturday Foursomes (a.m.)
D. Clarke and C. Montgomerie beat F. Couples and D. Love III 1 up   1

Sunday Singles
D. Clarke lost to P. Mickelson 2 and 1   0

Total 1

1999 Brookline, Boston, Massachusetts, US

Captain: Europe: M. James; US: B. Crenshaw

Friday Foursomes (a.m.)
D. Clarke and L. Westwood lost to J. Maggert and H. Sutton 3 and 2   0

Friday Fourballs (p.m.)
D. Clarke and L. Westwood beat T. Woods and D. Duval 1 up   1

Saturday Foursomes (a.m.)
D. Clarke and L. Westwood beat J. Furyk and M. O'Meara 3 and 2   1

Saturday Fourballs (p.m.)
D. Clarke and L. Westwood lost to P. Mickelson and T. Lehman 2 and 1   0

Sunday Singles

D. Clarke lost to H. Sutton 4 and 2   0

                                                              Total 2

2002 The Belfry, England

Captain: Europe: S. Torrance; US: C. Strange

Friday Fourballs (a.m.)

D. Clarke and T. Björn beat T. Woods and P. Azinger 1 up   1

Friday foursomes (p.m.)

D. Clarke and T. Björn lost to H. Sutton and S. Verplank 2 and 1   0

Saturday Foursomes (a.m.)

D. Clarke and T. Björn lost to T. Woods and D. Love III 4 and 3   0

Saturday Fourballs (p.m.)

D. Clarke and P. McGinley halved with S. Hoch and J. Furyk   ½

Sunday Singles

D. Clarke halved with D. Duval   ½

                                                              Total 2

2004 Oakland Hills, Michigan, US

Captain: Europe: B. Langer; US: H. Sutton

Friday Fourballs (a.m.)

D. Clarke and M.A. Jiménez beat D. Love III and C. Campbell 5 and 4   1

Friday Foursomes (p.m.)

D. Clarke and L. Westwood beat T. Woods and P. Mickelson 1 up   1

Saturday Fourballs (a.m.)

D. Clarke and I. Poulter lost to T. Woods and C. Riley 4 and 3   0

Saturday Foursomes (p.m.)

D. Clarke and L. Westwood beat J. Haas and C. DiMarco 5 and 4   1

Sunday Singles
D. Clarke halved with D. Love III   ½
                                                            Total 3½

FRED DALY PLAYED IN FOUR RYDER CUP MATCHES: 1947, 1949, 1951 AND 1953.

1947 Portland, Oregon, US

Captain: Great Britain and Ireland: T.H. Cotton; US: B. Hogan

Day 1 Foursomes
F. Daly and C.H. Ward lost to S. Snead and L. Mangrum 6 and 5   0

Day 2 Singles
F. Daly lost to E.J. Harrison 5 and 4   0
                                                            Total 0

1949 Scarborough, England

Captain: Great Britain and Ireland: C.A. Whitcombe; US: B. Hogan

Day 1 Foursomes
F. Daly and K. Bousfield beat R. Hamilton and S. Alexander 4 and 2   1

Day 2 Singles
F. Daly lost to L. Mangrum 4 and 3   0
                                                            Total 1

1951 Pinehurst, North Carolina, US

Captain: Great Britain and Ireland: A.J. Lacey; US: S. Snead

Day 1 Foursomes
F. Daly and K. Bousfield lost to B. Hogan and J. Demaret 5 and 4   0

Day 2 Singles
F. Daly halved with C. Heafner   ½
                                                            Total ½

1953 Surrey, England

Captain: Great Britain and Ireland: T.H. Cotton; US: L. Mangrum

Day 1 Foursomes
F. Daly and H. Bradshaw beat W. Burkemo and C. Middlecoff 1 up   1

Day 2 Singles
F. Daly beat T. Kroll 9 and 7   1

Total 2

EAMONN DARCY PLAYED IN FOUR RYDER CUP MATCHES: 1975, 1977, 1981 AND 1987.

1975 Pennsylvania, US

Captain: Great Britain and Ireland: B.J. Hunt; US: A. Palmer

Day 1 Fourballs (p.m.)
E. Darcy and C. O'Connor, Jr. lost to T. Weiskopf and L. Graham 3 and 2   0

Day 2 Fourballs (a.m.)
E. Darcy and G. Hunt halved with A. Geiberger and R. Floyd   ½

Day 2 Foursomes (p.m.)
E. Darcy and G. Hunt lost to A. Geiberger and L. Graham 3 and 2   0
Day 3 Singles
E. Darcy lost to W.J. Casper 3 and 2   0

Total ½

1977 St Anne's, England

Captain: Great Britain and Ireland: B. Huggett; US: D. Finsterwald

Day 1 Foursomes
E. Darcy and A. Jacklin halved with E. Sneed and D. January   ½

Day 2 Fourballs
E. Darcy and A. Jacklin lost to D. Hill and D. Stockton 5 and 3   0

Day 3 Singles
E. Darcy lost to H. Green 1 up   0
                                                        Total ½

1981 Surrey, England

Captain: Europe: J. Jacobs; US: D. Marr

Day 1 Fourballs (p.m.)
E. Darcy and B. Gallacher lost to H. Irwin and R. Floyd 2 and 1   0

Day 3 Singles
E. Darcy lost to J. Nicklaus 5 and 3   0
                                                        Total 0

1987 Ohio, US

Captain: Europe: A. Jacklin; US: J.M. Nicklaus

Day 2 Fourballs (p.m.)
E. Darcy and G. Brand, Jr. lost to A. Bean and P. Stewart 3 and 2   0

Day 3 Singles
E. Darcy beat B. Crenshaw 1 up   1
                                                        Total 1

NORMAN DREW PLAYED IN ONE RYDER CUP MATCH: 1959.

1959 California, US

Captain: Great Britain and Ireland: D.J. Rees; US: S. Snead

Day 2 Singles
N.V. Drew halved with D. Ford   ½
                                                        Total ½

DAVID FEHERTY PLAYED IN ONE RYDER CUP: 1991.

1991 South Carolina, US

Captain: Europe: B. Gallacher; US: D. Stockton

Day 1 Fourballs (p.m.)
D. Feherty and S. Torrance halved with L. Wadkins and M. O'Meara   ½

Day 2 Foursomes (a.m.)
D. Feherty and S. Torrance lost to H. Irwin and L. Wadkins 4 and 2   0

Day 3 Singles
D. Feherty beat P. Stewart 2 and 1   1

Total 1½

PADRAIG HARRINGTON HAS PLAYED IN THREE RYDER CUP MATCHES: 1999, 2002 AND 2004.

1999 Massachusetts, US

Captain: Europe: M. James; US: B. Crenshaw

Day 1 Foursomes (a.m.)
P. Harrington and M.A. Jiménez halved with D. Love III and P. Stewart ½

Day 2 Foursomes (a.m.)
P. Harrington and M.A. Jiménez lost to S. Pate and T. Woods 1 up   0

Day 3 Singles
P. Harrington beat M. O'Meara 1 up   1

Total 1½

2002 West Midlands, England

Captain: S. Torrance; US: C. Strange

Day 1 Fourballs (a.m.)
P. Harrington and N. Fasth lost to P. Mickelson and D. Toms 1 up   0

Day 1 Foursomes (p.m.)
P. Harrington and P. McGinley lost to S. Cink and J. Furyk 3 and 2   0

Day 2 Fourballs (p.m.)

P. Harrington and C. Montgomerie beat P. Mickelson and D. Toms 2 and 1 1

Day 3 Singles

P. Harrington beat M. Calcavecchia 5 and 4   1

           Total 2

2004 Michigan, US

Captain: Europe: B. Langer; US: H. Sutton

Day 1 Fourballs (a.m.)

P. Harrington and C. Montgomerie beat P. Mickelson and T. Woods 2 and 1 1

Day 1 Foursomes (p.m.)

P. Harrington and C. Montgomerie beat D. Love III and F. Funk 4 and 2 1

Day 2 Fourballs (a.m.)

P. Harrington and C. Montgomerie lost to S. Cink and D. Love III 3 and 2 0

Day 2 Foursomes (p.m.)

P. Harrington and P. McGinley beat D. Love III and T. Woods 4 and 3   1

Day 3 Singles

P. Harrington beat J. Haas 1 up   1

           Total 4

Jimmy Martin played in one Ryder Cup: 1965.

1965 Southport, England

Captain: Great Britain and Ireland: H. Weetman; US: B. Nelson

Day 1 Foursomes (p.m.)

J. Martin and J. Hitchcock lost to J. Boros and A. Lema 5 and 4   0

           Total 0

PAUL MCGINLEY PLAYED IN TWO RYDER CUPS: 2002 AND 2004.

2002 West Midlands, England

Captain: Europe: S. Torrance; US: C. Strange

Day 1 Foursomes (p.m.)
P. McGinley and P. Harrington lost to S. Cink and J. Furyk 3 and 2   0

Day 2 Fourballs (p.m.)
P. McGinley and D. Clarke halved with S. Hoch and J. Furyk   ½

Day 3 Singles
P. McGinley halved with J. Furyk   ½

Total 1

2004 Michigan, US

Captain: Europe: B. Langer; US: H. Sutton

Day 1 Fourballs (a.m.)
P. McGinley and L. Donald halved with C. Riley and S. Cink   ½

Day 2 Foursomes (p.m.)
P. McGinley and P. Harrington beat D. Love III and T. Woods 4 and 3   1

Day 3 Singles
P. McGinley beat S. Cink 3 and 2   1

Total 2½

CHRISTY O'CONNOR, JR. PLAYED IN TWO RYDER CUPS: 1975 AND 1989.

1975 Pennsylvania, US

Captain: Great Britain and Ireland: B.J. Hunt; US: A. Palmer

Day 1 Fourballs (p.m.)

C. O'Connor, Jr. and E. Darcy lost to T. Weiskopf and L. Graham 3 and 2   0

Day 2 Foursomes (p.m.)

C. O'Connor, Jr. and J. O'Leary lost to T. Weiskopf and J. Miller 5 and 3   0

Total 0

1989 West Midlands, England

Captain: Europe: A. Jacklin; US: R. Floyd

Day 2 Foursomes (a.m.)

C. O'Connor, Jr. and R. Rafferty lost to M. Calcavecchia and K. Green 3 and 2 0

Day 3 Singles

C. O'Connor, Jr. beat F. Couples 1 hole   1

Total 1

CHRISTY O'CONNOR, SR. PLAYED IN TEN RYDER CUPS: 1955, 1957, 1959, 1961, 1963, 1965, 1967, 1969, 1971 AND 1973.

1955 California, US

Captain: Great Britain and Ireland: D.J. Rees; US: C. Harbert

Day 2 Singles

C. O'Connor, Sr. lost to T. Bolt 4 and 2   0

Total 0

1957 Sheffield, England

Captain: Great Britain and Ireland: D.J. Rees; US: J. Burke

Day 1 Foursomes

C. O'Connor, Sr. and E.C. Brown lost to R. Mayer and T. Brown 7 and 5 0

Day 2 Singles

C. O'Connor, Sr. beat D. Finsterwald 7 and 6   1

Total 1

1959 California, US

Captain: Great Britain and Ireland: D.J. Rees; US: S. Snead

Day 1 Foursomes
C. O'Connor, Sr. and P. Alliss beat A. Wall and D. Ford 3 and 2   1

Day 2 Singles
C. O'Connor, Sr. lost to A. Wall 7 and 6   0

Total 1

1961 St Anne's, England

Captain: Great Britain and Ireland: D.J. Rees; US: J. Barber

Day 1 Foursomes (a.m.)
C. O'Connor, Sr. and P. Alliss beat D. Ford and G. Littler 4 and 3   1

Day 1 Foursomes (p.m.)
C. O'Connor, Sr. and P. Alliss lost to A. Wall and J. Hebert 1 up   0

Day 2 Singles (a.m.)
C. O'Connor, Sr. lost to D. Finsterwald 2 and 1   0

Day 2 Singles (p.m.)
C. O'Connor, Sr. halved with G. Littler   ½

Total 1½

1963 Georgia, US

Captain: Great Britain and Ireland: J. Fallon; US: A. Palmer

Day 1 Foursomes (a.m.)
C. O'Connor, Sr. and P. Alliss lost to W. Caspert and D. Ragan 1 up   0

Day 2 Fourballs (a.m.)
C. O'Connor, Sr. and N.C. Coles beat R. Goalby and D. Ragan 1 up   1

Day 2 Fourballs (p.m.)
C. O'Connor, Sr. and N.C. Coles lost to A. Palmer and D. Finsterwald 3 and 2 0

Day 3 Singles (a.m.)
C. O'Connor, Sr. lost to G. Littler 1 up 0

Day 3 Singles (p.m.)
C. O'Connor, Sr. lost to W. Maxwell 2 and 1 0

Total 1

1965 Southport, England

Captain: Great Britain and Ireland: H. Weetman; US: B. Nelson

Day 1 Foursomes (a.m.)
C. O'Connor, Sr. and P. Alliss beat K. Venturi and D. January 5 and 4 1

Day 1 Foursomes (p.m.)
C. O'Connor, Sr. and P. Alliss beat W. Casper and G. Littler 2 and 1 1

Day 2 Fourballs (a.m.)
C. O'Connor, Sr. and P. Alliss lost to A. Palmer and D. Marr 6 and 4 0

Day 2 Fourballs (p.m.)
C. O'Connor, Sr. and P. Alliss beat A. Palmer and D. Marr 1 up 1

Day 3 Singles (p.m.)
C. O'Connor, Sr. lost to A. Lema 6 and 4 0

Total 3

1967 Texas, US

Captain: Great Britain and Ireland: D.J. Rees; US: B. Hogan

Day 1 Foursomes (a.m.)
C. O'Connor, Sr. and P. Alliss lost to A. Palmer and G. Dickinson 2 and 1 0

Day 1 Foursomes (p.m.)
C. O'Connor, Sr. and P. Alliss lost to R. Nichols and J. Pott 2 and 1 0

Day 2 Fourballs (a.m.)
C. O'Connor, Sr. and P. Alliss lost to W. Casper and G. Brewer 3 and 2 0

Day 3 Singles (p.m.)
C. O'Connor, Sr. lost to R. Nichols 3 and 2   0

     Total 0

1969 Southport, England

Captain: Great Britain and Ireland: E.C. Brown; US: S. Snead

Day 1 Foursomes (a.m.)
C. O'Connor, Sr. and P. Alliss halved with W. Casper and F. Beard   ½

Day 2 Fourballs (a.m.)
C. O'Connor, Sr. and P. Townsend beat D. Hill and D. Douglass 1 up   1

Day 3 Singles (a.m.)
C. O'Connor, Sr. beat F. Beard 5 and 4   1

Day 3 Singles (p.m.)
C. O'Connor, Sr. lost to G. Littler 2 and 1   0

     Total 2½

1971 Missouri, US

Captain: Great Britain and Ireland: E.C. Brown; US: J. Hebert

Day 1 Foursomes (a.m.)
C. O'Connor, Sr. and N.C. Coles beat W. Casper and M. Barber 2 and 1   1

Day 2 Fourballs (a.m.)
C. O'Connor, Sr. and B. Barnes lost to L. Trevino and M. Rudolf 2 and 1 0

Day 2 Fourballs (p.m.)
C. O'Connor, Sr. and N.C. Coles halved with C. Coody and F. Beard   ½

Day 3 Singles (a.m.)
C. O'Connor, Sr. lost to G. Dickinson 5 and 4   0

     Total 1½

1973 Muirfield, Scotland

Captain: Great Britain and Ireland: B.J. Hunt; US: J. Burke

Day 1 Foursomes (a.m.)
C. O'Connor, Sr. and N.C. Coles beat T. Weiskopf and J.C. Snead 3 and 2   1

Day 1 Fourballs (p.m.)
C. O'Connor, Sr. and N.C. Coles lost to L. Trevino and H. Blancas 2 and 1   0

Day 2 Foursomes (a.m.)
C. O'Connor, Sr. and N.C. Coles lost to L. Trevino and W. Casper 2 and 1   0

Day 3 Singles (a.m.)
C. O'Connor, Sr. lost to J.C. Snead 1 up   0

Day 3 Singles (p.m.)
C. O'Connor, Sr. halved with T. Weiskopf   ½
Total 1½

JOHN O'LEARY PLAYED IN ONE RYDER CUP: 1975.

1975 Pennsylvania, US

Captain: Great Britain and Ireland: B.J. Hunt; US: A. Palmer

Day 1 Foursomes (a.m.)
J. O'Leary and T. Horton lost to L. Trevino and J.C. Snead 2 and 1   0

Day 1 Fourballs (p.m.)
J. O'Leary and T. Horton lost to L. Trevino and H. Irwin 2 and 1   0

Day 2 Foursomes (p.m.)
J. O'Leary and C. O'Connor, Jr. lost to T. Weiskopf and J. Miller 5 and 3   0

Day 3 Singles (p.m.)
J. O'Leary lost to H. Irwin 2 and 1   0
Total 0

EDDIE POLLAND PLAYED IN ONE RYDER CUP: 1973.

1973 Muirfield, Scotland

Captain: Great Britain and Ireland: B.J. Hunt; US: J. Burke

Day 1 Foursomes (a.m.)
E. Polland and M.E. Bembridge lost to J.W. Nicklaus and A. Palmer 6 and 5   0

Day 2 Fourballs (p.m.)
E. Polland and C. Clark lost to J.W. Nicklaus and T. Weiskopf 3 and 2   0
Total 0

RONAN RAFFERTY PLAYED IN ONE RYDER CUP: 1989.

1989 West Midlands, England

Captain: Europe: A. Jacklin; US: R. Floyd

Day 1 Foursomes (a.m.)
R. Rafferty and B. Langer lost to M. Calcavecchia and K. Green 2 and 1   0

Day 2 Foursomes (a.m.)
R. Rafferty and C. O'Connor, Jr. lost to M. Calcavecchia and K. Green 3 and 2 0

Day 3 Singles
R. Rafferty beat M. Calcavecchia 1 up   1
Total 1

DES SMYTH PLAYED IN TWO RYDER CUPS: 1979 AND 1981.

1979 West Virginia, US

Captain: Europe: J. Jacobs; US: W. Casper

Day 1 Foursomes (p.m.)
D. Smyth and K. Brown lost to H. Irwin and T. Kite 7 and 6   0

Day 3 Singles
D. Smyth lost to H. Irwin 5 and 3   0

Total 0

1981 Surrey, England

Captain: Europe: J. Jacobs; US: D. Marr

Day 1 Foursomes (a.m.)
D. Smyth and B. Gallacher beat H. Irwin and R. Floyd 3 and 2   1

Day 1 Fourballs (p.m.)
D. Smyth and J.M. Canizares beat B. Rogers and B. Lietzke 6 and 5   1

Day 2 Fourballs (a.m.)
D. Smyth and J.M. Canizares lost to J. Nicklaus and T. Watson 3 and 2   0

Day 2 Foursomes (p.m.)
D. Smyth and B. Gallacher lost to T. Kite and L. Nelson 3 and 2   0

Day 3 Singles
Des Smyth lost to B. Crenshaw 6 and 4   0

Total 2

PHILIP WALTON PLAYED IN ONE RYDER CUP: 1995.

1995 New York, US

Captain: Europe: B. Gallacher; US: L. Wadkins

Day 2 Foursomes (a.m.)
P. Walton and I. Woosnam lost to L. Roberts and P. Jacobsen 1 up   0

Day 3 Singles
P. Walton beat J. Haas 1 up   1

Total 1

APPENDIX 2

IAN WOOSNAM

Number of appearances:	8
Matches played:	31
Won:	14
Lost:	12
Halved:	5
Singles played:	8
Singles won:	0
Singles lost:	6
Singles halved:	2
Foursomes played:	9
Foursomes won:	4
Foursomes lost:	3
Foursomes halved:	2
Fourballs played:	14
Fourballs won:	10
Fourballs lost:	3
Fourballs halved:	1
Total points:	16.5

APPENDIX 3

RYDER CUP RECORD OF US CAPTAIN,

TOM LEHMAN

Number of appearances:	3
Matches played:	10
Won:	5
Lost:	3
Halved:	2
Singles played:	3
Singles won:	3
Singles lost:	0
Singles halved:	0
Foursomes played:	4
Foursomes won:	1
Foursomes lost:	2
Foursomes halved:	1
Fourballs played:	3
Fourballs won:	1
Fourballs lost:	1
Fourballs halved:	1
Total points:	7

APPENDIX 4

The 2006 European Ryder Cup Final Standings

World Points List PLAYERS	European Points List
1.	
2.	
3.	
4.	
5.	
6.	
7.	
8.	
9.	
10.	
11.	
12.	
13.	
14.	
15.	
16.	
17.	
18.	
19.	
20.	
21.	
22.	
23.	
24.	
25.	

2006 EUROPEAN RYDER CUP TEAM

1. _____
2. _____
3. _____
4. _____
5. _____
6. _____
7. _____
8. _____
9. _____
10. _____

11. _____
12. _____
13. _____
14. _____
15. _____
16. _____
17. _____
18. _____
19. _____
20. _____

*The leading five players qualify through the World's Point List. The next five players qualify through the European Points List. Positions 11 to 20 indicate the leading challengers for the European Ryder Cup Points List.

THE 2006 US RYDER CUP TEAM

1.

2.

3.

4.

5.

6.

7.

8.

9.

10.

11.

12.

13.

14.

15.

16.

17.

18.

19.

20.

APPENDIX 5

THE 2006 RYDER CUP TEAMS

EUROPE   UNITED STATES

PLAYERS

1.

2.

3.

4.

5.

6.

7.

8.

9.

10.

11.★

12.★

★Wild Card

APPENDIX 6

THE 2006 RYDER CUP AT THE K CLUB

EUROPE   USA

Fourballs: Morning

Foursomes: Afternoon

USA

EUROPE

Fourballs: Morning

Foursomes: Afternoon

USA

EUROPE

Singles

USA

EUROPE

INDEX

Ryder Cup Matches

A

Aaron, Tommy 30
Accenture Match Play Championship
  155
Adams, Jimmy 130
Alcan Tournament 133
Alexander, Skip 128
Alfred Dunhill Cup 92, 164, 168, 179
Alfred Dunhill Open 152
Allen, Bernard 115
Allen, Greg 101–105
Alliss, Percy 12
Alliss, Peter 12, 20, 21, 24–5, 27–9, 55,
  91, 111, 120–21, 133–4, 143–4,
  144–6
Amateur Championship 55
American Express Golf Championship
  ix, 62–3, 64–5
Arcapita Tour Champsionship 180
Arnett, Elizabeth 83, 84
Asian Open 164
Australian Match Play Championship
  177
Azinger, Paul 99, 102, 156, 169–70

B

Baker, Peter 182, 183
Ballesteros, Seve ix, 11, 36, 37–8, 39,
  42, 43, 45–6, 55, 102, 103, 106,
  113, 153, 157, 163, 173, 175, 181
Ballybunion Golf Club 53, 57, 67, 69,
  70, 97
Balmoral Golf Club 127
Baltray Golf Club 97, 104
Barber, Miller 31, 146
Barclays Classic 164
Barnes, Brian 146
Barter, Tim 96–100
Bean, Andy 160
Beard, Frank 29, 30, 145
Bedford, Joe 84–5
Bembridge, Maurice 118, 150
Benson & Hedges International Open
  48, 100, 152, 166, 168, 170

Berkemo, Walter 129
Björn, Thomas 46, 99, 155, 156
Blancas, Homero 146
BMW International Open 162, 168
Bolt, Tommy 21, 142
Bord Fáilte (Fáilte Ireland) xv, 58, 64,
  65, 66, 67, 69, 70, 72, 114
Boros, Julios 147, 149
Bousfield, Ken 18, 128
Boyle, Hugh 27–8, 147–8
Bradshaw, Breda 17, 129–30, 133, 135
Bradshaw, Harry 8, 10, 17–18, 20–23,
  35, 56–7, 107, 109, 118, 129–35,
  139–40, 142, 157, 164, 174
Bradshaw, Jr., Harry 17, 129, 135
Braid, James 5
Brand, Jr., Gordon 160
Brazil Open 164
Brewer, Gay 118, 145
British Ladies' Amateur Championship
  54
British Masters 130, 172
British Open 5, 29, 30, 31, 55, 128,
  130–31, 138, 140, 146, 148, 150,
  151, 152, 172, 175, 177, 178, 180
British PGA 11, 12, 13, 17–18, 21, 26,
  57, 58, 71, 118, 133
British Seniors 99, 150
Brown, Eric 31, 141, 142
Brown, Ken 35, 36, 95, 112, 181
Buick Open 164
Bundoran Golf Club 138, 139
Burke, Jack 135
Burke, Tim 80, 81
Burkemo, Walter 20, 134
Butler, Peter 11
Byrne, Gerry 73, 75–7, 84, 85
Byrne, Jim 75
Byrnes, Michael 80–81

C

Calcavecchia, Mark 42, 166, 173, 178
Campbell, Chad 156
Campbell, Michael 168